TOGETHER STRONGER

The Rise of Welsh Football's Golden Generation 2005-2015

Chris Wathan

St David's Press

Cardiff

Published in Wales by St. David's Press, an imprint of

Ashley Drake Publishing Ltd
PO Box 733
Cardiff
CF14 7ZY

www.st-davids-press.wales

First Impression – 2016

ISBN
978-1-902719-48-1

British Library Cataloguing-in-Publication Data.
A CIP catalogue for this book is available from the British Library.

Typeset by Replika Press Pvt Ltd, India
Printed by Akcent Media, Czech Republic

Contents

For Emilie & those who always believed

Foreword

It will be a proud moment for me when I lead the Welsh team out at the European Championship Finals in June 2016. The first time Wales have qualified on merit for a major championship finals, and the first time we've appeared at a tournament since 1958; far too long. The wait is finally over.

For as many years as I can remember the talk has been of Wales having a young group of players with the potential to end the qualification drought. Even when I first came into the team in 2008 there had been talk of a golden generation that were going to make history. It was easy to see why, with world class talents like Gareth Bale and Aaron Ramsey coming through alongside a group of genuinely talented and players. But in every campaign, the team came up just short – until now, that is. This current group has finally lived up to its potential.

It was a long, hard, but enjoyable qualification campaign. We made a solid start, which was key and the biggest thing for all of us, and the campaign seemed to gather momentum as we gained confidence and real belief as we progressed. It was new territory for us.

We always felt we were in with a chance of qualifying, but it really started to build when we got that 0-0 draw in Belgium and then it went up a level when we beat Israel out in Haifa. We knew that night we had a real chance. Then, beating Belgium at home in June, in a night none of us will forget, was when we knew qualification was in our own hands. If we didn't make it after that then we only had ourselves to blame.

I always felt we had the qualities to get over the line. The whole squad was in it together; the management and staff were in it together; we were 'Together Stronger'.

Everyone should be proud of what they've achieved. When you look back and see great Welsh players like Ryan Giggs, John Hartson, Ian Rush, Neville Southall, Kevin Ratcliffe and Mark Hughes all missing out on major finals, it makes you realise just how honoured and lucky you are.

More than anything, I am pleased for the Welsh fans that the pain of missing out on tournament finals every other summer has finally been eased. Nobody deserves to see their country in a major final more than them. The support they gave us over the qualifying campaign was amazing and they deserve to wear their Wales shirt with pride in France.

And you know it's a special time because even the journalists are smiling! Having watched so many campaigns falter over the years, they also get to cover a major tournament. Hopefully they will keep smiling because I know how much they want Wales to do well.

As captain of club and country, I've been lucky enough to get close to a few members of the Welsh media over the years. Chris Wathan is one of those that has constantly thrown his Dictaphone in my direction during international duty and my eight years with the Swans. I remember first speaking to him when I was first called up by John Toshack when I was still with Stockport; it's fair to say a lot has happened since.

We have a strong working relationship that has been built on trust. I prefer journalists who genuinely call it as they see it and Chris is one of those. He has covered the rise of this team over many years. He's been with us every step of the way over the past decade, reporting and sharing the highs and the lows for us as a side and as a football nation. He's covered every minute and knows the detail of how and why we succeeded in finally delivering an incredible qualification campaign.

It's why I was pleased to hear he wanted to tell the story of how this team (the players and management) has come together to achieve our goal. There are no writers who have been as close to the story as Chris over the last ten years. It is a story that's worth telling, worth reading and definitely worth enjoying!

It's been a story to remember – and one worth waiting for.

Ashley Williams
January 2016

Acknowledgements

There have been plenty of times where, in some far flung European city, the discussion around the journalists' dinner table has been that there was a good book to be done on the story of this Wales side. When Gareth Bale turned to celebrate and the anthem rang out against Belgium, it seemed as good a time as any to take the plunge and attempt it. Whether I have done the tale justice is up for others to decide but it goes without saying that it has been a fascinating period for Welsh football and hopefully, in covering it so closely for more than a decade, I have been able to convey some of that through these pages.

I am aware how privileged I have been to witness both the good and the bad times during that journey; certainly some of my greatest moments in this industry have come during this recent Euro 2016 qualifying campaign from Bale's goal in Andorra, to the raving in Belgium, that June night at Cardiff City Stadium and, of course, the moment the dream became a reality in Bosnia. I admit seeing the delight on the faces of fans I have grown to know over the years and players I have seen grow up, both as footballers and people, made it quite an emotional evening for those of us who are supposed to remain neutral. It is with some great fortune that, on a patch where there have been fine journalists before me, my time covering the national team has coincided with such success.

Putting this book together has not been about luck, however, but plenty of hard work, sacrifice and support from many who I must simply use this opportunity to thank. Firstly, my colleagues at Media Wales who have long been of great support on a day-to-day basis, from all on the sports desk with special thanks to Editor-in-Chief Alan Edmunds and Head of Sport Paul Abbandonato for their support both overall and with regards to this book.

Thanks also to those who have been on the end of a phone or e-mail for advice and to cast careful eyes and honest criticism of the project without whom I may have gone mad with doubt; Michael Pearlman, Phil Cadden, David Price and Ian Carbis, I am indebted to your help.

Ashley Drake from St David's Press deserves a special mention for making sure I did not forget a random conversation about this idea and gave me the belief and backing to press ahead.

To all who gave up their time for interviews and insight, I thank you: David Cotterill, Ian Davis, Brian Flynn, Jonathan Ford, Danny Gabbidon, Chris Gunter, John Hartson, Joe Ledley, Peter Rees, Osian Roberts, Carl Robinson, Dave Rowe, Neil Taylor, John Toshack – who was also someone fascinating to deal with during his time in charge where I learned a lot as a journalist – Jonny Williams and, with extra thanks to Ceri Barnett for the translation, Gabriel Riera.

Thanks to those journalists who accompanied me on the travels during Euro 2016, who offered great support to the idea as well as providing great company to make sure quite intense and stressful periods are as enjoyable as they are; you are too many to name but you know full well who you are.

Those supporters I have met along the way, with particular mention to 'stats guru' Gary Pritchard, I hope you enjoy this as much as I've enjoyed your company and appreciated your comments.

I am particularly grateful to those who have assisted in ensuring an extensive and attractive selection of images for this book, specifically: Dave Rawcliffe of Propaganda-Photos who also provided the cover image; Alex Gage for the majority of the Euro 2016 qualification campaign images; my colleagues at Media Wales Ltd for the reproductions of pages from the *Western Mail* and *Wales on Sunday*, and a special word of thanks to Gareth Bale and Chris Gunter who gave permission for the inclusion of their Tweets.

Great thanks to those at the Football Association of Wales with who I have long enjoyed a good working relationship, even in times of tension, and have been great support for a long time, including regarding this book, from Ian Gwyn Hughes, Peter Barnes and Mark Evans to name just a few.

I wish it was possible to say thanks to Gary Speed who was a pleasure to deal with in his all too brief time in charge and whose death impacted upon me like it did so many.

As documented here, Chris Coleman had a difficult time in picking up the pieces from a tragedy yet can be proud of his significant part in this story. There were times, as with most reporters and managers, when we crossed swords but it has been a joy to come out the other side with a handshake and history to be written about. It has been a pleasure, Cookie.

I'm not sure my wife Jen can say the same having had to put up with me spend time off tied to a computer, but her understanding and support was invaluable while I could not ask for a better motivator than my beautiful little girl, Emilie, who asked me each night for four months how many more words I had written. This book is for you, Ems, just as it is for my parents, Richie and Ann, without whom I would not be have been able to follow my dream in becoming a football writer.

Lastly, thanks to the team that made this a story worth telling. Again, I only hope I have done it justice.

Chris Wathan
January 2016

1

Gabriel Riera

"It has to be better, we will be better" – Chris Coleman

It takes more than ten thousand steps to climb a mountain. However small, however insignificant they may seem at the time, each step is one towards the peak and that triumph of standing above all others. However impossible the climb may seem at times, each step is one closer towards the goal, a summit that would have not been visible when starting out on the journey. You can imagine what it feels like to be there, to plant a flag where it touches the sky, but it remains in the imagination. You can only reach it through through thousands of steps.

As the Pyrenees looked down on Wales in Andorra la Vella, that peak, that dream of scaling the heights was as far away as ever. But then came that one step, that one movement forward.

Wales had stumbled so many times in the past, lost their footing, lost their way and, at times, lost their belief. The great names of the past had not managed to scale the heights reached by John Charles, Ivor Allchurch and others of a time long gone. Some had gone closer than others but Toshack, Yorath, Rush, Hughes, Southall, Giggs and so many more had been left looking on while other nations celebrated and competed. They had shaped history, they had weaved their significance into Welsh football, but they could not create history.

The hope in Andorra was that this time would be different, but France literally lay just beyond a mountain that Wales were staring up at, having once again stumbled.

But then came that one step, one movement forward. It seemed insignificant at the time, it might not be joyously recalled in the same way other moments along the way will be, but without it you wonder whether Wales' latest journey would have ended like so many before it.

It seemed as if it was going to be that way as Gabriel Riera looked around his surroundings. The car stereo fitter's forehead was glistening with sweat from the light kept alive by the floodlight pylons that disguised the fact the sun had long set behind the vast enveloping scenery in which Wales were suffocating.

Stood beneath the Pyrenean mountains, it was Wales upon which the landscape stared down ominously. Wales, in turn, looked for something that had avoided them in Andorra la Vella as it had done for more than half a century.

They had not found it when the lights failed at the Vetch in 1981, nor four years earlier than that when French referee Robert Wurtz had mistaken Joe Jordan's navy blue outstretched arm for that of the red-shirted David Jones. They had struggled to find it wherever they had turned, no matter the players nor the manager.

It was not so much luck they willed for but simply a minute turn of fate, the tiniest movement that could set off something bigger.

Many had given up, although the 1,250 supporters who had made the awkward trip to Andorra – first into Barcelona and then bussed through the winding mountain roads – had not swayed in their vocal support of the team. They rarely do.

A glance across into the away section at random European stadiums or strolls through various continental cities is returned by familiar faces, ones that have seen scores of defeats, optimism-crushing results. Many of them have shared the sometime anger and embarrassment caused by games such as the 7-1 beating in Eindhoven in 1996 – incredibly a result kept 'respectable' by the great Neville Southall in what he considers one of the best performances of his career – or countless other nights where Wales slipped into the stereotype of the team that inevitably disappoints, one that can snatch frustration from the jaws of hope and promise.

Those faces all have their memory of a game where they still shake their head, or promised on the trip home 'never again'; and yet the preference is to take pride in being among those that keep the faith and being among each other. As it was on the first steps towards Euro 2016.

The chance to 'shade in' another country's outline on their map of Europe with Wales' first fixture against the tiny landlocked Andorrans, not to mention the first game of a new qualifying campaign, had seen them take every available seat in the newly-opened Estadi Nacional.

The gallows humour had been in full flow beforehand, as it always is with Wales, but no-one truly believed an upset would be a concern against a team ranked behind only newly accepted Gibraltar in the UEFA standings, at 199th in FIFA's rankings, and had never registered a single point in Euro qualifiers. In their most recent World Cup qualifying campaign, they had failed to score even once.

As a result, there was almost a collective smile of acknowledgement among the disbelief that Wales were not about to do it the easy way when, after six minutes, the ball flashed across Neil Taylor who made the slightest of grabs on Ivan Lorenzo and Ildefons Lima converted the penalty.

The mutterings of worry did become louder when no-one had added to Gareth Bale's 22nd-minute leveller, but the frustration had been limited to a call for manager Chris Coleman to 'Sort it out'; even then it came against a backdrop of *Calon Lân*.

Those not in Andorra were not as forgiving. The social media sneering was deafening, the criticism of Coleman in particular was overwhelming, even when this was not the manager alone struggling; several of his players were clearly shaken out of their stride at the thought of going down in history for all the wrong reasons.

Even those fans who pleaded the same players for more, to stop this campaign ending before it had started, would have heard the mocking in their minds.

This was supposed to be the perfect start to things: the visit to the minnows, a chance of momentum that had evaded the national side in previous campaigns. The computerised draw for Group B of the European Championships qualifiers had handed Wales the opportunity to get a first win on the board in the September sunshine, long before domestic seasons started risking the fitness of key men.

Against a side full of part-timers and a side whose statistics propped up pretty much all others in European international football, anything other than victory was unthinkable, a notion accepted by the players and management in the build-up. Yet here they were not only thinking the worst but staring it in the face.

3

Indeed, the intros – those first damning paragraphs of a journalist's report – had been written as the clock arrived onto 81 minutes. The names of Georgia and Moldova were mentioned, even Leyton Orient who incredibly had recorded victory over a full-strength Wales team in 1996 during Bobby Gould's ill-fated time in charge. This would have been worse; the upsetting nature of a draw was bad enough in isolation but the prospect of the dropped points threatened to derail yet another bid for a major finals. No matter the spin, the reality was this would have been another campaign mortally undermined, another two years wasted for this group of players dubbed a golden generation.

The headlines no-one wanted to see were being readied. The deadlines of an evening kick-off were approaching as fast as the final whistle and were set to scream out the awful truth.

There was a pause in the press box as Slovenian referee Slavko Vinčić blew his whistle for a free-kick after Ildefons Lima had fouled substitute George Williams, the exciting Fulham rookie.

Gareth Bale, the most expensive player in the world, stood menacingly over the ball with the Wales supporters facing him, almost begging him to find the top corner and find a way out. The superstar was all set to provide salvation.

Only he didn't, his attempt was not quite whipped enough, not quite vicious enough and too central. Although it wasn't held comfortably by a nervous Ferran Pol in the Andorran goal, he quickly gathered the loose ball before a white Welsh shirt could lunge towards it, the attacking players in the box almost not expecting the Real Madrid Champions League winner to have found the denying hands of the part-time goalkeeper rather than the net he protected.

The mountain Wales needed to climb still remained and the steep Pyrenean landscape all too frustratingly fitted the well-read script of Welsh football woe.

Yet the one small movement the side needed suddenly came. Gabriel Riera looked forlornly around his surroundings but Vinčić's whistle had sounded, a flash of yellow in his direction confirming his indiscretion.

It was a matter of inches too quickly, a second too soon, but that one step was all Wales needed to take their stride forward. Perhaps it was panic, perhaps the exhaustion of trying to protect one of his nation's greatest sporting triumphs, a desperation to try and make it as difficult as possible for Bale as he lined up the goal with nine minutes remaining. Perhaps Riera, that man who stood in that spotlight, can't quite answer himself why he moved out of the defensive wall. Not by much, but enough.

Bale, who had done so much throughout the fixture to try and take the game by the scruff of the neck and prove his talismanic qualities, did not need to be asked twice.

The moment he connected with the ball for the second time it felt different from the first, those fans in the small stand of seats behind the goal recognising the brilliance well before the goalkeeper's all-too-late dive followed the sound and sight of the ball reaching its intended destination.

Riera, who had been pushed out of the wall by his teammates before the second attempt, looked around once more. Andorrans shouted at each other, bellowed at the referee, but the truth is no-one was watching them. Eyes were on Bale and the celebrations, ones that were as if Wales had qualified there and then rather than taking so long to secure a victory bookmakers struggled to find appropriate odds for.

Bale had sprinted into the corner, roaring towards the fans and the night air with as much relief as joy. Several players raced towards him, throwing themselves around his upper body while others had celebrated with fans as if they had scored themselves. It made for an unusual sight; the togetherness that had already been cited by the squad and that would become a theme over the next year was as much about the team and its supporters as with fellow teammates. Every Welshman in that stadium knew what it meant.

It included those in Football Association of Wales suits, the worried looks at half-time replaced with knowing smiles about the awkward situation that had been avoided. No-one had said it – even if several would write it over the next few days – but had Coleman's future been in the balance that evening? Quite possibly, even with a new contract behind him.

He knew he had got away with one.

"I was looking at my watch thinking 'This is not a night to have one of those nights'," said the former defender as he addressed the small media contingent sat on the school chairs of the gymnasium that doubled-up for the stadium's press conference room. There was

5

no need for translation, the locals knew everything from the body language that this was a relieved man.

Yet although he had clearly gone through the mill, the Wales manager had the smile of someone who had got what he came for. As he left, he shook a hand and exchanged glances that accepted he had come close but, as he had stressed beforehand, he was taking the three points back home on the plane with him.

And that's how fickle football can be. From bleakness to brightness in the space of a few moments.

There were misgivings about the performance – rightly so, former captain Kevin Ratcliffe making it loudly clear about what he thought as he gave a cuttingly honest appraisal at the final whistle as part of his broadcast duties.

"It has to be better, we will be better," said Coleman, under no illusions himself.

And yet there was a refreshing element as players spoke in the mixed zone area between the rear of the stand and the team bus, bookended by school-age Real Madrid-clad autograph hunters and the anonymous Andorran street the stadium was housed on.

For so long, for many years of painfully slow progress and the lowering of expectations, it had become customary to hear about positives of performances, to be told that results would follow. Here there was an insight to the ruthless determination of players experienced in the unsympathetic surroundings of top level football; they knew the performance wasn't good enough but they had the win. To them, to Wales, that's all that mattered.

It seemed to be a feeling shared by supporters, some of whom had smothered Bale as he celebrated, others dancing wildly as emotions and exuberance took over them and took some over the advertising hoardings and onto the pitch. While some fans were punished, even UEFA suits accepted the FAW defence that this was pure joy rather than anything sinister.

It was a joy to witness, an incredible moment where something so innocuous on paper became so much more in the moment, under those mountains when there appeared no way out. The record books will not tell of the struggle, just the result.

Few remember that the iconic free-kick scored late on by David Beckham for England against Greece was an equaliser rather than a winner; plenty vividly remember it as a goal that took his team to the World Cup. For those who remained in the café bars of Andorra la Vella rather than heading back to Barcelona, as the team did, through the night, there was enough optimism to wonder if Bale's goal could soon be recalled as fondly and as importantly.

The headlines did not shy away from Bale's winning contribution; Riera's guilty part ignored.

Because history is written by the winners, by those who stand at the top of the mountain. It is why the Romania side of 1994 will talk more of Georghe Hagi and Gica Popescu and their run to the World Cup quarter-finals rather than Paul Bodin and penalties hitting the crossbar, as it did that November night at the National Stadium. Scotland remember simply reaching the 1978 World Cup more than the controversy that got them there, the argued-over Anfield win over Wales a footnote at best. The hard-luck stories and the heartache that has littered the history of the Welsh national side mean little outside Wales, the same as Riera's minuscule movement does not make the internet clips of Bale's winner.

But it is the smallest details that often add up, as they had done with this Wales side. The inching forward in the climbing of the mountain after a journey that had already long put faith to the test.

2

Heroes & Hope; Heartbreak & Humiliation

"We don't want any more glorious failures" – Mark Hughes

It was an odd question to finish on, but it prompted perhaps the most revealing answer.

John Toshack, sat in a room of microphones, cameras and scribbled shorthand, had spent the best part of an hour already outlining what he hoped his tenure would bring after the worst-kept secret in Welsh football was formally c onfirmed.

"On top of everything you've achieved, would you say leading your country to qualification would be the zenith of your career?"

Having covered all manner of topics during the inquisition of his November 2004 appointment to replace Mark Hughes as Wales manager, it was the only time the well-travelled Toshack seemed to be caught for words. Then, with a pause and a smile once he had double-checked the meaning of the word zenith, he was happy to oblige.

For all his success in Spain with Real Madrid, for his name-making promotions with Swansea, for all his European experiences, the difficulties and challenge ahead found him in an element of agreement with the awkwardly-worded question that had come from the back of the room.

For a man who had little need to improve a CV many managers

would struggle to match, the then 55-year-old accepted that doing something which had not been done before had been both a major attraction to the job and the motivation for doing it.

It was the equivalent of wanting to climb Everest just because it was there to be climbed.

Six men had failed in the attempt since Jimmy Murphy had taken a team to the World Cup in 1958, one man – Mike Smith – failing twice. Toshack himself had been lured to the challenge ten years earlier only to quit after one game in charge, citing too much of an overhaul being needed for him to perform while sharing his time between his country and his club at the time, Real Sociedad.

"Well, we haven't got a game for three months, so that's more than 47 days anyway," Toshack said with a smile; a pre-prepared answer seeing off the first question of whether he was going to last longer than his first appointment, having initially replaced Terry Yorath in 1994 but walking away after one friendly defeat to Norway.

"We are ten years further on, I have more knowledge of the game and I feel now is the right time for me.

"After 26 years in six different countries, I have won honours as a player and manager, but taking a national team to a European finals or World Cup finals is something I haven't been able to do. It is one of the few things left which motivates me and I hope this time around I will be able to do it. Put it this way, I would be bitterly disappointed if I was not able to produce the goods this time around."

And yet he would have been aware that disappointment had remained a by-word of the national team. He would have been aware because he had been a part of it himself.

Even the revered Wales side that reached the World Cup did not directly qualify before making it to Sweden in 1958. They'd booked their place at the finals as representatives of the Africa/Asia group after being drawn, as a 'lucky loser' from Europe, for a FIFA-contrived play-off against Israel which had been boycotted by other sides. Without the intervention of politics into sport, the Welsh players would have been relaxing by Mediterranean swimming pools that summer rather than making history in Scandinavia.

Toshack had been part of the team that did top their group on the way to the 1976 European Championships, losing over two legs to Yugoslavia in the quarter-finals. Yet with the competition, at the time, being a home-and-away knock-out until the semi-finals rather than the major summer tournament it is today, it is not – fairly or otherwise – regarded as the exception to what seems to be a Welsh football rule to rue missed opportunities.

Because there had been so many of those missed chances, perhaps explaining why the mood around the national team is so often polarised; it is either the extreme of excited hope and optimism or apathetic disillusionment. The huge fluctuations in the numbers of supporters coming together to see Wales play out their fortunes over their 50-year tournament exile is testament to that.

If such an issue has an air of familiarity, it is not alone. All the way through the sometimes heartbreaking, sometimes hapless story of Wales' wish for a major tournament are tales of problems that were as prevalent following Murphy's men's return from Sweden as they have been in the Premier League era and beyond.

As Wales tried to follow up on the 1958 success with qualification for Chile in 1962, the talismanic John Charles was denied permission by club Juventus to feature in a two-legged game with Spain. With another star name, Tottenham's double-winning Cliff Jones, also missing for the 1961 games through injury, defeat at home and a draw in Madrid denied them a chance of playing-off against Morocco.

The national team's battle with clubs to be able to call upon the best players raged as frustratingly in the sixties as it has done in recent times, not so much a modern ill but a lengthy sickness of which a smaller nation is always more likely to suffer.

It helped ensure a bid for the 1966 World Cup finals, just over the border in England, never really materialised; impressively beating the Soviet Union when qualification was already impossible in that group was another trait Wales have repeated down the years.

Some disappointments have been hidden by history, not having the same impact down the generations as others. The bid to qualify for the 1972 European Championships, for example, came down to the final two fixtures. The first was a clash against Czechoslovakia, when Wales were refused the services of key players because of domestic fixtures being played in England and duly losing narrowly 1-0 in Prague.

So too in 1974, as Toshack emerged in a side also containing the likes of Leighton James and Terry Yorath, the closeness to qualification has been somewhat forgotten. Needing to beat Poland in their final game to leave their fate in the hands of England, they lost 3-0 in what was described as a brutal game in Chorzów with Trevor Hockey becoming the first Wales player ever to be sent off. For the record, Poland and their 'keeper Jan Tomaszewski, famously called a 'clown' by Brian Clough, qualified when they held England at Wembley three weeks later, a result that would have been good enough to send Wales to West Germany.

Even relative success came tinged with sadness when, for the 1976 European Championships, Wales had done superbly to top a group containing Austria, Hungary and Luxembourg with a new side of considerable talent, only to concede after 45 seconds of that quarter-final clash with Yugoslavia in Zagreb on the way to a 2-0 defeat. A 1-1 home draw against a backdrop of disallowed goals, crowd disturbances, refereeing controversy and a missed Yorath penalty saw the visitors progress to the Championship finals held in their own country.

Wearing the now iconic Admiral shirt with its yellow and green trim, the hard-luck tales of that era are just as well-known. Wales had lost once to Scotland in their three-man group for Argentina '78 but an unexpected and impressive 3-0 win in Wrexham over Czechoslovakia encouraged dreams of qualification – only for them to turn to nightmares at Anfield.

Playing in Liverpool – financial need as well as health and safety restrictions ruling out both the Racecourse and Ninian Park – the Tartan Army invaded to turn Anfield into Hampden South. Victory would have meant simply needing to avoid heavy defeat in the final game in Prague, yet Norwich defender David Jones – a late selection to the side – Wurtz, Jordan and Don Masson combined to ensure that Alan Rough's earlier brilliant save from Toshack and Kenny Dalglish's late header were little more than footnotes among the tears.

More supporter saltwater followed four years later, a campaign remembered for the lights failing but with greater actual context in a group from which two qualified. The bid for the World Cup in Spain under Mike England had actually begun with four wins over Iceland, the Czechs and Turkey (twice) before a respectable 0-0 draw with the USSR left Wales three points clear with three games remaining. A team containing the talents of Robbie James and Joey

Jones and buoyed by club success from Toshack's First Division-bound Swans had given genuine belief that Wales had, once again, a side that could compete at the top table, a belief hardened from the 1981 Home Championships where England had been torn apart in Wrexham in a 4-1 victory. The impact of that victory has lived long into fan culture and folklore. The photo of the team, standing proud in the white-sleeved adidas shirt, would later make its way onto iconic t-shirts above the block-lettering boast that Wales were *Gwell Na Lloegr* – Better Than England.

The hope surged through those initial results as Wales entered the decisive period of three fixtures in a fortnight in November 1981. It began with a 2-0 defeat in Prague, including an unfortunate own goal from goalkeeper Dai Davies, but thoughts of Spain '82 remained providing they could beat Iceland at home before a final game in Tiblisi. It is remembered here as the night the lights went out yet, in Iceland, the reason for the failure is less metaphorical.

"Mickey Thomas," said the long-serving Icelandic journalist in disagreement when the floodlight failure of Swansea in 1981 is put to him, uttered with a strange mix of anger at the midfielder's antics and smiling pride at the end result. Thomas, as it turned out, had agreed to be persuaded by a tabloid newspaper to dress up in an ape costume to service the headline of 'making monkeys' out of the unfancied visitors. The aim to win with a qualifying-boosting goal difference of six had already looked shaky when a small fire in the Vetch's electricity generator saw the lights go just before half-time. They then looked foolish when Iceland levelled in the second-half, delayed by a 45-minute half-time break, equalising once more after Alan Curtis had restored the host's lead.

Despite the disappointment of the 2-2 draw, there was still a decider to play against the USSR, but a straight-forward 3-0 defeat left Wales fans waiting for news from Eastern Europe 11 days later in the hope the Soviets would beat Czechoslovakia in the final game in Tiblisi. The news the fans received was not good: a 1-1 draw in Bratislava saw Wales stay at home by the virtue of goal difference.

The by now familiar 'so close yet so far' recurring theme returned only two years later. With two group games remaining, a team now with the potency of rookie poacher Ian Rush needed just two points to qualify for France's 1984 European Championships. Unbeaten in their first four games, they lost in Bulgaria and conceded a late leveller against old foes Yugoslavia at Ninian Park. Even then, a draw or slender Bulgarian victory against the Yugoslavs in Split one week later would give Wales a pathway to Paris that no-one would turn down.

Even without the current methods of live blogs or rolling score updates from 24-hour sports channels, there were ways and means – mainly through radio reports – of hoping against hope that Bulgaria could gift wrap Welsh progress just a few days before Christmas 1983. Going into the final minute, it seemed they had delivered with the 2-2 scoreline, enough for Wales to top the group by virtue of a plus one goal difference. Little more than thirty seconds before the final whistle sounded, Partizan Belgrade defender Ljubomir Radanović headed a winner to leave the Mike England-managed Wales side heartbroken once more.

It was a huge disappointment, one compounded by the FAW's financial worries following the ending, by England and Scotland in 1984, of the World's oldest international tournament, the British Home Championship, which in turn saw hopes to make the Wales manager's role a full-time one, shelved. The mood did not lighten when, again hampered by end of season absentees, they began the bid for Mexico 1986 with an embarrassing 1-0 defeat in Iceland in June, the hosts way short of the strength they have displayed in more modern times.

The absence of Ian Rush meant a lack of goals and defeat in Spain promptly followed, although the emergence of a young Mark Hughes at least gave something to hold onto in the four-team group, he and Icelandic anti-hero Mickey Thomas earned a 2-1 win against the side from the Nordic island going into the second-half of the campaign.

With Neville Southall and Kevin Ratcliffe also among the ranks, Rush's goal in Glasgow sealed a 1-0 win over Scotland before Sparky sealed a place in history, and highlight videos for decades to come, as Spain visited the Racecourse. The volley in front of the Kop still defies belief as much as the scoreline, the 3-0 success one of those nights often recalled by fans when describing their own 'I was there' moments, even if they could only have dreamed to have seen Hughes' acrobatics in person.

It built towards another Scottish showdown, a Welsh win enough to book a two-legged play-off against Australia, the winners of the Oceanic group, with Spain likely to gain a big enough win over Iceland to take the only automatic spot. A Ninian Park draw, though, would be enough for Jock Stein's side and, on a night of genuine tragedy as opposed to simply a sporting one, they got what they came for. In a horrible flashback of the agonies of Anfield, it was another penalty that would do for Wales. They had taken the lead and, seemingly, the control of the game and their destiny when Hughes opened early on. Yet, with ten minutes to go, David Phillips could not get away from the ball blasted at him inside his own box and, while more debatable than Jordan's 'Hand of Jaws' incident, Davie Cooper's resulting score could not stop the self-pity of the denied thousands inside Cardiff City's home.

What they couldn't have known at the time was the toll the drama had taken on Stein, the legendary former Celtic manager who had once played for Llanelli Town before becoming of the very best of 'Bhoys'. Already said to be suffering with poor health, he never recovered from the heart attack he suffered soon after Scotland's decisive goal and was pronounced dead in the ambulance outside the ground. Mike England could not have known this as he was held back from remonstrating with the referee in the dressing room area immediately after the game.

Scotland would go to the World Cup under the stewardship of Stein's assistant, Alex Ferguson, while Wales would look towards the 1988 Euros for their next hope of changing fortunes. They found none, even if their bid took them closer than many may recall.

The outstanding talents of Southall, Rush and Hughes always gave a chance and, with two games remaining, Wales definitely had a realistic one after an unbeaten start included a draw in Czechoslovakia and a win over a Denmark side that had captured the attention of the world in Mexico, courtesy of Michael Laudrup and Preben Elkjær. Coupled with Finland's surprise win over the Czechs, Wales faced two games in the final month knowing a draw in Denmark and something similar in Prague would suffice. A suspect offside goal from Elkjær in Copenhagen and a injury crisis that would force Hughes to play for Wales in the afternoon and new club Bayern Munich the same evening led to the inevitable in Czechoslovakia. Wales were out and so was manager England.

After initially courting Clough the FAW turned to Yorath, although guiding the team to qualification for Italia '90 after being paired with the European champions the Netherlands and world champions elect West Germany would probably have proven to be beyond any managerial mind.

So it turned out, despite brave performances against the Ruud Gullit-fuelled Dutch and a 0-0 draw with the Germans at Welsh football's new home at the National Stadium. Though the move to the home of Welsh rugby only saw a slow take-up from fans, there was a platform for something better and even an uninspiring friendly against Costa Rica, ahead of the Euro '92 qualifiers, offered a glimpse of the future as a young midfielder from Leeds United made his debut. Gary Speed fitted the burgeoning new image of football that the World Cup in Italy had sparked, the brightness out of the gloom of the eighties, yet his poster-boy looks of himself and those of another teenager who would come onto the Welsh scene by the end of the campaign were all underpinned by the fact he was a superb footballer.

He was, though, still raw for the group opener where the trinity of Hughes, Rush and Dean Saunders all scored in a 3-1 win over a Belgium side that had taken England so close in the summer tournament just a few months earlier.

The momentum and excitement continued with a hard-fought win in Luxembourg and a draw in Brussels. It all led to an Arms Park sell-out in June 1991, where the newly unified Germany were beaten for the first time since winning the World Cup 12 months earlier, Paul Bodin's searching pass devoured by Rush as he raced past Guido Buchwald and slotted past Bodo Illgner.

Football's arguably greater profile saw Wales' victory gain global attention which piled on greater hope and expectation amongst the fans, a sense only heightened when Brazil were beaten in a Cardiff friendly at the start of the following season. Yet the truth of Welsh fragility was exposed when, missing a glut of experienced, if not star, players, a 4-1 defeat ensued in Nuremberg with Saunders being sent off.

It marked the end of any realistic chances of qualification – Germany's win in Brussels after Wales' win over Luxembourg through a Bodin penalty confirming it – but it also marked the first cap for Ryan Giggs, breaking John Charles' record as Wales' youngest international when he joined Speed off the bench in Germany.

Attention turned to the new horizon of America and the 1994 World Cup, but on the same night that most watched Barcelona's 1992 Dream Team capture the European Cup at Wembley, Wales suffered an opening nightmare in Romania as their own exciting side, led by the irresistible Gheorghe Hagi, cantered to a 5-1 win in Bucharest.

Yet, as the game came and went, the qualifying group would see-saw. Wales exchanged 2-0 scorelines with Belgium, the Republic of Czechs and Slovaks (RCS) were held to draws twice, and the minnows of the Faroe Islands and Cyprus both dispatched.

With Speed now a central figure along with established stars Rush, Hughes, Saunders and Southall, and Ratcliffe having rolled back the years – despite by this time playing among the lower tiers with Cardiff – while the likes of Barry Horne added the steel, Wales had a competitive and settled side. Most significantly they had Giggs, with Yorath having little compunction in allowing him a freedom to attack sides and the Manchester United headline grabber only too willing to do so with his goals against Belgium and the RCS illustrating as much.

With the strains of *'Can't Take My Eyes Off You'* used in BBC promotions, the Wales supporters were only too happy to tell this side *'I Love You Baby'* as the excitement and unity of the squad oozed out towards the date with destiny on November 17, 1993.

Four sides – Wales, Belgium, RCS and Romania – could all qualify and, while the mathematics had been made clear, there was a sense that the workings out could come later given that Yorath's side needed to win first and foremost before worrying about needing to boost their goal difference. Had the RCS beaten Belgium by one goal, Wales would need to win by two, yet no-one was in any doubt that simply getting past the talented Romanians would be a tough enough, especially with Hughes suspended.

Yet the state of euphoria and belief around the country suggested that, surely, things would fall into place this time. It is perhaps why there was such eerie silence when Hagi struck after the half-hour mark, the incredulity of both the script not being followed and the usually faultless Southall seemingly letting the shot slip past him, striking dumb the capacity crowd.

Wales rallied, levelling through Saunders and then, as Speed burst into the crowded area soon after, winning the penalty that all believed had the passport to the World Cup final stamped upon it. The rattle of the bar and a thousand 'what if' stories told the tale of Bodin's smashed attempt. Instead of Romania collapsing, they countered and scored the reality-dawning second with seven minutes remaining.

Again, the disappointment became intertwined with real tragedy when a fan was killed by a flare set off at the final whistle. This offered a sense of perspective, but even then there was a feeling that the sporting disappointment had hit harder than many of the previous 'so near and yet so far' failures.

Yorath would be axed – cueing the 47-day stay of Toshack – and the problems the Spanish-based boss spoke of became apparent as the side failed to rise above a continuing slump.

Indeed, if anything spelt out what was to follow, it came at the very start of their Euro '96 bid, where it was not so much 'Football's Coming Home' as the ramming home of the point that qualification was to be as far off as ever.

Wales did not catch the eye as they expectedly beat Albania in the home opener, Chris Coleman marking his move from reserve to regular centre-back with his first goal in a 2-0 win, but eyes were certainly opened with two trips from hell.

Moldova had never hosted a competitive international game before Wales, now back under the charge of 1970s manager Mike Smith, travelled to capital Chişinău, the city historically known as Kishinev. The problems had begun long before the withdrawals of Giggs, Rush, Saunders and Hughes through a mixture of injury and suspension. There had been issues even getting to the country for the standard reconnaissance trips and it was only by chance that then general secretary Alun Evans had been selected as a delegate for a UEFA Cup game in the city in the month before the October 1994 game. Evans had opted out of eating some of the food offered and it was perhaps not a coincidence he avoided the food poisoning that befell some of his colleagues. He returned to Cardiff with information of the poverty experienced, but without some of the items he had packed in his suitcase.

The FAW opted to send a private chef for the first time and took nothing for granted by packing items such as toilet rolls and bath plugs. Players had been primed for what to expect and yet they still were shocked as they slept in their team tracksuits and shared their mattresses with cockroaches, with one star's sleep interrupted by an intruder looking for valuables.

Training had to be scheduled to fit with when the hotel could provide running water – "And when it did come out of the shower it was brown," recalled striker Nathan Blake – while there had even been arguments about the gas being turned off before the team's meals were prepared as the hotel's quota had been used up.

Still, Wales had been expected to ease to victory through a mixture of the remaining confidence in the side that had gone so close less than 12 months earlier and ignorance of the strength of the new national sides emerging from the old Eastern Bloc.

But Wales did not help themselves. While the lack of information about their hosts was perhaps understandable, players went into the game with frustration over their preparation and with a desire to get back home as soon as possible.

"If ever poor preparation led to a poor performance this was it," said Barry Horne, the captain at the time. "We were confident in ourselves but I'm not sure we had the confidence in the infrastructure. We hadn't wanted Terry to go and after John left, Mike Smith got the job almost by default. He was a lovely man, make no mistake, but he was probably out of his depth."

While Horne's words came after the benefit of two decades of reflection, the 5-0 defeat in the war-zone of Georgia a month later meant plenty were willing to make a similar assessment as the yearning for the Yorath days went on, even if the Georgians had proven themselves to be far too technically gifted to be considered a minnow.

An experienced, ageing squad was supplemented by the likes of John Hartson coming through, but little could put a shine on the slide into embarrassment with not even a battling draw with Germany allowing anyone to pretend all was well. The final insult to supporters came as the controversial Vinnie Jones, new dragon tattoo and all after the discovery of a Welsh grandfather, was sent off for stamping in the home game with Georgia. The match marked the end of manager Smith, though not of the dark days of disappointment.

If supporters had spent their time discussing a new manager, the name of Bobby Gould had probably not come up in the conversation. It appeared it had with the FAW decision-makers, said to have been won over in an impassioned interview after he was encouraged to throw his hat into the ring on a chance visit to Cardiff.

Though it did not appear so in the final death throes of the European qualifiers – Wales finishing bottom having been unable to beat Albania away – there was a glimpse of why Gould might have impressed. He was bubbly, forever with a smile which the national side had seen little of, and he recognised the need to try and freshen things up, even if picking a fight with Rush and Hughes did little to endear him to the Welsh public. Both had been dropped for the Albania game and Rush's career came to an almost unwilling end when he was substituted early on in a 3-0 friendly defeat in Italy. The striker had gone from being tipped as the people's choice for the manager's job to that of an ex-player. Hughes managed to inch his way back in after what Gould delightfully called a meeting of "controlled aggression".

There was even a defeat to Leyton Orient as a full-strength Wales – Giggs *et al* – lost to the lowly fourth-tier side in a game designed as a warm-up for the first France '98 qualifier against San Marino. So it was to pass that on 25 May 1996, after John Robinson had cancelled out teenager Lee Shearer's opener with ten minutes to go, a trialist by the name of Peter Garland who had been released by Charlton made history and provided headline writers with an unexpected treat. The Daily Mirror's 'O's Stuff the Tragic Dragon' was one of the kinder ones.

At least the national side managed to beat Cwmbrân later that summer, with Gould unbelievably taking the place of Speed to score one of the goals in a 6-1 warm-up win over the Welsh League side. Incredibly, the Welsh press pack had also served as opposition at the National Stadium a few days before one qualifier.

Regardless, back-to-back wins over San Marino either side of the off-season at least gave reason for some optimism, even if reality suggested that the Dutch would cruise to qualification to leave Gould's Wales facing the unlikely challenge of bettering both Belgium and Turkey.

Granted, Saunders' early goal against the Netherlands in Cardiff had pointed towards chances of one of those scalps that campaigns can be built upon, but the truth was Wales were reliant on Southall and three goals inside seven minutes meant the game edged away as the class of the Oranje told.

Gould decided he needed something different for the return match in Eindhoven a month later in November 1996, namely a new captain due to Horne's absence. The decision was made following a secret ballot cast amongst players, though even now it is a struggle to find a player who is prepared to concede to voting for the eventual winner and wearer of the armband on a night that is remembered as among the worst in the national side's history of extremes.

Desperate measures in desperate times, new skipper Vinnie Jones reportedly issued a rallying cry in the tunnel of the Philips Stadion, perhaps in an attempt to unsettle the Dutch in the same way that he and other Crazy Gang members had done to more gifted rivals in domestic football with Wimbledon. Dennis Bergkamp, in that ice cold manner he had, stared straight ahead.

"They gave us a difficult game for five or six minutes," said Guus Hiddink, cuttingly accurate. Southall described it as his greatest game and, indeed, it could have been a lot worse were it not for the goalkeeping great. Gould blamed the education of both coaches and players in British football in a glimpse of understanding of the greater problem facing Wales. He had a valid point but it was difficult to show too much empathy alongside the embarrassment as Gould's good intentions also foundered, his laughs not disguising the feeling of many Welsh football fans that their pride had become a laughing stock. The manager once wore a Max Wall mask at a press conference in a bid to show he could poke fun at himself, trying not to take to heart the 'Muppet' jibes he faced when finding himself locked in the changing rooms after strangely organising the Wales team to train at Usk prison where, to his credit, the facilities were seen as better than many others in the area.

There was the more ugly fall-out with Nathan Blake over alleged racist jibes about the colour of his training top, for which Gould apologised and denied being racist. There was an allegation he ordered Hartson to grapple with him inside a circle of players after a fall-out to clear the air, which left the manager with scratches and the striker uncomfortable with the bizarre situation.

Players found it a struggle and withdrawals were increasingly commonplace, Horne retiring and the criticism flooding in. Toshack was among his critics as Wales lost 6-4 in Istanbul, where Southall's Wales career ended in similar fashion to that of Rush when he was hauled off before time by Gould.

Toshack had bluntly questioned the naïve defending and the sudden change of tactics mid-way through the first-half, prompting Gould to study the tapes and ask for a right of reply on the BBC. It was granted with Gould's well-meaning defence undermined by the need to correct him for calling his questioner John Fashanu rather than John Toshack.

The verve and national confidence of Cool Cymru was building and yet there were no signs of the buzz being replicated by the nation's football team, with the cries of the Manic Street Preachers – who had changed the chorus lyrics at Welsh concerts from '*Everything Must Go*' to '*Bobby Gould Must Go*' – falling on deaf ears.

Indirectly the blame can be partly laid at the door of Craig Bellamy. Tensions were rising between Gould and his players. New captain Speed had torn into his manager after a 4-0 defeat to Tunisia ahead of the Euro 2000 campaign and there had been several senior players allegedly rushing to confront Gould when he publicly admonished and banned Robbie Savage from the team hotel after a TV skit where he had thrown away a Paulo Maldini shirt.

Gould, though, was to enjoy arguably his finest moment as manager just a month after the opening 2-0 defeat to the Azzuri, when a teenage Bellamy showed the talent he would showcase for years to come as he headed Wales to a shock 2-1 win in Denmark. Dean Saunders, an arch-critic of the manager, said to the young goalscorer, perhaps only half-joking, that he had kept Gould in a job.

A pulsating win over Belarus at Ninian Park followed four days later and suddenly Gould's escape door to keeping his job had opened.

By the March it had closed a little as Wales went down quite dismally to Switzerland in Zürich. By June it had slammed shut, both for qualification and on Gould.

There are various claims of players picking the team in Bologna, of Gould leaving players out by mistake and correcting the teamsheet when it was pointed out inside the dressing room, but the only known fact was that, after a 4-0 defeat, Gould faced up to his own shortcomings and quit. It is not unfair to say the news had sparked smiles and celebrations among players as much as there had been among supporters.

And so to Sparky, the man who Gould had gone against so early into his reign and yet who had remained. It was he who the FAW turned to, after initial links with Terry Venables and Roy Hodgson, taking the job part-time as he continued playing in the Premier League with Southampton and then Blackburn.

It all meant a new millennium, a new hope – literally as the 74,500 Millennium Stadium opened its doors to football and saw crowds flood in to watch friendly defeats to Finland and Brazil. At that point, fans were simply keen to sample the atmosphere of the impressive new venue lodged in the centre of the capital city.

They were not alone, with Giggs playing his first friendly since first pulling on a Wales shirt. He would be injured for the defeat to Brazil but still joined up with the squad with the hope his relationship with former club and country teammate Hughes would lead to a revival of his form and talismanic capabilities in the coming campaign. The mouth-watering combination of Hughes and Giggs had already been witnessed, with the pair celebrating together as the previous turbulent campaign's penultimate game finished with victory in Belarus, Giggs grabbing the winner.

Progress was to be slow, however.

While Gould won some praise from some for trying to look at the set-up below the senior team, critics of Hughes suggested he focussed too much on the senior squad. Yet it is hard to fault that Hughes saw obvious things at senior level that needed to be addressed in the first instance, a lack of perceived professionalism in the national team being among them whether it was from training, preparation, travel and even clothing. The phrase 'Ragbag Rovers' had cropped up in conversation around Wales more than once, Hughes among those using it.

"It's something I was always aware of when I was a player," Hughes said after settling into the role. "International football should be the pinnacle. Yet when I was a player, I would team up from a top club and not necessarily feel it was a step up. I used to think to myself, 'There's something totally wrong here'."

Hughes' mantra was to keep the top-level players comfortable with familiar surroundings and inspire the lower-level ones, or young hopefuls, by opening their eyes to what off-the-field standards should have been like. At the very least, it proved popular with players who had a growing sense they finally had the tools they needed for success and enjoying the thought of representing their country following the years where there was a sense of simply doing their duty.

Gould had attempted change but it was Hughes who had the power to implement it fully, both with his recent experience of what was required at the top level for players to perform, and also his status. While suggestions that Gould was not helped by his Englishness perhaps miss his various other perceived failings, it is no mistake that Hughes' position as a hero to fans – and even to many in his dressing room – helped him make things happen.

Things weren't quite happening on the field however, certainly not as quick as some would have liked. A string of friendly losses was followed by defeat to Belarus, again a qualifying opponent, in a group for World Cup 2002 that had no big name but big challenges in the shape of Ukraine, Poland and Norway as well as the awkward Belarussians and Armenia.

One month on, in October 2000, the feeling was Wales needed to beat Norway to create the momentum missing in their last three campaigns. A 50,000-plus crowd were willing it to come when Blake opened the scoring on the hour with a towering header to meet Speed's cross, only for the visitors to level in the final ten minutes and the criticism to flow.

Dai Davies and Mark Aizelwood were among those delivering it but Toshack was the one that provided the headlines, especially when it was Giggs who received particular attention as he asked: "Is it too much to ask for him to get to the bye-line six times?"

Players responded to the criticism following the draw, as did Hughes when he suggested there was now a growing siege mentality in his ranks that he would try and use to his advantage.

"They are very together as a group and deserve to succeed," said Hughes of his players. "They read criticism that is unjust but they have to use it to motivate themselves. If people want to criticise easy targets then they have to live with it. People are entitled to their opinions but it doesn't mean I must respect them."

A 0-0 draw in Warsaw four days later, albeit one that had little attacking thrust, was a better response.

"Many people did not believe that we could do this and it is testimony to my players' will that we have got a result to be proud of," said Hughes.

"I did not have to motivate them but I will admit there have been emotional things said about certain subjects in the dressing-room afterwards. I don't really want to dwell on it, as the manner of their performance said everything."

Disappointing draws in Armenia and Ukraine followed, the latter after Wales had taken the lead through Hartson who had also bagged a brace in difficult conditions in the Armenia capital, Yerevan. Then Wales took on group leaders Poland where another lead came but another loss followed, though an impressive draw in Kiev at least kept the slim hopes of qualification brewing into the following season.

They did not last long with Giggs sent off in a 3-2 defeat to Norway in Oslo, the first red card in his career sparked after two cautions, the first of which was somewhat softly given for questioning the referee.

It might be too much to say pressure was building on Hughes but the way he questioned the decision – "I'm sure the referee will go home to his wife and boast about sending off Ryan Giggs" – suggested he was at least feeling the strain that the efforts and expectation of something better was not turning into results.

Only 18,000 had watched the preceding 0-0 draw with Armenia at the Millennium and, while this was an upturn on the 5,064 that had witnessed Hughes' first game in charge, it was a sign that some of that millennial optimism had sagged as the team equalled the unwanted record of a dozen games without a win.

Hughes was aware that the tag of the worst Wales side in history – undoubtedly unfair in terms of quality if not statistics – would dog him if they could not provide victory over Belarus in the final qualifier, and thankfully his players finally delivered. Hartson showed he could lead a line with his power and fourth goal of the campaign, while Speed's move to left-back helped steady a defence to provide a platform for the creativity of Simon Davies, with the knowledge that Bellamy and Giggs could spur a fully fit side going into the Euro 2004 qualifiers. More than anything, while leads had been squandered, they appeared a more organised team on the field that had begun to reflect similar standards off it. They had won just once, but had drawn six and just needed to push themselves a stride or so in the right direction to fully put the depression of the Smith and Gould eras behind them.

What really pressed home Hughes' point, that lying ahead was perhaps better times than those suggested by the 101st position in the FIFA rankings, came in a February friendly with Argentina. Arranged so the South Americans could experience atmosphere under a closed roof as they would face in that summer's World Cup in Japan – and against old rivals England – Wales in turn used the game for their own advantage. The 1-1 draw did not give a pretence that Wales could match the class of the likes of Juan Sebastian Veron or Juan Román Riquelme, but the battle and energy of Savage was typical of what Wales could offer when quality was lacking, while Bellamy's goal underlined what a threat he and they could also be.

The fans came back for the glamour game – 65,000 of them – meaning a feel-good surge flowed into a friendly draw with the Czech Republic the following month, a game where the calm and classy centre-back Danny Gabbidon offered hope he had the top-level ability to flourish despite playing third tier football with Cardiff City, and thus seemingly solving a problem position.

And then, one month before yet another World Cup without Wales, Gabbidon's fellow and free-scoring Bluebird Robert Earnshaw helped sink Germany 1-0 just shy of 11 years on from Rush's similar feat. Earnshaw liked to be called the Zambian Prince to reflect his African background, though his Caerphilly upbringing, perma-smile and passion in grabbing the higher-level opportunity after his efforts with his club left no-one in doubt his happiness being able to represent the 'Land of My Fathers'. The 21-year-old debutant's expression was in stark contrast to the stern features of beaten German goalkeeper Oliver Khan who was to win the FIFA Golden Ball for best player at the World Cup two months later, and Earnshaw's trademarked somersault celebration after beating him was used by marketing men in the Far East ahead of the tournament. Suddenly Wales were getting the kind of publicity they had wanted rather than dreaded over the previous decade.

Hughes wanted to show his team meant business, an idea given further backing with a warm-up draw in Croatia where Simon Davies scored a superb solo effort; the lack of footage of which unfairly robbed him of internet immortality. Still, a win was needed in Finland to really throw things forward towards a Euro 2004 group also containing perennial superpowers Italy, Serbia & Montenegro – the remaining nations of the old Yugoslavia team – and the unknowns of Azerbaijan.

The fitness and availability of Bellamy did cause concern, the livewire having played limited football for Newcastle because of a knee problem, but he was ready to argue his case with Sir Bobby Robson and Hughes was ready to get firm and utilise FIFA call-up rules. Robson relented and even a missed flight connection did not stop Bellamy arriving in Helsinki. An £8,000 charter flight later and Bellamy was on the bench, emerging from it after an hour to help ensure Davies added to Hartson's opener that had set the ball rolling.

A month later and both the buzz and the belief that had been so longed for had returned. A sell-out for the visit of the Italians ensured an emotionally-charged evening, made even more so by the presentation of John Charles – Wales' great and Juventus' *Il Gigante Buono* (The Gentle Giant) – before kick-off. There was a sense something special was in the air and Hughes had done much to try and calm his men to not let the occasion overawe them – it having been so long since any of them had tasted such an atmosphere, in their country's colours at any rate.

"There was a buzz around the build-up to the game, so Sparky was pretty relaxed about letting us go out and having a few beers on the Sunday as long as we didn't go overboard," recalled John Hartson in 2012, explaining the unlikely role the Halfway Inn public house near his Trallwn home on the outskirts of Swansea had in the famous night. "So I took a few of the boys, about six or seven, down to my mate's pub and we relaxed over a couple.

"I can remember me and Gary Speed up on the karaoke singing a couple of Stereophonics songs.

"It was a great way for us to unwind a bit, let off steam ahead of all the build-up – and then get on with the job.

"We didn't have to get up for it, you never do playing for Wales, let alone against a side like Italy at a packed Millennium, but Sparky had this trick where he had arranged for a video to be made for the bus journey from the hotel to the ground. It featured clips of all of us playing: me and Bellas scoring goals, Speedo making a great pass, Sav getting stuck in, Giggsy beating a man, defenders clearing off the line. It made you feel 10 feet tall, reminding you that you could do it, but it also made you feel good about the others around you.

"You looked around and saw this group of players, such a strong side, lads in their prime or with experience of having been there and done it. It was all timed, so by the time it finished we were right in the city centre, seeing all the fans and ready to take on the world. Then the atmosphere when we got on the pitch was incredible. It's not often the Italians are intimidated."

They appeared to be; suggestions of all not being well in the Azzurri camp were one thing but the way in which Wales went about them was quite another. Davies opened the scoring after 20 minutes from a tight angle and, after a deflected Alessandro del Piero equaliser, Bellamy expertly rounded Gianluigi Buffon having collected a knock-down from Hartson that would have made Charles smile.

Wales refused to be slowed by the difficult trip to Azerbaijan, Hughes taking on former boss Ferguson for the availability of Giggs for the November fixture and attempting to ease the difficulty of the travelling by keeping players and staff on British time rather than counter the four-hour difference following the 3,000 mile trip. It helped an injury-hit side ease to a fairly uncomplicated 2-0 win in Baku.

It was even more straightforward when the Azeris arrived in a sun-kissed Cardiff the following March, the visitors dispatched 4-0 with fans singing songs of Portugal aware of the fact they were five points ahead of Italy with four games remaining.

Certainly no-one was particularly perturbed by the fact the second fixture of that week had been postponed, the trip to Belgrade cancelled after the assassination of Prime Minister Zoran Đinđić and rescheduled for August.

What they weren't to know was that they would be hampered by injury and lack of preparation time in the early season affair, with Hartson a significant loss. Yet it was more Hughes' tactics that fingers pointed at, deemed too negative against subdued hosts and then caught when Dragan Mladenović scored with 17 minutes remaining.

Toshack was again forthright, saying that Wales had been "lulled into a false sense of security".

"If we had gone in with a little bit more ambition, we could have won," the former Real Madrid manager had said. "There were inroads there for people to make."

To his credit, Bellamy had admitted that Wales – and he – could have done more going forward, but Hughes was having little of it.

"Perhaps people have been waiting this long to have their say," said Hughes, referring to Toshack and the defeat being Wales' first in competitive football in a little less than two years.

It appeared to bristle with Hughes who failed to grasp why the approach would attract criticism. To some it was a risk to rely on other fixtures rather than seizing the moment, but perhaps Hughes' confidence in himself and his team extended to the forthcoming fixture with Italy in Milan.

It was misplaced, Wales eventually outclassed after holding out for 59 minutes before Filippo Inzaghi scored three times inside 11 minutes with del Piero converting a penalty for good measure and added Millennium revenge.

Bellamy, as so often, pulled no punches when asked for his thoughts before leaving the San Siro. "We got battered out there."

Hughes had produced a dressing room dressing down his old Manchester United manager might have been proud of, but quickly spent the Sunday back in south Wales attempting to pick up players who had fallen hard from the high expectations and higher hopes.

"The way I felt after the game on Saturday was the worst I have ever felt," said skipper Speed, who admitted the occasion of his 34th birthday the day after the defeat had passed him by. "After a defeat like that, you don't feel physically dreadful, but mentally you do. It is complete shock, quite hard to describe really. But it is part of my job as captain to pick everybody up."

And yet the sneaking suspicion was that Wales would struggle to do so as they faced Finland in Cardiff just a few days later. Deep down the sense was that Italy would now win the group and Wales just needed the point to guarantee a play-off place, something that easily would have been considered a success before the start of the campaign. A predictable 1-1 draw followed, a result that rendered Italy's own dropping of points in Belgrade meaningless.

Wales would stumble further over the finish line as they lost 3-2 to Serbia & Montenegro a month later in the final game. Wales were without momentum going into the play-offs and also without Bellamy who had pushed his knee problems as far as they could go to make the games against Italy and Finland.

The celebrations were hardly that of securing the play-off berth, both Bellamy and Speed almost speaking the fans' words and concerns for them as the striker noted the sides in the draw included Spain and the Netherlands, while the captain was much more cutting regardless of potential opponents. "If we carry on as we are we won't get through the play-offs," Speed said ominously.

Hughes was more upbeat as Wales were paired with Russia in the draw two days later with the potentially crucial second-leg at home. Russian media spoke of their luck at being drawn with Wales – Hughes even claimed the Russian delegate was whispering 'Wales, Wales' under his breath once his country's name came out of the hat – and their coach Georgi Yartsev claimed it would be "unthinkable" not to qualify but, by the time Hughes' side travelled to Moscow, the belief had crept back for such do-or-die circumstances.

"Four years' hard work comes down to the outcome of 180 minutes' of football," said Hughes reflecting on the journey to this point. "Two initial years were a case of trying to get us to where we needed to be for this campaign, and so it's been a long period in which we've worked very hard. We want to make sure that we complete the job now."

Despite such stern warnings of the stakes, there were smiles from the team as they donned the traditional *ushanka* and strolled around the sights of Red Square, more so than some of the fans that had encountered plenty of intimidation with one hotel coming under something of a siege in the hours before kick-off at Locomotiv Stadium.

Inside, the atmosphere could have easily daunted, the Russian national anthem itself serving to unnerve, while flares emerged from every part of the ground. Wales stood tall though, several such as Darren Barnard of Grimsby playing beyond themselves while Jason Koumas – so talented but often so frustrating – offered a far more mature performance.

Only one player seemed shaken, though it came with just cause. Yartsev had already said Giggs, Wales' most obvious target and threat, had to be "neutralised" and several visiting players had been left angered by his treatment. One challenge from Vadim Evseev saw Giggs snap and aim a throw of an elbow at the right-back. He escaped punishment before the second-leg in Cardiff where Hughes had hoped the hard work in Moscow would set-up for the end of the seemingly ever-lasting cycle of hope and heartbreak.

"Each and every one of the players knew they had to produce a big performance," said Hughes of the 0-0, revving his men up for what laid in store in Cardiff. "You only get so many chances. We've had false dawns before and we don't want any more glorious failures. It's time Welsh football qualified for something."

And yet all that was found on November 19 2003, ten years and two days after Romania, was another near miss.

It was an Evseev header after 22 minutes which decided this would be a night to forget rather than remember, the game even denied the drama of the 1993 'so close, but yet so far' failure.

There were three chances, Giggs going closest when he clipped a post, but Russia had been worthy winners. The atmosphere at the Millennium, initially one of fervour and hope, quickly turned into one of resignation and regret.

Self-belief had seeped out of Welsh shirts as the visitors appeared to rise to the occasion and above the physical demands of playing two tension-filled games in the space of four days.

Hughes again faced criticism for refusing to be more adventurous as it became obvious the chance was slipping away. The question being begged to ask was for how long, given the age of some of Wales' loyal servants and – despite some of his critics – Hughes attracting the attention of Premier League clubs, would it take for him to land a first role in club management.

There was an appeal when it emerged Yigor Titov, the Spartak Moscow midfielder, failed a drugs test for use of a stimulant named Bromantan. He did not play in the first leg but started the decisive Cardiff match and played for 59 minutes, the FAW appealing to UEFA to have the result overturned and Hughes even backing the bid to take it to the Court of Arbitration for Sport after the initial appeal was rejected. The sense from many, though, was it was a wasted exercise and simply another story of hard-luck, almost bordering on self-pity, to add to the heartbreak that had gone before. The mountain of missed opportunities had been added to. Everest remained unclimbed.

3

The Darkness Before The Dawn

"Another five-star hotel boys. Look out the window, if the waves are making a noise in the evening, just phone down and we'll see if we can move you over to one of the rooms on the other side of the hotel"
– John Toshack

There wasn't an appetite for change.

As Wales began the bid to reach the 2006 World Cup in Germany – that mountain still there – few wanted much change to the set-up and side that had come so close a mere 11 months earlier; fewer still saw the need for it.

John Toshack wasn't among them. Rarely was he shy in letting that standpoint be known, either.

As Wales kicked-off in the Saturday evening heat of September in Baku, it had not escaped the manager turned pundit that the average age of the side had crept steadily beyond the 30 mark.

It had not concerned many, even if some of the spark of Sparky's reign had seemingly waned with the winless end to the previous campaign.

The idea that the side had become negative, or at the very least cautious, wasn't one held by the majority and, given the repetitive speculation of a move into club football, nor it seemed were Premier League chairmen worried.

But something wasn't quite right as the side drew in Azerbaijan and then drew at home to Northern Ireland in a match that included elements of the comical and farcical, from James Collins' slip on his competitive debut that saw David Healy add to Jeff Whitley's opener, to Robbie Savage's ninth-minute sending off for squaring up to Michael Hughes having been wound up by his opponent. It would not be the last time the midfielder would fall so easily into a trap laid for him.

The groans returned, even if the full stadium had remained, and it may well have been the final straw for Hughes who agreed to take over from Graeme Souness at Blackburn Rovers a week later, the club he had been playing for just months before the start of the Euro 2004 campaign. At the time, the promise to remain in charge for the final two fixtures of the year a month later seemed a sensible one for the FAW to agree with, one to enable them good time to prepare a proper search for a successor.

And yet it is difficult to ignore the wondering whether the situation would have been the same had one of those final fixtures not been the old enemy at Old Trafford.

When the draw was made in December 2003, the excitement of a 'Battle of Britain' buzzed around Wales, a first match with England in 20 years since the Three Lions were tamed 1-0 at the Racecourse in May 1984, with Hughes himself the only goalscorer.

When the game approached, the feeling was one of a cup final but the sense that this was a match of equals was misplaced. An injury to the veteran Andy Melville in the warm-up did not aid Wales' situation and ultimately, while it still needed a spectacular goal from David Beckham to seal things after Frank Lampard's deflected opener, it was a straightforward win for Sven-Göran Eriksson's side with Hughes thankful for goalkeeper Paul Jones' ability to keep it a contest for as long as he could.

England were a side moving steadily towards qualification, Wales were sliding towards uncertainty.

A defeat to Poland did not aid matters. In the lead-up to the game, players spoke more in the media about who they wanted to replace Hughes than the qualifying campaign that remained in front of them. Or, perhaps more pertinently, who they didn't want.

It became even clearer after the defeat that summed up the end of Hughes' reign, the disappointment rising as much as a fear of what was next. Whether it was just typical of his full-on commitment and desire to win for his country or a more significant sign of the feeling at the time, it was difficult not to take note of Craig Bellamy sat in the centre-circle removing his boots before slowly making his way to the tunnel in his socks, head bowed.

By this point Toshack was the favourite to replace Hughes, although only with bookmakers, with plenty of fans sharing what seemed to be the concerns of senior players in appointing the former centre-forward. Speed was the man many wanted, the midfielder having retired from international football on 85 caps on that October night. It says much about his influence even at 35 that Wales were still level when he was withdrawn to the standing ovation his efforts deserved.

That the same kind of gamble taken on Hughes should be followed by one taken on the then Bolton midfielder was made quite clear by players speaking out at the Millennium that evening. Change was coming, but the call was for it to be minimal.

The decision-makers did not – nor the man they would appoint – see it the same way.

Speed was not so sure. Whether it was a genuine feeling he was not ready, or that he still felt he had more to give as a Premier League player – something backed up by the further four years he would play in the top-flight, reaching 614 appearances in the highest division – or an inkling that the FAW were not truly prepared to consider 'another Sparky', was not clear. Neither, in the end, was it relevant.

There are some suggestions that he at least discussed the possibility with club manager Sam Allardyce before going public with his feelings. "If you've got aspirations to be a manager, obviously coaching your country would be a great honour," Speed said. "But you only get one shot at it and for me this time I don't think I could give it my full attention. We want the best man for the job and I don't think that's me at the moment. I definitely won't be applying for it."

With no FAW approach forthcoming, there were suggestions Speed would follow Hughes to Blackburn as an assistant, though ultimately Speed remained at Bolton – the club he had joined from Newcastle that summer – and would observe Wales as a fan for the next few years.

Instead, Hughes took with him coach Eddie Niedzwiecki and former Wales No. 2 Mark Bowen meaning this now appeared a full rebuild job for whoever took over, though he would be able to have a back room team to call his own.

Few were surprised that Brian Flynn and Ian Rush – who had

tasted a morsel of management life in the bottom tier with former club Chester – placed their hats into the ring that October, though the emergence of Gérard Houllier as a candidate raised both eyebrows and expectations.

Houllier had enjoyed success in international football, his technical director post at the French FA coinciding with their World Cup triumph in 1998, while he had won a string of cups during a six-year tenure at Liverpool. He could even associate with the Millennium Stadium, the Welsh team's home since 2000 where the Anfield giants had also won the FA Cup and League Cup during Wembley's rebuild.

Toshack's arrival, though, quickly appeared to be a *fait accompli*. Houllier pulled out, replaced as the alternative choice on the FAW interview list by Phillipe Troussier, the much travelled Frenchman whose international CV included spells with Nigeria, South Africa and Japan.

Dean Saunders was among those interviewed by the 11-man international committee at a Heathrow hotel, though the fact Toshack was the manager-elect was underlined by the unanimous decision to recommend his appointment on a four-year deal.

Not all were as convinced. Toshack's impending arrival had split sections of support. On the one hand his career achievements screamed out, certainly to an association unable to pay the kind of salary that would tempt anyone with rival credentials to consider the post. For years, as he succeeded and survived the scrutiny in Spain, adding trophies with Real and Sociedad along the way, he was the manager fans would not think twice about when naming their preferred choice. His unobtainable status as the national team struggled in the Gould years was the quick-fix solution in pub debates, his tactical nous seen as ideal for the international stage and perhaps the difference needed to climb that mountain.

Yet his BBC barbs at Hughes' team and the obvious resentment returned from the dressing room had left many fearing at splits rather than salvation. His halo had slipped, his attractiveness diminished with his most recent posts at Catania and Real Murcia leaving plenty wondering if he was the same Toshack that had led *Los Blancos* to a record-breaking *La Liga* title in 1990. This was quarter of a century on; Wales did not have a Hugo Sánchez.

34

Such misgivings were on display during the unease of that Poland game, a banner draped from the upper tier reading: "Thanks Sparky, No Thanks Tosh".

Not all were of the same mindset, certainly not those tasked with securing Hughes' replacement and the Toshack the FAW were attracted to was not the manager who who had such success at the Bernabéu the first time around, but the one who had had a more subtle success in his second spell.

In February 1999, less than nine years after he'd left Madrid only three months into his title defence following three successive defeats, Real again turned to Toshack as the axe fell on Guus Hiddink.

John Benjamin – as he was often known in Spain, with his middle name taken as a first surname and therefore used in the local custom – still had credit at the club. His initial spell had been seen as an obvious success and he could be considered unfortunate that his champions were paired with the timeless AC Milan side of that period in the European Cup; Gullit, van Basten, Rijkaard, Baresi and Maldini ensured a 2-1 defeat for Real and, as remains the case with Madridistas, without the holy grail of Europe then there is little else.

Toshack tells of being called in for a 5pm meeting with president Ramón Mendonza. He had already arranged for his belongings to be taken back to his adopted Basque home of San Sebastián before he walked in to hear the inevitable.

This second time, the call to Toshack had been one to sort out problems in the Bernabéu dressing room, the player power of the 'Ferrari Boys' of Predrag Mijatović, Davor Šuker and Clarence Seedorf.

"The dressing room resembled Baghdad," Toshack would later state in typical fashion.

He cleared them from the side, living up to the *Latigo* – the whip – role placed upon him to install discipline in a disorganised, almost archaic side. He did that but, most pertinently, he did so by looking towards younger, rising stars as he had done at Sociedad where the club's pro-Basque transfer policy meant he had little other option.

Though he – or at least the club – still sanctioned high-profile signings including that of Nicolas Anelka from Arsenal for £22m, the likes of Samuel Eto'o and Iker Casillas were unearthed from the Madrid *cantera*. Whether those looking to appoint Toshack could ever

35

have known there was equally impressive young talent in Wales to turn to is doubtful, but it was the veteran's stubbornness to persist with his faith in them that may have caught the eye. Even when it came at his expense.

The Bernabéu board had shelled out for the expensive Argentina international goalkeeper Albano Bizzarri with the message clear that Toshack should select him over Casillas. When Bizarri conceded goals that Toshack stated "made me weep", it wasn't the first time the Cardiffian had spoken with cutting Castilian.

Having helped them to Champions League qualification upon his arrival, Toshack's Real had subsequently made their worst start to a *La Liga* season and, even after victory over Rayo Vallecano that kept pressure momentarily at bay, he had remarked: "I close my eyes every time the ball comes near our area."

Captain Fernando Hierro spoke up for the players, saying that such issues should be sorted out in the dressing room rather than in the newspapers, but that was not Tosh, something that ultimately proved his undoing.

Asked to apologise, Toshack continued his use of English idioms in Spanish that didn't always translate as they should have.

He told the media there was more chance of pigs flying over the Bernabéu than him taking back his criticism of the team. The following day, the front page of influential Madrid sportspaper *Marca* featured president Lorenzo Sanz's head superimposed on a pig doing exactly that.

There was no press conference called to announce his second sacking, just simple A4 notes given out at the Bernabéu instead, no chance for a final word. Without one, Toshack had to be content with his own belief, only later acknowledged by others, that his groundwork had helped replacement Vicente del Bosque lead the team to the Champions League later that season. In goal for the 3-0 final win over Valencia was Iker Casillas.

Six years on, Toshack had no need to spell out such stories of legacy, the men wearing the dragon blazers all too aware of the experience and achievements of the man in front of them. Similarly, they were all too aware that the players' misgivings came at a time where options were scarce in more ways than one.

"We had obviously enjoyed some success under Mark but we could see ourselves that not only did we have a finite number of people to look at, but that the team was coming to an end and we'd have to look past that," says Peter Rees, a member of the sub-committee charged with identifying the new man and who would go on to serve as FAW president for much of Toshack's subsequent reign. "But in terms of Tosh himself, it wasn't a case of misgivings – here was someone who wanted the job and had been one of the most outstanding managers of the past decade or so.

"He had taken Swansea from nothing to the First Division, managed Real Madrid twice and gained experience from all over Europe. He was someone who had real respect all around the world and wanted to take on this challenge."

Toshack had a clear view on the future, one the FAW power-brokers accepted, that success could be a long time coming. To give credit, where it could be easy to criticise the association's hierarchy for looking to associate themselves and their decisions with immediate success, their move was one of long-term faith.

"He didn't say he wanted to invest in youth, he said he had no option but to," continues Rees. "While Mark's team had got us so far, there was nothing coming behind it and it was obvious that many of the side's international playing careers were coming to an end if they hadn't already. We may have hung onto that for a while but where would it have left us?

"John made the point many were playing for their last contracts at their clubs and we simply had to look at the players coming through. We then saw a lot of them retire, although it's no secret the one player he would have liked to have stayed on was Gary Speed.

"He was very open with us, that this would be a long-term thing and that he had to blood the kids and give them a chance of being better than what we had, to develop them into the players we needed with the experience he was prepared to give them."

Indirectly, Troussier may well have strengthened the belief that Toshack was the obvious appointment. The Frenchman flew into London and gave a similar indication of how he saw the job, that success could be ten years away. The repetition would have only underlined the fact that change was on the menu, even if there was little outside appetite for it.

Yet it would be too simplistic to say there had been a squad consensus about the new man, even from the senior players. Still, at the very least, there was tension.

Ryan Giggs did not surprise when he revealed that several had reservations about Toshack, something seemingly centred on his criticism of the side under Hughes. Perhaps with a nod to the Manchester United star's talent, Toshack would often cite the need for more from Giggs, the lack of times he featured and how he performed when he did, all of which the player deemed to appear non-constructive.

"When we got back into the dressing room after a game, the telly was on and there he'd be, slaughtering us," Giggs revealed in his autobiography. "Emotions were high. The adrenaline was still running and it didn't sit too well. We called him every name under the sun, hurling abuse at the TV."

It had clearly stuck with Sparky. On the impending announcement of Toshack as his successor, Hughes admitted surprise his chief critic was now putting "his head above the parapet" as he put it.

"Obviously he's been highly critical of the efforts of others, but I will have more respect for him because he's put his head on the line and is trying to move Welsh football forward," Hughes said, while wishing him luck. "In the past he hampered it."

If Giggs' feelings didn't come to light until after the event, Savage was less subtle.

While Robert Earnshaw, one of the younger members of the squad, said that he would be willing to work under whoever the FAW thought the best man available but "sometimes it's good to take into account the players' opinions", Savage left little room for misinterpretation.

While also giving Speed and Flynn full-blooded backing, Savage didn't name Toshack but didn't have to in a column for North Wales' *Daily Post*.

"Some pundits haven't helped themselves by media comments about Hughes and Wales – if they get the job they will soon find the boot is on the other foot," before adding: "I don't know a great deal about Toshack, he's not been involved in British football for 20 years or so since his successful spell at Swansea and seems to spend a lot of time in Spain nowadays."

Hughes had also stated Speed would have been a good appointment but Savage went further following the Poland game, claiming the

FAW were risking "a few players looking long and hard at their future" if they went with the favourite as they clearly were. It was notable that Savage did not name himself as one of them but he only served to stir up emotions as well as receive a stern word from Speed who told him – privately and then publicly – he was not helping matters.

Still, if Toshack walked into a dressing room of anarchy at the Bernabéu it could be easy to think he was about to encounter something similar with Wales.

And yet it wasn't so black and white.

"Personally I liked him and was all for it," says John Hartson, the side's main striker under Sparky who was still a regular goalscorer at Celtic and under 30 years of age at the time. "I'd obviously grown up a Swansea fan and I'd remembered standing on the North Bank at the old Vetch watching his side. I had massive respect for him stemming back from then and obviously for what he had done in Spain and in Europe since.

"Look, of course there was tension from what he had said about the team, certainly from a few of the senior players. Some of them felt there'd been a little lack of respect about the side and Sparky, but he was a pundit and had to give his opinions like a few others have gone on to do themselves.

"But I was interested to hear what he had to say and what his plans were for the team. Everyone has their own reasons for calling it a day and you'd have to ask each one but I had a respect for him and had no intention of quitting just because he had come in. I was looking forward to it."

Not all were as willing to give Toshack time or even the benefit of the doubt.

Just before his appointment, *The Western Mail*, the national newspaper of Wales with a historically strong influence, made room for a back page editorial to cite Toshack as the only prospective candidate "big enough, strong enough and bold enough" to rip up the side arguably slightly before the end of its cycle and start again.

Whether news of such a plan impacted on their decisions or it simply felt the right time, it sparked a series of international retirements. On top of Speed, veteran centre-half Andy Melville walked away as well as midfielder Andy Johnson. On the very day the full FAW council met to rubber stamp the international committee's recommendations to appoint Toshack, Mark Pembridge made it four.

Holding court at that press conference at the Vale hotel resort, it hardly warranted a mention from Toshack who made clear his manifesto.

"How many international teams have an average age of 30?," he asked. "I see no point in playing a player of 30-32 plus who is not going to be available for a tournament in two years' time.

"When Wales played Azerbaijan, the average age of the team was 30. That needs to be brought down – it's too old, too high.

"If you fail to qualify with players aged around 24-25, then you can still get something from the experience. The worst scenario is failing with players aged 30 plus – that has to be changed."

It resonated. While some had difficulty getting to grips with almost giving up on the chances of achieving in the short-term – Toshack had already mentioned the word "fail" in his first press meeting – there were plenty who agreed Wales could not afford to simply sit around and wait for success to come.

Neville Southall, never shy of speaking his mind, immediately called for Toshack to take a greater interest in the age-grade sides that the likes of he and Rush were in charge of to start shaping a pathway for development, adding: "The length of Tosh's contract shows me that we could be in for a lean time in the short term as he reshapes everything and puts right what he sees as being wrong from the previous regime, but I'm quite optimistic that towards the end of that time we could find ourselves talking about a very good Welsh team."

Toshack's intentions for the feeder teams became apparent less than a month after his unveiling, with Southall among a series of former players to suffer at the hands of it.

Southall, Rush, Mark Aizlewood, Kevin Ratcliffe and Glyn Hodges were all to make way in one of the most innovative and significant acts of Toshack's entire six year tenure.

Toshack had already gone back to Sociedad when appointing Salva Iriate as his No. 2, describing his former assistant at Anoeta as the best assessor of opposition he had worked with. He paired him with Liverpool 'Boot Room' graduate Roy Evans; a combination that almost perfectly illustrated Toshack's own mix of Anfield and Spanish football education.

But it was adopting *La Real*'s youth structure that proved one of his earliest decisions to be one of his greatest.

Having combined as a forward partnership for Wales in their 1970s playing days, Brian Flynn – a rival for the senior post – was the ideal man with whom to renew the link-up and serve as foot soldier for the kind of war Toshack wanted to wage.

Flynn had twice been a contender for the Wales job and had been a real tip for it while Wrexham manager before Bobby Gould's appointment, but at this stage he had been out of work having been shown the door at Swansea less than nine months after being credited with keeping them in the Football League following a memorable last-day victory against Hull in May 2003.

He was also a previous Wales Under-21 manager, a role he held until Gould's time in charge, but his task this time was more than simply overseeing the team's own attempts at qualifying for an age-grade tournament.

The thought process was simple: instead of separate individuals taking care of the separate age teams from Under-16s through to Under-21s, Flynn would be in charge of them all. The theory was that not only was Flynn, a long-time advocate of youth, comfortable enough with his role and previous achievements in management to put the players' developments ahead of his own, but that there was now one voice for both Toshack and the players in his care to listen to. Age-grade sides would play the same style and systems as the senior wherever possible, smoothing potential transitions and allowing a fast-track of talent when the opportunities arose. It was holistic before it became hip and fashionable in today's Premier League set-ups.

"They worked tremendously well together," says Peter Rees. "They trusted each other and were both on the same page as to what they wanted to do."

It was on Flynn's appointment that the first signs of the length of the job became clear, the 2010 World Cup qualifying campaign mentioned as the target to drop the average age of the team down to 25. It hadn't escaped their notice that the previous five World Cup winners had sides with an average age of 28.

The Under-21s themselves had struggled to convince there was enough talent coming through to inspire. Leaving his post a year before Hughes, Jimmy Shoulder had overseen a record number of continuous defeats, winning just two of their previous 33 by November 2013 including an 8-1 hammering at the hands of Italy during the 2004 campaign.

Flynn was undeterred, quickly looking at younger players to identify not so much which players could help him win then, but those who could help Wales win later down the line. In his first match in charge of the Under-21s, a 16-year-old Wayne Hennessey was named on the bench.

The other side of the job entrusted to Flynn was that of spotting the diamonds to polish that Wales didn't even know they had. It was not senior games Flynn spent his Saturdays at but at academy fixtures across the country, showing little care for getting knocked back if his questions about their heritage didn't get positive responses at the time or after a bit of digging around family trees. It has been claimed that it was at a Reading game that Flynn approached a player with a surname – be it Hughes, Jones or Evans – in wondering if there was a Welsh qualification to be found, only to be told 'no' but cheekily suggesting the exotically named Hal Robson-Kanu would have.

Flynn would see no issue in becoming a regular at motorway services in seeking out lower league games to attend to check out the progress of a potential young gun.

And with the work of the Welsh Football Trust going on below him – the development arm of the FAW charged with players still at school-age – Flynn quickly got to grips with bringing through "his boys" as he would often say with the same kind of smile a parent would give.

"When I first spoke to John the basic aim was first to get the average age down within five years," says Flynn. "It was obvious he was thinking long-term even then and it was something I was comfortable with because I'd done something similar in building a team at Wrexham, just as John had done with Sociedad.

"He obviously had all the experience he needed. Tactically he was light years ahead of anybody else and knew what he needed to do to draft in the players he wanted.

"And for all people want to say about the training and whatever, the game doesn't change when you get on the field. He knew what he wanted to do and he was happy with me establishing a model and letting me get on with things. He didn't set me any parameters, just told me to get on with the job and the only instruction was that, when I had a player that was ready, I had to tell him and he would pick him.

"The phrase he used when we first discussed this just showed what he was prepared for. He told me what he had planned would mean we would have to suffer some 'car crashes' along the way – but we can handle that.

"And we did. We knew we would need time and patience and that we would have to trust the players we turned to, but that it was the right thing to do."

Of course, while Flynn wasted little time getting to work, Toshack would have to bide his.

Indeed, for the first year or so of his time in charge, there was little evidence of the revolution he had hinted at apart from the slow erosion of the previous squad as more senior players ended their time in Welsh red.

That is not to say Toshack did not make an immediate mark.

"Being honest, after all the talk just before Mark Hughes left, I wasn't sure what to expect or what he would be like," says Danny Gabbidon. The classy centre-back had taken to the international stage under Hughes with the kind of unruffled coolness that was so obvious in his game, hailed for his role in handling Alessandro del Piero in the watermark win over Italy. Still 25 at the time of Hughes' departure, it was clear he would be a key part of the team under Toshack.

"I had a fairly open mind and I was quite pleased when he got in touch with Cardiff to set up a chat. He had called meetings with a few of the players and I remember me and Earnie (Robert Earnshaw) going to a small Italian restaurant opposite the Millennium.

"It was the first time I'd actually met him and got to know what he was about. Before then I'd only known what I'd seen on the TV or what he had said in the papers.

"And the first impressions were good. I was pleased he'd gone to the effort to speak to us and to try and get his view across about what he wanted to do. He spoke of the kind of formation he was thinking of playing and even then he was talking about the younger players coming through and how he wanted them get into the team.

43

"We'd seen quite a few retirements already and although I was one of the younger ones I had quite a few caps, and he saw me and Earnie as part of the group that would be mainstays in the side.

"It was obvious it was going to be a time of transition but I remember coming away thinking I was happy enough with what he had to say and it was a case of seeing how it goes.

"But at the same time you had all the stuff going on with Sav who had been a teammate of mine a few weeks earlier and it seemed to me as if he was trying to finish him off."

Toshack had also contacted Savage, the midfielder later claiming that the words from the man he had spoken out against were ones promising "a fresh start".

Though it could be considered by some as being said with a spiked tongue, Toshack had said as much in public previously.

"I saw one player coming out after the Poland game saying people would have to look at their futures," he had stated. "But players eligible to play for Wales have a clean slate – one man's meat is another man's poison."

The food analogy would become ironic but for the time being the truce appeared to be genuine. Savage, despite his public protestations over Toshack prior to his appointment, was named in the first post-Hughes squad, a Millennium Stadium friendly against Hungary in February 2005.

Yet, like several others, there was no Savage in the side that eventually beat the Magyars 2-0 courtesy of two Craig Bellamy goals. Savage had by then followed Hughes to Blackburn, angering Birmingham fans by claiming the reason was to be closer to his parents' home in Wrexham, seemingly ignoring the fact the distance to from St Andrew's to north Wales was less than from Ewood Park. Within a few days of Toshack's first camp, the midfielder was travelling back to Lancashire having withdrawn – along with Ryan Giggs and John Hartson – with a groin strain.

It would be the last time he donned a Welsh tracksuit.

Before the squad sheets containing the 21 names selected for Toshack's first competitive games in charge – a home-and-away double header with Austria – the news that Savage's name was not among them had already broken. A statement on Blackburn's website detailed his decision to retire from international football at the age of

30 and with 39 caps, citing family time and concentrating on club duties as his reasons.

Toshack was prepared for the inquest, quickly revealing how he had already informed the player he was not being called-up and the snap response it prompted.

Impressed with how Carl Robinson and Carl Fletcher had performed against Hungary, Toshack claimed: "I told him (Savage) I wanted to have a look at something else. I told him he wouldn't be involved. He said he was retiring anyway and the line went dead."

The row did not rest in peace, however.

It's impossible for anyone other than Toshack to know whether it had been his intention all along to antagonise Savage into his own exile.

While he had been a popular member of the senior group – Speed claiming his bubbly presence and wind-ups combined with a passion for the shirt would be much missed – there were those in the camp who saw him as difficult and a potential poor influence on the youngsters Toshack wanted to rear. As one member of the backroom team put it, Toshack set the trap and Savage fell into it.

Of course, the wily manager left it for others to speculate and kept the moral high ground Savage had fallen off when he reacted with retirement at a younger age than Mark Crossley and Nathan Blake who had also opted to call it a day by this stage.

Toshack opted not to include the "You can stick it up your arse" of Savage's short retirement speech that the player included in his autobiography, but it didn't take long to work out that the fallen star was simmering.

Following the initial calmly-worded club website statement – that made no reference to Toshack – Savage went on the front foot.

Claiming he could accept being dropped from the side but that being axed completely was "a statement of intent", Savage went on to heavily criticise what he had seen in his limited time in camp with Toshack.

"We had fried bananas to start the meals, which no-one's ever heard of. There were no carbohydrates before the game," Savage told BBC Wales two days after.

"The training methods were embarrassing – I think he's (Toshack)

45

totally lost touch with the times. Most of the lads agreed with me and I was the spokesperson, I stuck up for the lads but it backfired."

By the time the games with Austria rolled around, Toshack – as you would expect from the experience of the countless Spanish inquisitions formed by Madrid media – was all too prepared.

Following up on Savage's claim that he was speaking for the squad, one questioner asked whether Toshack indeed had the backing of the whole squad.

"That's potentially a fried banana skin of a question," he said with a knowing smile.

It was suggested that Toshack had won a first battle as Wales boss, though Speed was quick to put it into perspective as he was asked for his opinion from afar.

"Nobody has won. The only loser is Welsh football because whatever your thoughts on Savage's style of play, he is an established Premiership player and he's Welsh," said Speed.

Savage would not let it go, the war of words resurfacing a year down the line, although it was Savage firing most of the bullets and Toshack either electing not to rise to it – constantly saying he'd prefer to talk about players who were in the squad rather than those who were not – or letting others fight back for him. One such soldier was Leighton James, the former Swansea and Wales winger going head-to-head and head-on with Savage on a south Wales radio phone-in that was one of those laugh or cry moments surrounding the fortunes of the national team.

It ranged from Savage saying he would be back under the next manager, that Toshack would not last the term but he would not get on his hands and knees to ask him to play again, to James maintaining he simply wasn't good enough for a recall. James queried why a phone-call wouldn't suffice – only for Savage to complain that he didn't have a mobile phone and calls to the FAW went unreturned. Suffice to say, a suggestion from James that he should write to him fell on deaf ears. "Do you think I'm in school?"

The way it descended into name calling made you wonder.

If the radio row had everyone talking, it was ignored by both the FAW and Toshack himself. The only word from the camp came from Roy Evans who conceded – as Savage had claimed – he had told the player in a chance meeting he would like to see him back involved, but added that a lot of caveats in the conversation had been left out.

Yet Savage's grumbles weren't baseless. If Hughes had won praise for dragging Wales into a more modern set-up after the days of Gould there was a sense of concern from some that they were taking a step backwards off the field even if the intention was to plough towards a long-term future on it.

"It did change," admits Hartson. "There was less of an emphasis on the sports science we had seen and got used to under Sparky. With all the physios, the masseur, video analysis that have come in, it's certainly not what you would expect now. It was a bit more old school."

It is a term that often crops up.

"It was quite different," adds Gabbidon. "He was older and a bit more old school to go with it. Under Mark I think we had definitely been more forward thinking. Things had started to change in football and he had done a lot to try and get the FAW invest in more things off the field to get us better prepared and it seemed like they understood what we needed a bit more.

"I remember walking into the dressing room in the first game and normally when you went in you'd see a table in the middle with the energy drinks lined up, bananas, that type of stuff that had become standard. In that match I think there was only water there. It's only a little thing but straight away it felt a bit of a throwback."

Regardless, things were moving on with Toshack – something illustrated by even his early squads.

His first match set the tone. There were debuts for Sam Ricketts of then fourth-tier Swansea, Sunderland's Danny Collins – both of whom had played for England's non-league representative side. Wrexham's Stephen Roberts also featured to win his only cap, an example of a number of players who sprang up on the international scene under Toshack but did not stay for long.

David Partridge was another, a former West Ham scholar and Wales Under-21 cap who had impressed in salvaging a career in Scotland with Motherwell and initially did not look completely out of place at international level, going on to win seven caps in 18 months. By the time Wales faced Trinidad & Tobago in 2006, his time in the red shirt was over, sentenced to two months in prison for his part in a brawl outside a nightclub after joining Bristol City and taking on a nomadic career after his release.

All in all, by the end of his time in charge Toshack handed out 43 debuts – not including those called into squads and not capped – in the space of 53 matches.

For every one of 'Flynny's Fledglings' there was a player making up the numbers, never quite good enough to establish themselves as an international.

Toshack, though, was keen to give opportunities. There was an element of belief that players might be able to raise their game on the international stage, that the pace and poise of the game might encourage more from them and provide an answer to problems within the squad.

A painful search for a striker was one such problem. The dearth of goalscoring options was often bemoaned by the ex-Liverpool striker, especially when it came to his old No. 9 shirt.

After John Hartson decided to retire a year into Toshack's time in charge and those found by Flynn not ready to be called upon, there were turns for Daniel Nardiello, the Manchester United graduate who had resisted previous attempts to pledge allegiance to the land of his father, the twice capped Donato Nardiello. His son would muster half of his appearances.

Freddy Eastwood had impressed in the lower leagues with Southend. His Romany background provided an avenue to exploit, used when a birth certificate for his maternal grandfather confirmed him to be born in a caravan in Pontyberem near Llanelli. He at least managed to offer hope before losing his way, scoring an eye-catching strike on his debut in Bulgaria in 2007 and, by the time of his last appearance four years later, had scored four times in 11 appearances.

But it does sum up the difficulty in finding talent where there was little that the last debut handed out by Toshack in his penultimate game was to another striker – Steve Morison – who scored once in ten outings beyond the Tosh tenure. Fans accepted his limitations with the chant "He used to be shite/But now he's alright/Walking in a Morison wonderland...". His physical if ungainly presence had been welcome, but he was no Hartson.

"It had been my time to retire," says Hartson of his exit one year on from Toshack's appointment, right-back Mark Delaney also by then unavailable for selection after a string of injury problems eventually forced the decision upon him. "There were younger players coming through but I felt it was the right point for me. I'd had injuries and with 51 caps I felt I played my part.

"I'd got on well with John and I had been delighted to see him come in and he did ask me to stay on because he wanted my experience.

"But I'd felt I played my part and, while others had their own reasons, I had thought that a few of them maybe should have hung on for a couple more games, a dozen more caps and it might have helped."

It might have at least helped them through a difficult first campaign – or half campaign – for Toshack. After defeat in Cardiff to Austria, there would be no vengeance in Vienna four days later despite an impressive performance that saw Giggs and Bellamy miss chances before an error from goalkeeper Danny Coyne handed the hosts victory.

A drab 0-0 draw at Slovenia – the first international fixture at the Liberty – was followed by defeat to England at a sold-out Millennium. Toshack's use of a five-man defence, something that would become a feature of his reign, did restrict Wayne Rooney but not a 'quarter-back' David Beckham who helped Joe Cole to the winning goal. Paul Robinson's superb save from a Hartson header kept Wales not only looking for a first qualifying win under Toshack but a first goal, finding neither in the follow-up game in Warsaw as Poland booked qualification with a 1-0 win.

They then mustered three in a spirited display in Belfast to beat Northern Ireland 3-2, finishing the campaign with an easy enough 2-0 win over Azerbaijan to at least offer hints of slow progress towards the next campaign.

But the Toshack transition was far from complete. Joe Ledley had already come in for his debut in Poland, so too Richard Duffy, the highly-rated Swansea right-back soon to be snapped up by Harry Redknapp at Portsmouth. The 18-year-old David Cotterill was another before the first real leap of faith came on St David's Day 2006 when the little-known Lewin Nyatanga was capped against Paraguay to become Wales' youngest player at the age of 17 years and 195 days. The Burton-born centre-back had stood out for Flynn's Under-21s yet had hardly entered double figures in terms of professional football.

It was a statement, both of the fact that Toshack knew he needed to have better depth than he had at the time, and that he would be prepared to place his faith in potential, regardless of the various mentions of Ryan Green, the player Bobby Gould had capped in 1998 to take Giggs' record as Wales' youngest international only for him to languish in the lower leagues ever after.

"It was quite an easy transition for us coming into the senior squad," says Cotterill, one of the first draft of young hopefuls to be included. "There were so many of us from the Under-21s coming in to at least train with the first team, if not play, that it almost felt like an extension of the Under-21 squad.

"Of course, you had the big players, the big names like Giggsy, Bellamy and Gabbidon, so it was a little bit separated. The youngsters kept themselves to themselves around that time, but we didn't feel out of place. As it went on, a lot of the youngsters were better than a lot of the senior players either still there or who had been talked about. Most of us were doing well with our clubs so who else was there to look towards?"

In May 2006 Toshack would look younger still, Bale making his debut against Trinidad & Tobago before the Euro 2008 campaign kicked-off against the Czech Republic in Teplice with Ledley, Nyatanga and Cotterill all involved and all unlucky not to get more than the late 2-1 defeat suffered in the final minute.

Bale did enough against Brazil in the subsequent friendly to start against Slovakia at the Millennium in October 2006, a game that would mark Paul Jones' 50th appearance and that he would mark by shaving the number 50 in the side of his head.

But if the performance against the Cezchs had brought hope without points, everything that happened against their neighbours in Cardiff took it away.

Not even Bale's sublime free-kick – a goal that would make him the country's youngest goalscorer to go with the youngest cap record he took from Nyatanga – could stop the boos and the gnashing of the teeth. When the then left-back's left-footed curler found the net to half the two goal lead the Slovaks had breezed to within half an hour, the glimmer was dimmed thirty seconds later when Marek Mintál made it 3-1. A further two goals from the visitors after the break left Wales with their heaviest home defeat since 1908, a 7-1 thrashing by England.

Toshack was asked to take a quick question from the Slovak media before they raced off to catch their plane. "I'll come with you," he replied. Toshack had not lost his sense of humour, even if he did not see the funny side of a defeat that was painfully plainly no laughing matter.

Young side or not, he was not holding back in describing it as the worst international performance he had seen, comparing some players to headless chickens.

"We took over a side that had gone 10 competitive games without a win," he said. "Eleven players have retired and we've lost five injured since Teplice (including Giggs, absent through injury and illness).

"These are facts, not excuses, but it doesn't mean we should have made the mistakes we did.

"You can't just give [the young players] a pat on the back. Pats on the back soften up champions, punches on the jaw don't soften up champions.

"We will all be having to take some punches on the jaw over the next few days and we will do. I have already delivered one or two uppercuts."

Dušan Galis, the Slovakia manager, delivered a low blow of his own when he was asked about Wales' chances against Cyprus in Cardiff a few days later, a team his own side had beaten 6-1.

"With or without Ryan Giggs?" he asked. There was no surprise that he indicated Wales would find it difficult when he was informed the man Toshack had made captain would again be missing.

Toshack had made Bellamy his stand-in skipper who failed to hide his hurt on a day he called "disastrous" even if he did cede that the gap for some players to go from reserve football to international football was too big.

The firebrand, whether it was justified or not, was rarely far away from the headlines but it could never be questioned that he genuinely cared for the side and for the will to make it come good.

Still, he had warned that a long 18 months would lie in wait if Wales could not deliver from their back-to-back home matches and few were doubting his assessment even after a pride-restoring 3-1 win over the Cypriots.

It had already been a long road and there were at least some players struggling with the way Wales were travelling along it with Toshack at the wheel.

One of the key areas of frustration were the team meetings that some say both dragged on but didn't have the level of detail they felt was needed, such as the videos of the opponents being unedited – including every stoppage and even the anthems – rather than focussing on pertinent points.

"Every manager is different and perhaps it was up to us to adapt and there was a willingness for that," adds Gabbidon.

"But it was frustrating at times. You'd go back to your clubs and it felt like football was moving on – as we felt we had been doing under Sparky – but you couldn't help but feel you were stepping back at times, certainly in the build-up to matches.

"Tosh wanted to play a different game, one more about possession and keeping the ball and I was a fan of that. We tried to play some good football, bringing out of the back which suited me and there's no doubt a few of the lads benefited from it. It was that continental approach that he'd gone for from his time in Spain and at Madrid and it was something I thought was a big plus.

"But in my view, in the build-up to games, there wasn't the focus on tactics, the videos of the opposition and how we might able to affect them. I wouldn't say it was less professional but, in my opinion, the level of detail wasn't the same as it had been under Mark Hughes and what a lot of us were getting at our clubs. It took a lot of getting used to."

There had been a change in terms of the preparation for games but, as suggested, also in the way Wales played. There was a slower tempo to things, a determination to make players comfortable on the ball and often three central defenders used that covered the inexperience of some but also led to criticism of safety-first. Slovakia at home aside, Wales could never be accused of taking the kind of beatings that would have abandoned all hope and rocked the fragile confidence of the teenagers he was promoting.

Toshack used to regularly cite a metaphor about his issues being a blanket not quite big enough to fully serve its purpose: "When you pull it over your feet, your head gets cold – but when you pull it over your head, your feet get cold."

There would be no quick-fix – "There are no transfer windows in international football," he would regularly say as a reminder of the time needed for younger players to mature – and the idea was to build towards success rather than race to short-term victories. When the up-and-at-em approach of Northern Ireland in the previous campaign had brought them a win over England and suggestions they could qualify, Toshack was dismissive of suggestions to adopt a similar approach and adamant that his way would bring more chance of consistent glory rather than one-off nights akin to FA Cup shocks.

It certainly struck a note with some.

"I fell between the groups really when John came in; I was younger than Ryan and Gary and a bit older than the lads who had just come through under Sparky," says Carl Robinson, the central midfielder whose service as a steady, intelligent midfielder often went unnoticed but was a key part of the transition under Toshack. "People had their thoughts but I was probably more of my own person really.

"We were all obviously disappointed Mark had left after we had gone so close but Tosh coming in was an eye opener for me and I honestly think it was the best thing that could have happened.

"We needed a steady hand, an old head to do what we needed to do. He tried to build something and we knew, for a while, it might have to come at a cost of some results.

"Some players decided to call it a day but in some ways it benefited us because it meant we had to develop something different.

"There was a pathway being created with Brian Flynn underneath John that he trusted and the players coming up knew they had a chance and could see the rewards for them – and when they did that the team was rewarded. It was a structure that could fast-track and identify the players we needed for the future.

"I accepted at the time, like John probably did, that it might take some time but I felt with him there was plenty of reason to have faith in what he was doing.

"He had great experience – you were talking about an ex-manager of Real Madrid. Every time I sat down with him I wanted to pick his brain. I was like a sponge and took on board everything he had to say. The sessions could be long, there was an old school element to things but he knew every tactical trick in the book."

Not all were as convinced, not even by his esteemed past.

"I remember early on someone telling me as we were warming up about him being at Real and I thought to myself at the time 'Bloody hell, this guy has managed Madrid, surely training should be better'," recalls David Cotterill.

"It was a personal view, I don't know about others, but at the time I remember thinking that with him having been at the highest level I was expecting more.

"The younger lads probably didn't know what to expect but I remember some of the senior players coming out of some meetings in a sort of disbelief.

"We were all wanting to do well but a lot of us felt the preparation just wasn't there and it said everything.

"My frustration was that we'd go through one or two players of the opposition and about how we'd have to be aware of them but, more often than not, they'd be from lesser countries who in all honesty couldn't lace the boots of some of the lads like Giggs and Bellamy.

"A lot of us thought we should be spending more time on us and how the opposition would be scared of the players we had who were on fire in the Premier League and how to make the most of it.

"The atmosphere was still good – the older lads were always great and we had a good group in the camp. When Giggs and Bellamy were there training you wanted to be there to learn from them, but you could sense there was a frustration in coming from the clubs they were at to what we were doing. We could see it ourselves; I think we all found it difficult coming from high intensity training to practically walking around for most of the week.

"With all the problems with withdrawals we had, perhaps the thinking was not to get any more knocks which was fair enough because of the small pool of players we had.

"But you were in camp for a long time and training would get you down. It wasn't what was happening at our clubs, not even the warm-ups. It was so different to what we would experience most weeks and a world away from what we have now. I think for a lot of the lads it became a bit of a grind."

Wales would plod along in a manner that would be a fairly neat summing up of results under Toshack. The win over Cyprus was followed up by a convincing and confidence-building 4-0 Wrexham friendly win over Liechtenstein and a healthy enough 0-0 work-out in Northern Ireland to ramp up the hope going to Dublin where remaining hopes of a qualification challenge rested on beating the Republic of Ireland.

The first game at Croke Park was set-up for Wales; the pressure on the unpopular Irish boss Steve Staunton was as obvious in the city's air as the aroma from the Guinness brewery and Bale was slowly becoming a player who was getting plenty outside of the hardcore Wales fans excited. Come the game Bale himself was poor – no disgrace for an inexperienced 17 year-old – but the team as a whole could not impose themselves in front of a crowd of 72,539. It was no surprise Wales looked vulnerable as James Collins started as sweeper between a still raw Nyatanga and Steve Evans, the 28-year-old Wrexham centre-back who had been playing Welsh Premier League football with TNS the previous season.

Giggs played and would be among the scorers as San Marino were routinely beaten 3-0 later that week but, unbeknown at the time, it was a landmark that pointed to even further change.

Come the end of the season, following a 2-2 draw with New Zealand in Wrexham where yet more kids were capped – Chris Gunter and Wayne Hennessey – Giggs announced his retirement from international football, signalling that the game against the Czechs in Cardiff would be his last.

Toshack did not fight it. In private he had brought up the subject of Giggs' lack of influence in games, laying the foundations with a few journalists that the unthinkable may be on the cards.

In truth, Giggs had become more of an icon than an inspiration. While Wales needed every drop of experience they could muster, let alone that so great and gifted as Giggs', the player himself admitted he was "not performing as well as he could have" for his country.

Whether Toshack would have followed through with his musings over the then 33-year-old is another thing – certainly, regardless of Giggs' form in Welsh rather than Manchester red, it would have added to the fan grumblings over the fortunes of the national side.

But, when Giggs first told teammates and then leaked the news out, Toshack didn't shy away from at least hinting to his thoughts.

"People say Ryan hasn't performed as well at international level as club level and I feel retirement probably is the right decision for him, United and Wales," said Toshack who had, in fairness, managed to get a level of commitment from the player criticised for his international turn-outs in the past, placating Sir Alex Ferguson at the appropriate times, with a half-time withdrawal against Brazil when he was clearly Wales' star man, an obvious example.

"At least I will never have to say to Ryan I will have to leave him out because I have handled and managed numerous big players with big egos and had to do it.

"I have taken lots of criticism in the past over those decisions and I wouldn't have been looking forward to doing it with this one."

In the end, Giggs went on his terms, taking the standing ovation of the 30,714 at the Millennium where, in his 64th and final appearance coming a little less than 16 years after his debut in Germany, a 0-0 draw with the Czech Republic at least gave some momentum towards the second-half of the campaign if without chance of qualification.

The fact Giggs went onto something of an Indian summer with his club suggested he made the right call as far as his Old Trafford pay-masters were concerned. Within two years he had regained the Champions League, the Premier League, broken Sir Bobby Charlton's United appearance record and won the PFA Player of the Year award. It, of course, left plenty wondering and wishing over a return and, in March 2010, Giggs opened the door saying he was "open minded" about a comeback if Toshack contacted him. The headlines hit the stands overnight but, by mid-morning and Ferguson's United press briefing, it was bluntly dismissed in withering style as the Scot responded to the idea with: "You must be joking. It must have been a weak moment for Ryan."

Toshack's weak moment was to come.

A friendly win in Bulgaria in the first post-Giggs match led to a home clash with Germany, a game won at ease by the heavyweight group favourites with Bastian Schweinsteiger giving a performance of complete midfield control.

What followed, four days later, was one of the highlights – in terms of results at least – of Toshack's reign as revenge over Slovakia was inspired by Bellamy in a 5-2 hammering of the hosts in Bratislava. A brilliant Bellamy scored twice but was unplayable at times in a convincing counter-attacking display with his manager admitting the now full-time captain had reached new levels.

"You normally have 22 players battling away out there, pretty evenly matched. This game saw 21 players and one who was just unbelievable," Toshack said after the September 2007 win. "It was a scintillating performance – I cannot recall the last time I saw such an individual performance."

Yet, again, the optimism was not to last. One month on, at the same Nicosia venue that Wales would succeed with such significance in 2015, the blanket Toshack so often referred to threatened to come apart at the seams in a 3-1 defeat.

A late Saturday evening game, the FAW press officer had asked beforehand for the travelling Welsh journalists not to ask questions in the main press conference that followed the loss, one that blew away hopes of a third-placed finish and much needed momentum towards the next campaign. With the need for deadlines to be hit and formal press conferences translated from English to aid the assembled host media, the notion was that Toshack would speak in a huddle afterwards at the side of the room.

He briefly answered that he was "bitterly disappointed" as the one question came but, as the pack awaited a chance to inquire just what had happened, Toshack left them waiting and turned back to the dressing rooms. His thoughts, though, had been written over his face before a flash television interview to the BBC that the "debacle" had left him needing "a long hard look at myself and what I am doing here."

The looks from FAW suits and players emerging from the dressing room only added to the sense Toshack had appeared to have had enough.

"I was on my way back to the hotel after the game and I had taken a call to turn around and go and see John," says Peter Rees. "When I got there he was sat in the changing room. It was clear what he was thinking but I said to him 'You've taken us into this situation, you've had what you wanted, now you bloody see it out'.

"All he said to me was 'You're right' and that was that. Nothing had changed in terms of what we wanted to do but I think he needed someone to take some of the weight off his shoulders".

Toshack's manner, his almost stubbornness that he was taking the right course, made it seem strange that he was suddenly seeming to questioning his own stomach for the fight if not what he was doing.

57

There were at least some questions from the players, meetings called the next day between staff and senior men.

"It was a low point," says Gabbidon. "As players we knew he could go. He called some of us in one at a time, wanting to know what had happened the night before and for us to voice our opinions.

"I couldn't tell you what others said but I felt I had bitten my tongue and wanted to tell him what was on my mind.

"I'd felt training had become monotonous. It had been quite intense under Sparky where you couldn't slack off and everyone was sharp. As time went on under Tosh we'd be doing the same things, we all knew what was coming and it became frustrating that we weren't mixing it up more – but he was set in what he wanted. You didn't feel as prepared as you wanted to.

"We didn't really have the know-how to win games or to close them out. It would be so frustrating because we'd do well for 60 minutes but couldn't finish the job, or make a mistake and it would go to waste.

"It happens when you bring through youngsters and it wasn't easy – especially when you looked at some of the groups we were in and teams we were up against – but it felt at times it wasn't just that and that the lack of intensity and the game-plan to attack teams wasn't there because we'd go through the same stuff every camp."

It wasn't that Toshack was disliked. Several speak of his humour, the witty put downs that became a staple fare for his press conferences found the mark with players who enjoyed his dry humour and enjoyed his company. But there was a sense from some that the enjoyment of the camp itself was seeping away and the laid-back nature of a man who had seen it all was not having the right kind of effect.

"When you had the chance to sit down and spend some time chatting he was a good bloke, a funny guy," adds Gabbidon. "He was very laid-back and I don't know whether it was to protect some of the younger players, to take the pressure out of the camps, but I didn't think it was what we needed as a team at that time.

"He wasn't bothered what a lot of other people thought about what he wanted to do with the team and he didn't have any fear when it came to bringing the young players in if he thought they would be worth a chance, even if it was for later down the line.

"He'd have almost a stubbornness to stick with them when others might not have because he saw the potential and knew what we needed to do and, looking back, he deserves credit because if he hadn't have had that bravery to go with the youngsters they wouldn't have the experience they have now.

"But at the time, even with that in mind, I felt there were things that we could have done differently and might have helped us along the way.

"Like I said, he would be quite laid-back and it reflected in the camp. It had been a very different atmosphere under the previous manager. I was younger then and when me and Earnie had come in we kept our heads down, you didn't dare want to step out of line. I remember racing back from town once having gone for a coffee, panicking we were going to be late for a meeting. You didn't have that with Tosh.

"I felt we were slipping into bad habits because there was a feeling standards were slipping and we weren't quite motivated and prepared as I and others thought we should have been, and me and some of the other senior players weren't setting the example we should have.

"Looking back now, I don't think I would ever have done some of the things under Gary Speed or Chris Coleman – they were only little things but we'd still go out when we were told we weren't supposed to leave the hotel, but it was just because that focus was lost that so was the discipline. You felt if the set-up wasn't as good as it should be you'd find yourself wondering 'why should we?'

"It was wrong and it wasn't that we didn't want to be there but, to us, the enjoyment was missing. You're there to work and be professional but that extra edge was missing and it was making a difference.

"I can guarantee there would be no danger of similar things now because everything is so focused on the job at hand and qualifying, which we didn't have at that time.

"It was tough to get an atmosphere going with the squad having gone through so much change and there'd be times where you'd find yourself wondering where it was going, or come out of a session wondering what we had gained from it and it was showing on the pitch.

"I brought a lot of it up in that meeting because he had wanted me to be honest and I told him I believed a lot of things were wrong, that our preparation needed to be better and some players just weren't enjoying things.

59

"He took it on board, said he was glad I'd told him and that was that."

Only it wasn't. The day before the next game of the double-header, an away fixture in San Marino, Toshack went on the front foot as claims he had been ready to resign were dismissed.

Instead of questioning himself, Toshack questioned the players.

"Another five-star hotel boys, here we are in Rimini now. Look out the window, if the waves are making a noise in the evening, just phone down and we'll see if we can move you over to one of the rooms on the other side of the hotel," Toshack told reporters.

"When I came in at half-time the other day, I looked and thought to myself: 'Some of these look as if they don't want to go out'. We were winning 1-0 and were 45 minutes away from being in with a shout of finishing third and getting a big crowd for the next game.

"I looked around and I thought: 'Some of these aren't enjoying themselves'. Sometimes I feel that some of these take it for granted. And I won't accept that.

"The players will say they do care and it is rubbish to say they don't. But did it look like they cared? It didn't look like it to me."

Over time, Gabbidon's name for some reason became associated with being the mystery – perhaps mythical – player asking to change rooms.

"It didn't happen, not from me anyway," he says. "I don't know whether he was making a general point or if it was aimed at me, but I do remember feeling disappointed because he'd asked for honesty and the next minute he was having a go at some of us for being prima donnas. I guess we just got on with it."

Wales won in San Marino – scraping a 2-1 win – the tension obvious between fans and those on the pitch, with captain Bellamy making it known in a touchline interview after the game, refusing bluntly to get dragged into questions around Toshack's comments over what he perceived as 'pampered' players.

"I've played for Wales for a number of years and this was one of the worst atmospheres I've been in," Bellamy said. "The Welsh crowd here were very vicious, which is rare. It was an uncomfortable night to play in. The chanting early on was vicious and I think that took its toll on the players as well. It wasn't nice."

Bellamy had also avoided getting caught up in the heightened scrutiny over Toshack's role before the game, claiming it wasn't his place to say whether Wales were heading in the right direction.

But regardless, with renewed support and firmer faith from the man overseeing it, it was a direction they would continue in – at even greater pace.

4

A Golden Generation

"What we've done since is all down to something he started"
– Chris Gunter

It is difficult to pin down exactly when the term 'golden generation' was first attached to them.

But many had long been taking notice that something was stirring beneath the mediocrity of the senior side's results.

Ryan Giggs, before his retirement, had been aware as he made the surprise decision to travel to Northern Ireland for a February 2007 friendly despite being injured, watching Brian Flynn's Under-21 side in the bitter Belfast wind. In one corner of The Oval, home of Glentoran, is a sponsorship hoarding that simply reads: Jesus. As Welsh football looked for salvation, there was a growing sense that some of the youngsters in the side which won 4-0 that late afternoon might just be able to help provide it.

Already several had been called upon – notably Gareth Bale who, by the time of Giggs' retirement at the end of that season, underlined his stature with a £10m move from Southampton to Tottenham.

But there were others being unearthed by Flynn as he revelled in the responsibility bestowed upon him by Toshack.

By the August of that year Flynn took a team to Sweden, winning 4-3 with a side containing rookie goalkeeper Owain Fôn Williams, the then Wrexham defender Neil Taylor, up-and-coming Swansea playmaker Joe Allen, Shrewsbury midfielder David Edwards, striker Simon Church who had been impressing at Reading, Wigan's £2m teenager David Cotterill, powerful Bournemouth forward Sam Vokes,

Swansea's Shaun MacDonald and young Cardiff City talent Aaron Ramsey – all of whom would feature eight years later in Coleman's qualifying charge to Euro 2016.

Three months later and France were taken apart at Ninian Park, this time with midfielder Jack Collison thrown into the mix. Collison had been seen as a real star in the making at West Ham, courted by England but convinced by Flynn that his future could lie with the nation of his maternal grandfather.

Craig Bellamy, like Giggs before him, could see the potential both in Collison and the rest of the clutch of players who were being told the future was theirs, speaking in the dressing room before the 4-2 win.

Midfielder Collison was one of a number of dual-qualified players that Wales were suddenly being proactive in reaching out to, not simply waiting until an agent or administrator let the FAW know about potential heritage; they were prepared to try and discover at source.

"I think I knew the road to every training ground in the Championship and Premier League," laughs Flynn of his efforts to boost eligible options with Vokes, Edwards, Church and, later, the likes of Andy King; all dual-qualified 'Anglos' who were quickly identified as being able to deepen Wales' player pool. "It was all about contacts. I knew the vast majority of development coaches at clubs and I would make sure we stayed in touch about players coming through.

"The contracts players sign at that age only ask to stipulate where your parents were born not the grandparents so we would often ask the coaches to ask the question to players – and if they weren't sure, for them to go and check and we would then follow it up and do the research.

"Obviously, then they'd have to pass the football test and I would go and watch them to see whether we thought they had what it took.

"But we did the ground work on their background first so we didn't miss out on potential players because we knew the talent was out there – we just had to go looking for it."

And when they found it, the pathway created by Toshack was encouraging players who might have scorned the opportunities in the past to follow it.

"When we approached Hal Robson-Kanu he wasn't sure – he had

played for England Under-19s at that stage – so I told him to take his time, but I would be like a rash," recalls Flynn. "I had a good relationship with his manager at the time, Brian McDermott, and every time I'd be in London I'd go over to Reading's Hogwood Park, checking in on Jake Taylor and Churchy and then just to see how Hal was doing.

"That's what it was like, doing whatever we could to see what players were out there and clubs welcomed it. We were taking a positive interest in their players but it wasn't as if we were a rival club coming to poach them, we wanted to promote them and it would benefit the club for the player to get the chance to develop with us.

"And these young players would see others getting their chance with John and realising there was a great opportunity for them. They could see what we were trying to build."

The promotion of the production line was no lip-service sales pitch. Chris Gunter had made his senior debut against New Zealand in May 2007, but by the time the final games of the Euro 2008 qualifying campaign – the first fixtures since the Cyprus and San Marino fall-out – he had been back on the fringes of the first team at Cardiff City.

"I'd been called up for the games against Ireland and Germany but as far as I was concerned I wasn't going to be playing," recalls Gunter, still only 18 at the time and with less than 20 Football League appearances to his name.

"I can remember coming out of the shower after one training session on the Wednesday ahead of the first game on the weekend and John Toshack was sat on the edge of my bed. I was sharing with Joe Ledley at the time and John was there chatting to Joe asking what formation he would be comfortable in and what others thought. We had been down to play 3-5-2, as we quite often did, but Joe told him the general feeling among the boys was that we preferred a 4-4-2 or at least a back four.

"We'd still been lining up with a 3-5-2 but come the Friday morning, Tosh came up to me before training asking if I 'fancied a game tomorrow?' At that age, those of us young enough would quite often train with the seniors but then go and play for the Under-21s so that was my thought and I said I'd travel up to Wrexham after training to join up with Flynny.

"He turned to me and said: 'What the hell are you on about? I mean for us. Left-back okay?' And that was that; I played left-back against Ireland, wing-back in Germany where we got a draw and I didn't really come out of the side."

A Cardiff reserve before that week, by the turn of the year he had moved to Tottenham and the Premier League in a £2m move.

"If they were good enough, they were old enough," adds Flynn. "And we knew a lot of them could be good enough if we gave them the right chance."

Some were clearly good enough. One more than others.

Aaron Ramsey had already been making people sit up and take notice. He had, by coincidence, taken Toshack's record as Cardiff City's youngest player at the age of 16 when he played a Championship fixture against Hull in April 2007, before underlining his class with Flynn's Under-21s and as a key part of the Bluebirds' 2008 run to the FA Cup final.

Understandably shy off the field, on the field he was a buzz of belief and ability even at that stage of his career, his demand for the ball belying his tender years. It was of little wonder that Everton were among clubs that had tried to lure him from Cardiff even before he had signed full terms; even less of a surprise that Arsenal and Manchester United battled it out for his signature after his breakthrough year. While there may have been some gambles taken on others in Toshack's youth revolution, there was simply no risk in predicting the impact this kid from Caerphilly would make.

"I think that it was when we knew Gareth and Aaron were coming through at the age of 15, 16 that we knew this group could be something special," says Flynn. "Gareth had already moved on quickly at that stage and there was never any doubt Aaron would do the same."

It could be argued that the two stand-out talents of their generation were the firmest justification Toshack needed to carry on as he had been, a two-part symbol to strengthen his resolve in building a team for tomorrow rather than for today.

As a minor earthquake interrupted their stay in Iceland for an end-of-season friendly, the 1-0 win in Reykjavik did not exactly send out shockwaves, but the fact the side sent out was the youngest-ever fielded by Wales in modern times was a further statement of intent from Toshack. It would not be the last time journalists gathered to compare scribbled notes and numbers to check whether the average age of the side selected was lower than ever before.

It could have been younger still. The 17-year-old Ramsey remained in reserve having travelled and trained ahead of a £5m move to Arsenal, but there were first caps for Vokes, Collison and Ched Evans, the striker who kept up a Jimmy Greaves-esque record of scoring on his debuts with a delightful flick. It was a particular frustration that the north Wales Manchester City product did not fulfil his career potential even before the incident that saw him create more headlines on the front pages than he ever managed on the back.

Hennessey, Edwards, Gunter and Ledley were all part of the team too, now given an extra defensive boost with the arrival of Ashley Williams into the set-up, and even Toshack's fieriest critics had to accept, that despite a 2-0 defeat to the Euro 2008-bound Netherlands in their next June fixture, the future now looked brighter than it had done for some time. There was a greater faith in that future too when it came to the World Cup 2010 qualifiers. It had been this campaign Toshack had originally targeted when appointed and set out to reach his Everest.

It provided edgy home wins over Azerbaijan and Liechtenstein both before away defeats to group favourites Russia and Germany, though the performances in both those narrow losses gave encouragement that, as well as the steep learning curve, a corner was about to be turned.

It was with this in mind that Ramsey made his first start, capped as part of a fresh-faced Wales side that deservedly won in Denmark, Craig Bellamy scoring in Brondby just as he had done in Copenhagen all those years ago. Bellamy, now the elder statesman trying to nurture the new kids on the block, did sound a warning amid the optimism that one friendly win did not mean that the team had arrived, yet even he could not help but get caught up in the hype and hope surrounding Ramsey.

"We don't want to put too much pressure on him but we have every right to feel excited about him," Bellamy said. "I just thank God he's Welsh."

As ever, though, there was a punch to the stomach to bring such wide-eyed optimism to its knees.

In fact, it was a double blow. If the second was unavoidable, the first saw a return to the grumblings around Toshack's ability to get the best out of the team he had developed.

In a game where only a win would turn the second-half of the campaign into one where qualification could be a possibility, an ageing Finland side put Wales to the sword in a 2-0 win in Cardiff. The bubble had not so much been burst but obliterated and Bellamy, with his usual brutal honesty, was not prepared to tiptoe around the fact.

"What is promise? It means nothing," said Bellamy, clearly hurting but unflinchingly honest. "You have to fulfil it. You can only do that here and now.

"We're in the same situation where we're playing for pride again. We have never done anything; we are not going to do anything – certainly in this campaign.

"We never passed quick enough, we never got forward quick enough and we let people get back and then what do you do? You invite crosses against a defence in which the smallest person is 6ft 1in. We played to their strengths and we fell into a trap. It is frustrating as they were there to be got at. They are not a good side. And obviously neither are we."

Toshack did not offer much of a defence, aside from reminding all – as was his way – to the fact that no Wales side since 1976 had topped a group, let alone one with the rawness of his side, a team he said was still in transition.

"But, as they get older, other teams will have to go through the same process and, hopefully, these players will be doing to other teams what other teams are doing to them now," he said. "It probably won't be me here who will see it. But I think it is the only way forward because this just shows again that this current crop isn't ready. It hurts and it's frustrating but that's the truth of it."

Not all were as accepting, especially with Ramsey kept on the bench until the damage was done, most of it caused by the veteran Jari Litmanen who, as one reporter brilliantly put it, 'stood Wales ragged'.

Even with the previous promise shown, crowds were now down to 22,000 for a Saturday fixture at the Millennium, 50,000 empty seats staring in silence – and boos echoing from many others – at a manager who had been handed a two-year-contract extension and a remit to carry on regardless just a few months earlier. The performance had, some felt, summed up how things had become: all potential and no end product.

"Look, the mentality was to win every game," argues Carl Robinson. "But the reality was the side was still developing so on some occasions there were games where there was an element more about not getting beat.

"But there was nothing wrong in developing that side and understanding that a 0-0 draw in international football can be good. I totally understood why we did it; not to be negative but to try and give nothing away because we still had talented players who might just be able to offer a little bit of magic.

"I think some people wanted us to run before we could walk but, even while there was the odd result that would set us back, I still felt we were moving forward.

"The building blocks were in place and the success that came later just wouldn't have happened if Tosh hadn't have done what he had done."

Nevertheless, whether Toshack was being accurate or not in his assessments, the lowering of expectation was taking its toll as a feeling of apathy built up among the wider public who either would not, or could not, see the bigger picture that the manager was keeping in his focus.

When Wales went to Liechtenstein towards the end of the group, angry at suggestions his side were facing international football's version of a pub team, Toshack talked up the opposition. The contrast with the constant reminders of the difficulties his inexperienced side still faced wore thin on fans beginning to wonder whether the wait for the golden generation was ever going to be worth it.

"He was just protecting young players who needed it," says Robinson of the period. "We all wanted these players to fulfil their potential but he knew that they weren't ready at that point and just had to go through the process. He was lowering expectations but only as a means of taking the pressure off. Ultimately he gave these players the opportunities that they benefited from later. I'm not sure he's had the full appreciation for that.

"It was hard at the time – probably more for people on the outside – but when you spoke to him and looked past the short-term, you could see what he was trying to do and that it was the right thing for the right reasons."

Robinson stood down during the campaign having moved to North America and Major League Soccer, where his time in a developing team has now aided his own move into management having won much admiration for the building work with the new Vancouver Whitecaps franchise.

And while he had told Toshack he would be happy to accept a call-up if injuries struck – hopping across the Atlantic during a playing spell with Toronto in one such case – he had already foreseen his exit.

"I knew all about Rambo coming through," he says of Ramsey. Robinson's brother Lee had been in charge of Cardiff City's academy and done much to help ease Ramsey's path to the recognition that was quickly coming his way. "He must have been about 15 when Lee had told me this kid had a real chance. By the time he got into the squad he had it all – technical ability, he could carry the ball, an engine that would run all day. The only thing he was missing was experience but you didn't have to know much to know he was the future for us."

There was a tantalising glimpse at it as a supremely young side, missing all manner of senior players, travelled to Azerbaijan in June 2009. On a hard pitch in the heat and hostility of Baku, there was more than a feel of an Under-21 side to the team captained by Joe Ledley and anchored by Ramsey. The will for the team to do well was an early sign of what would eventually follow much later down the line, many eager for obviously inexperienced players to come good and prepared to overlook mistakes because of the understandable rawness; a rawness illustrated delightfully in the pre-match press conference where Ledley, still 22, looked around the room in desperate search of a friendly prompt when a local Azeri journalist asked which of the home players he was most wary of. He soon composed himself and gave the standard, easy escape answer of not singling out one player and that Wales were focussing on themselves.

Which is what Wales did, answering the questions being asked both by Azerbaijan and those not so sympathetic to the cause of Toshack's twentysomethings with a 1-0 win courtesy of a David Edwards goal before half-time.

That they came through together, prompting the youthful joy of the players who felt they had done it by themselves, gave a real fillip at a time when many were willing to give up on Wales grabbing the nation's attention any time soon.

"I remember seeing the squad and realising just how many of the senior players were missing," said Ledley, still at Cardiff City at the time, his hometown club where he had quickly broken into the first team at the age of 17 and immediately impressed with his ability and industry. "I can't be sure why the squad was as it was – perhaps the game being at the end of the season didn't help – but you became used to it. None of us had that much experience, certainly not in places like that where you had the heat and the poor pitch and all the hassle that comes with travelling to places you're not used to.

"It was a huge honour but I had to rely on myself a little; I'd come through with Cardiff at 17 so had played a bit more than a few others and I'd been in the Wales set-up longer than most. To be honest, Tosh could have probably picked anyone because the choice wasn't huge for him, but it was one of the best occasions of my career.

"Not just for being captain either. It was the fact we felt really together out there, most of us being the same age getting a first taste of things. We were sharing it all and, later on, it was good to be able to look around the dressing room knowing you'd had that same experience. You could look around knowing you all knew what it took sometimes, that places like that were always going to be difficult no matter who was playing, that you would have to roll your sleeves up and it might not be nice football.

"Slowly things started becoming second nature; we weren't too experienced in football as a whole but we were at least becoming experienced at international level and the differences it had to club football. You got used to the fact you'd be facing a lot slower tempo and how to adapt to it, which was tough especially coming from playing Championship football week-in, week-out. On a Saturday, if you gave the ball away you still had a good chance of not getting punished for it – do it for Wales and you were asking for trouble.

"And regardless of the teams we were playing, you started to realise you were playing against the best players of that country and you had to give them that respect. It was a higher level and you had to get things right no matter if you were playing one of the major nations or one of the minnows. We all learned that together; we all had moments like when we were in Baku together, where we fought so hard to get that win; it didn't mean much to the qualifying group but meant a lot to us.

"We enjoyed the night because it was the end of the season and moments like that helped us as well. It was a real high for us, but even the lows we had around the time and afterwards all added to what made the spirit so strong because we were all sharing it with lads you knew and liked. We were in it together and while every team needs those individual players, the biggest thing is that spirit and tightness as a group. Nights like that built ours."

It was perhaps a neat summing up of the second half of Toshack's time in charge: devoid of experience and hit by injuries, but still managing to hint that something good was to come from it.

"We'd lost Gareth in unbelievable circumstances really and it was a very young side, even by our standards in a competitive game," recalls Toshack in 2015. "But they came through it and really pulled together. After the game Ramsey couldn't speak; he'd been ill, he had a temperature so we just asked him to give us what he could. He gave everything and by the end he was coughing, spewing, but they came through it together.

"Look, people can ask 'who are Azerbaijan?' and that Wales should be beating them, but circumstances such as those, and other ones we often found ourselves in, gave results like that different meanings for us."

Of course, Wales being Wales at that time, even success couldn't be straightforward. Bale had not travelled because of a knee injury, incredibly either sustained or aggravated when playing with a young relative in the back garden of his family home the day before the team were due to travel, leaving him sidelined for several months.

It was nothing, though, compared to the sickening blow that would follow.

Bale was back for a November 2009 friendly with Scotland, the World Cup campaign having edged to its inevitable conclusion. Led out by Ashley Williams for the first time, Toshack's side looked the real deal in a 3-0 stroll over the Scots with Ramsey at the heart of it. He had provided goals for former Under-21 teammates Edwards and Church before adding his own for good measure, one that displayed the tenacity and technique that underlined his growing stature with Arsenal.

His only problem, Brian Flynn said at the time, was working out exactly what type of midfielder he wanted to be because he had the attributes to perform them all.

Three months later, before Wales would play again, the images of Ramsey's twice fractured leg placed knots in the stomachs of those far beyond Wales fans interested in the fortunes of their national team. In action for Arsenal against Stoke, a lunge from Ryan Shawcross left the midfielder writhing in agony and onlookers uncomfortably witnessing the pain and suffering of the young star. The unease the scenes in the driving rain of the Britannia prompted were worse for Wales – and Arsenal – followers knowing there was a gut-wrenching acceptance needed that Ramsey could only concentrate on his own recovery, rather than their team's revival, for the next 12 months at least.

"I'm shocked. That wasn't football. If I have to live with that, I don't want to be involved in the game," Arsenal manager Arsene Wenger said of the incident. His words resonated in Wales, the disappointment lurching between compassion for the player and the renewed wondering whether their quest for the national team's glory was cursed.

"I was sat in the Vale hotel on a Saturday evening with the players due to report on the Sunday," says Toshack remembering the night of February 27 2010, just a few days before a Liberty friendly with Sweden. "I was doing the usual ring-around, waiting for news about who may have problems after their games. I phoned Gareth to check all was okay as Tottenham were playing Everton the following day. He said he was fine and mentioned he was watching Aaron play and I said I had been keeping an eye on it too. I wished him luck, 'See you tomorrow', put the phone down and walked back into the room with the television.

"As I did I could see the ambulance on the side of the pitch, players all huddled around and concerned and someone on a stretcher. I tried to count through the players and thought 'It can't be him'. Then I could hear the commentator's words saying Ramsey appeared to be in some distress. My heart sank.

"I phoned Gareth back straight away and he was the same. It was very difficult to take, for us and for the player. It felt a real blow."

As with all such horror injuries, there were initial doubts

over Ramsey's ability to recover, but those who knew the steely determination of a 20-year-old mature beyond his years felt that he would be back.

Still, it was the setback that Toshack perhaps never really recovered from, something he referred to at the end of his time.

Pivotal, he called it. He had been extra patient with Ramsey, more so than with many of the other rookies rushed into international responsibility, and thought he had been rewarded. The Scotland game had been a benchmark, finding a system where Ramsey could dictate Wales' creative game which had been frustratingly missing for so long amid the caution he had placed upon the young team.

Injuries to Collison and Allen would follow while Bale would also spend sporadic time on the sidelines. When Toshack travelled to Croatia for an end-of-season friendly, 15 players were missing and the inevitable defeat took its toll.

"That game knocked me for six," he now admits. "I'd spoken to the players and arranged this game because of the fact we were starting the next campaign away in Montenegro so they would provide a similar test, but when we turned up for training there were only ten players to start with.

"We gave a debut to Neil Taylor in that game and that was a positive – he was a tough little bugger, taking a big knock on his ankle but carrying on – but he was playing non-league at the time and we had no option. Looking back now, when you compare it to the most recent campaign and the players available, it was a ridiculous situation to be in.

"I had always been a believer that you make your own luck in football but there always seemed to be something, always a knock back whenever we looked to be taking a step forward. It felt we were just forever swimming against the tide.

"I still look back to that game against Scotland; we had reached a stage at that point where we were looking good. Ashley Williams had been captain for the first time and in the midfield we had Edwards, Ramsey, Ledley and Bale. We won 3-0, looked good for it and I came away thinking we have just got to keep our fingers crossed because I really felt we could do something.

"Within six months of that game, Edwards and Ledley both had operations, Ramsey had broken his leg and Jack Collison, who had come on off the bench, was out for a year.

"The older players who had been there – the likes of Carl Fletcher, Robinson, Koumas, Simon Davies – they had seen what was happening with this group coming through, seen the way we were progressing and decided to call it a day for different reasons. When those injuries came, we were without them all.

"I think it showed the difficulties. We had been in place for four or five years by then and it had felt like we had been getting to a point where we could kick on, but the culmination of those difficulties just hit us."

Deflated, Toshack privately told the FAW that he would be willing to review his situation at the end of the calendar year and the first four games of the Euro 2012 qualifiers. It never reached that stage.

After defeat to Montenegro in the opening game, Toshack was seen in conversation with the incumbent FAW president Phil Pritchard on the flight home. By the Monday he was gone, his departure agreed by mutual consent though the veteran did go onto claim he had not wanted to leave quite at that moment.

"John had been around a long time and I respected him – I was of a generation who remembered him as a player and I still keep in contact now," says Jonathan Ford, the former Coca-Cola sponsorship director who had been appointed as the FAW's chief executive ten months earlier.

"There is a lot of credit owed to him because he put the foundations down to help us build to where we wanted to go. He put in a lot of work and absolutely put our focus where it needed to be.

"But from a national team point of view, we needed to galvanise the team, to be passionate in what they were doing, to be hungry and to bring people together to work harmoniously. By that stage, unfortunately, I don't think he was managing to do that.

"I wouldn't call it in-fighting, but people could see it; players weren't turning up, some players appeared not to want to be there and, unfortunately, by his own admission he had taken the team as far as he could take it.

"We had started putting the wheels in motion after the chat and as much as he positioned it in the press conference that he might have stayed and said he hadn't used the word 'resign', he would not have signed those forms to go if it really was the case."

Ultimately Ford would have known a change was needed and there was little chance the FAW were going to pass on the opportunity of pushing it through. If players' faith, or lack of it, hadn't been raised vocally, it had with a growing section of fans who had grown tired. Many who were prepared to be patient, backing his ideas and plans, had seen that patience run thin. Toshack himself, as he had suggested, had looked beaten at times with the injury to Ramsey taking its toll. The fight he so often enjoyed had appeared to have seeped away.

"Personally I would have liked him to have stayed," says Peter Rees. "I think if he had been sat down as he was in Cyprus and had some sense talked into him it would have not got to that stage."

But it had and there was a general sense that, for all the groundwork, something new was needed. The players he had brought through were not clamouring for his exit, but they were part of a new generation. Toshack had fast-tracked the development of players but the team and the set-up, in the eyes of many, was not keeping pace.

"I was still so young I never really had an opinion one way or the other," says Gunter. "When you're that age, looking around at where you were, if you were told to run here or do this or that, you did it. I hung off every word because this was Wales and this was the national manager. It could have been the chef and I would have listened.

"I think a lot of the boys respected him, certainly the younger ones, because he had brought us through. I'd buy into the sessions because I'd think this is what he would have done with Real Madrid and all their stars – but as the years went on, we would do the same sessions, we knew what was coming up and things didn't change. It wasn't something I questioned because I was so young and there were a lot of us like that.

"He was someone we liked and got on with. He-was quite funny and the squad still talk about him now and the witty lines he would come up with.

"But football did move on. The sports science side of things has changed even since I've started and perhaps a younger coach may have helped him. I have wondered since if another coach more in touch with the changes happening in club football might well have made a difference.

"Whether it was the right time in the end, I don't know. All I know is what he did for my career and a lot of others here. He knew what he wanted and the faith he put into us was amazing. He could've played all sorts of other players, especially when the pressure came on him, but he stuck with us."

There is the question though, after the clean broom and ensuing fall-outs – Ben Thatcher, Jason Koumas and Danny Collins all also walked away from the squad at varying points – did he have any other choice? Was not the talent of Bale, Ramsey and others in the golden generation something that would have always risen to the top?

"Probably," admits Flynn. "But would some of the others? It's difficult to say but one thing I have no doubts about is that John accelerated their progress. We brought through players and gave them a chance to become the players they are at a time where they would have more caps than league appearances. There's no doubt there was a golden period; we knew when we saw Bale and Ramsey coming through that something could happen for us and their arrival was a key factor.

"But the group was bigger and for about two or three years there was a good bunch who we knew could really strengthen us. I think you saw that with the way the Under-21s almost qualified [Flynn's side would be edged out by England in the play-offs for the 2009 Championships despite having topped their group above France] and on top of their talent they were a pleasure to coach, good friends who all felt they were going somewhere together.

"John had made sure they felt they had a chance of doing something as a group and he didn't back away from his belief that, with some time and trust and continuity, it would happen, even if it was later down the line.

"He would keep saying to me that we were doing this for someone else to get the benefit. He meant it sincerely and I think he's been proven right."

Toshack is quick to credit Flynn as much as anyone for that. "No-one can overstate the impact Brian had," Toshack says. "The amount of miles he put in, the research he did, the background work, you just can't underestimate the fantastic job he did."

That 11 of the 13 players who took to the field against Belgium in June 2015 were given their first caps by Toshack suggests there is sound evidence to the theory. Indeed, as the much-travelled manager watched that game from Morocco, his latest place of residence, he wasn't oblivious to the fact so many who celebrated that night had first emerged under him. Having led Wydad Casablanca to the Moroccan championship – his sixth frontline trophy in management – he sat with a degree of satisfaction and, in contrast to all those years of well-intended, thick-skinned stubbornness, some introspection.

"I think seeing so many of them we helped bring through out there tells its own story," says Toshack of the rewards amid the regrets of his time. "People can say as much as they want but that statistic is everything you need to know, despite all the difficulties. And we've been gone five years, don't forget.

"I know Chris [Coleman] – I coached him when he was a 12-year-old at Swansea schoolboys with my son Cameron – and I spoke to him a couple of times after we got there. He came in with very difficult circumstances after Gary Speed and has done fantastically well, but I do think the job has been easier for him because of the work we had put in.

"It was tough. We had to start again almost. The team that had gone before had grown old together and we needed a new one to come through together. We needed to find it from somewhere, we couldn't just go and buy players ready-made. It took a lot of time and, being honest, we blooded players before they were ready because the circumstances dictated it.

"I found it difficult, to be honest. It wasn't like ripping up a club side you could do in six or 12 months; we had seven, maybe ten matches a year.

"We picked Wayne Hennessey when he was on loan at Stockport with Ashley Williams. Some were in reserve football, Aaron and Gareth were still both in the Championship and others were lower, all teenagers or just turned 20.

"And there were times I went into games doing something I had never ever done in football management. I took no pleasure from it but I found myself sat down before a match thinking about damage limitation. I'll admit it. There was no point being daft, we couldn't go out against some of these teams with the age of the players we had and not think like it.

"Coming through at Liverpool, I'd never been one to think a goalless draw was anything to write home about whoever it was against, but when we picked up a 0-0 with the Czech Republic in Giggsy's last match and the one in Germany, from all my time in football those results gave me as much satisfaction as a lot of my other achievements.

"We had to go through that and, perhaps as a result, Chris hasn't had to give out too many debuts, he hasn't had the battles which it felt like we had every time you named a squad.

"I'm sure the difficulties we went through just finding and sticking with those players had a role in the success that followed.

"Yes, I took criticism and perhaps I was a bit of a punchbag and I could take it because I was comfortable with what I had achieved in my career, but we had to do it. What was the alternative? And I'd like to think people saw what we were doing and saw the difficulties."

There can be no doubting the fact that Toshack could never field a side in successive games without the absence of one player or another with an injury, and that the longer-term lay-offs knocked things – and himself it seems – psychologically. The belief could never find its momentum.

But one of the overriding themes to come out from those involved as staff and players at the time is that Toshack may well have been able to do more and, in most cases, there was a will and a wish that he had looked to others for support.

He was never going to embrace the modern, fine detailed and scientific approach to the level of his successors, but there remains a wondering whether stronger support – and a readiness to listen to it – might have helped in those latter years.

"People can always be wise after the event but of course there were mistakes," he says with a fair amount of honest reflection. "There are always ways to improve and maybe there were a few things I could have done differently, regarding the staff and things. Maybe I took on too much myself. A number of people have said that to me since and, looking back, maybe I did.

"But I always took responsibility for whatever team I had been in charge of and what I have or haven't done.

"And as much as I accept I could have done things a little differently, I have won six trophies with six clubs across four countries and I never felt the need to use the number of staff some managers have now, where I feel clubs are doing wonders for the government's

78

unemployment numbers. I remember overhearing a young boy telling his father when I was with Wales that I couldn't have been any good because I'd been sacked by Real Madrid twice. He's right, but I must have done okay to have been appointed twice too.

"People can ask about managing in Morocco and what a title means here but there are difficulties wherever you manage and I put my track record out there to defend myself because I still think, everything else aside and whatever people want to say, what really killed us were the injuries.

"Like I say, maybe there were things I could have done differently, but it was six long, hard years and there were times I felt impotent, that my hands were tied. I'll be honest and say, especially by the end, I found it very difficult.

"But I take great pleasure at seeing those lads we picked lower down and at a very young age not just doing what they've done with Wales but just that they are playing in the Premier League. It's why, with all due respect, and I do mean that, I think one of the main reasons we have done what we have now is because those players were able to gain the experience to do it. "There is a satisfaction about that and I was delighted for all of them to see them do it. It genuinely was terrific.

"But it was perhaps harder than I had expected, international management. I remember the previous manager after the Russia game saying it could take ten years. In the end he was spot on."

But was it through a revolution of design or default? Probably a mixture of both, just as the difficulties faced were caused by a blend of a hesitation in embracing fresh ideas in the same way he had embraced fresh-faced talent, and the long-term injuries that might have undermined it all anyway. Having dug deeper than most to find a new seam of stars, there was still an element of fortune in having a clutch of clearly capable contemporaries – but it is hard to ignore the lamentable luck with injuries that slowed their progress. The Welsh Football Trust had already been doing its bit to create more technically-gifted footballers – this era perhaps the first beneficiary of the switch to smaller-sided games at junior level – but would it have made a difference if the pathway to early experience was not clearly marked out by both Flynn and Toshack?

The extent of his impact divides opinion, but even those who struggled with many aspects of his reign cannot deny the role he played and the platform he provided for what followed. There was plenty of reason to be critical over elements of his time in charge, but the overall achievement is in the bigger picture he painted that would only be fully admired after his time.

"Of course, we didn't play just because we were young – a good few of us had been doing well at our clubs and went on to do well for him too," reminds Gunter, one of that 'Golden Generation'.

"But I'm sure a lot of managers, especially when results weren't always great, would have not done the same thing. It would have been the easy thing to do to leave us out and gone for older heads but he stayed true to what he believed in and was never going to change, no matter what anyone thought of it. What we've done since is all down to something he started."

5

A New Hope

"I couldn't have got into this side" – Gary Speed

It was the surprise, obvious choice. Or the obvious, surprise choice.

Obvious in that Gary Speed's name was the one being mentioned by both those wearing scarves and suits the moment the plane from Montenegro landed in Cardiff and news of Toshack's fateful conversation spread like wildfire through texts and hushed tones.

It had been the fantasy appointment, romantic perhaps, that many had wanted before Toshack had succeeded Hughes.

Here, six years on, was the chance. Speed, the man who had captained the country more than any other player, had not only been popular with Wales fans – indeed, with football fans in general – but he had long been one of those who had been tipped to be a natural manager of the future.

His leadership qualities were there for even the casual observer to take notice of through his time in the top-flight with Leeds, Everton, Newcastle and Bolton, but perhaps more striking when in the red of Wales.

It was why Bobby Gould had made him captain at the age of 27, taking the armband for a friendly against Scotland in 1997 and keeping it for a further 43 games until he walked off that Millennium pitch for the final time in 2004.

Gould – who claims he was greeted with a smile and a 'What took you so long?' when he informed Speed of his decision to replace Barry Horne as skipper – leaned on his skipper, although it's doubtful the midfielder from Mancot would have given him much choice not to receive the nudges, be they harsh in their honesty or not.

It was in a game against Tunisia in 1998 that Speed famously let rip towards Gould about the standards being set inside the camp "Everything was getting to people, someone had to say something and Gary did. He was like a volcano, he was disappointed about the result and he just exploded. It was a game too far," said Gould's assistant at the time, Graham Williams.

"But he talks sense and is very knowledgeable about his football. When he speaks you listen because even as a coach I can learn from him. When we played Belarus he was on the bench and it was interesting to watch him. He was analysing the match, he was analysing Bobby and myself and how we work and thinking about how things can improve.

"He'll be a coach in the future, I'm sure of that. He's still young, of course, but I'm sure he could be a future Wales manager."

It had been that obvious for some time, and even more so now given the new man driving the FAW.

Jonathan Ford had himself been an unknown choice when he stepped into the association. Though his CV contained work for MTV and Coca-Cola with a heavy marketing background, he wasn't new to football administration having headed up the soft drinks giant's Euro 2004 partnership.

It led to suggestions Ford wanted to influence the decision-making blazers in the FAW council to appoint a marketable manager, one that could help him in his aim to bury the apathy that had grown around a team that couldn't even be sold to its own public at that stage, as attendances testified.

It wasn't lost on Toshack. As the veteran fleshed out his disappointment and reasons for stepping down to a huddle of Sunday paper journalists following his farewell press conference, Ford came over to shake hands and say goodbye. Toshack's response was a warning that succeeding in football was tougher than selling cola bottles.

"Tosh was older and some of the councillors in that room were the age my parents would be if they were still with us," recalls Ford with a smile. "I was the younger one and the easy shot in an industry where it can sometimes be 'where's your medals?'.

"But football had become more than what's on the field, it's a multi-million pound business. You only need to look at the last

82

20 years and the influx of professionals coming into the sporting industry.

"Look, I'm not the type to ask why substitutions were made, as much as I try to understand decisions being taken by the manager, because it's not my expertise. Like any business, you employ people with the relevant expertise to do the job, be it an accountant for finances or a lawyer for legal inquiries.

"The business needed a business person to run it and my feeling was that we needed a manager that, yes, was someone who could help us try and boost the profile of the association but that was more the case of being a modern manager, someone who could engage.

"More importantly, because of the progression at that senior level in Premier League clubs, things had developed and progressed so much in the way you oversaw a team. Things like sports science, analysis, fitness – all things that were being done at the Premier League clubs and some Championship clubs our players were at, but we weren't doing. We weren't replicating what was happening elsewhere or providing a home from home to the standards that players expected. We needed that and wanted someone who would instil it."

In Speed, there was a chance for Ford to bring in a man who was the dream ticket in that sense; the poster boy with the smile to beam off the back pages, the leader who could bridge an age gap and galvanise a team, and the forward-thinking individual who had bought into the added extras professionals needed to gain those small margins that can often separate success and the same old, same old.

He had been interviewed for the Swansea City job in 2009 and had been approached by the upwardly-mobile Liberty Stadium club again 12 months on after Paulo Sousa's short reign. Speed was said to be interested but, as far as Swansea hierarchy were concerned, not enough to force the issue when then employers Sheffield United blocked their advances.

Wales would surely be different. Unlike Ryan Giggs, whose name was again mentioned but quickly dismissed from contention, Ford and the FAW could even be confident Speed wanted it.

Back in 2003, in a more candid moment before Hughes' departure, Speed had said of whether he wanted the national job in the future: "If everything in life was perfect, yeah, but it's not."

And yet, when Speed was finally unveiled as Wales' 11th manager since Jimmy Murphy, it was still something of a surprise.

Publicly at least, Speed had ruled himself out of the running. He had not long been promoted to his first manager's post at Championship club Sheffield United, succeeding Kevin Blackwell, having served as his coach and assistant when a back problem eventually ended his playing days at the age of 40.

"I am only three weeks into being a manager with Sheffield United and that's the only job I am interested in right now," was the message given out by Speed, and that – as far as most were concerned – was that.

Still, the FAW international committee – the select few whose job it was to come up with the name to make the difference – had bought time. Brian Flynn had immediately been given the chance to press his own open claims for the role he coveted by taking caretaker charge of the side for the games with Bulgaria and Switzerland one month later.

Wales lost both games, looking feeble in a 1-0 October loss to Bulgaria in Cardiff and although were spirited in a 4-1 defeat against an impressive Switzerland side in Basel a few days later, the writing appeared on the wall. Unprompted, and possibly unsurprisingly, many of the players he had helped bring through voiced their support of Flynn, the man who had been previously overlooked in hopes to lead his country. Even in defeat he could take some pride in fulfilling his aim, albeit for just two games.

Flynn was granted an interview, although there were some at the FAW who, if they hadn't made their mind up already, were said to have been far from impressed as the Under-21s lost a game they needed to win to qualify in Italy that same month. For the record, an Under-21 side containing Neil Taylor, Sam Vokes, Andy King and Simon Church, had beaten the junior *Azzurri* 2-1 the previous year with Darcy Blake marking Mario Balotelli out of the game and Aaron Ramsey winning the Swansea clash with a stunning volley.

Nevertheless, Flynn made a shortlist that soon became public knowledge, leaving punters and pundits to make judgements and select their favourites well before they were presented to the committee.

Among the other names were Dean Saunders, who had come in

as Toshack's No. 2 midway through his reign, the former Wimbledon midfielder Lawrie Sanchez, who had overseen some up-and-at-'em success with Northern Ireland, and Lars Lagerbäck, the former Sweden manager who had most recently been in charge of Nigeria and had a track record in international football better than most. The remaining candidate was Chris Coleman, the former Wales defender who had impressed as boss at Premier League Fulham after a car crash had eventually forced early retirement from playing, but whose stock had fallen after spells at Real Sociedad and, amid financial issues, Coventry City. Coleman was unsure about applying before getting a call of support from his old international room-mate, a certain Gary Speed.

Speed would make a further phone-call to Coleman, though not before one to Ford who was given the opening he and Welsh football had been hoping for. The surprise obvious choice was available.

"We had spent a lot of time working on it not coming out," explains Ford. "Gary was still in employment and we wanted to follow the protocol of getting permission to talk; it's not a legal requirement but it is the gentlemanly thing. We kept it very much to ourselves out of respect to Gary and Sheffield United with whom we'd not had very long conversations at that point, but also in the knowledge that confidential shortlists don't tend to stay confidential very long. We produced all the biogs, the materials you would for any appointment and interview process, but we kept Gary off the list. It was only until that afternoon when I told the others we had one more candidate to interview that we opened the door and Gary came in. No-one knew. Not even those on the panel."

Sheffield United accepted they could hardly stand in Speed's way and accepted the £200,000 compensation offered well after the bookmakers had stopped taking bets on Speed becoming the next Wales manager as – just as Ford predicted – the secret didn't stay secret for long.

Yet it mattered little at that point. Speed had been assured enough that he could make the changes he felt were needed and, not that it needed spelling out, his desire to put his country's cause first meant he was prepared to take a reported 50% pay cut to fall in line with the relatively restricted FAW finances.

It was December 2010 when a smiling Speed was formally

presented as Wales manager, speaking of his ultimate pride, his chance to ease the regret of not making a major finals as a player but – most pertinently – "lifting Welsh football from top to bottom" and of the things he wanted to put into place to make it happen. That he had only four months of frontline managerial experience – where he lost half of his games at Bramall Lane – was washed away in a wave of optimism as Speed's natural charisma and reputation as a winner shone through even in his first hours in front of a camera. Only Ford's smile was wider than Speed's as the photographers' flashes filled the room.

Players were equally pleased. Those who knew Speed were already convinced they had the right man in front of them; those who didn't know him, even if already immediately full of respect for the player they had watched and imagined being in childhood, were quickly told of his attributes in the usual squad ring-arounds that accompany such significant decisions.

There was good reason for the mood, aside from the initial euphoria of both Speed and Ford – and many others – in getting what they wanted.

While a long road remained ahead, both had already gained important victories. Speed had quickly grabbed the kind of support he knew he would need to implement what he wanted, and Ford the backing from within the association to grant it to him, not to mention the necessary financial wherewithal.

"It was a conscious decision to support him as much as we could, and there were clearly a lot of things he wanted to do," says Ford. "We had a good partnership very early on but, while technically I was his boss as chief executive, he had to report to a committee with regards to the football side of things.

"But that partnership worked and it allowed us to root and branch the backroom set-up. There was some internal challenge, but the new broom gave us the opportunity to do it.

"And we also had the support of the president at the time, Phil Pritchard, who would bang the table and demand we were listened to when it came to presenting what we wanted to do.

"It was difficult because while the senior side is responsible for bringing in nigh-on three-quarters of the association's income, the budget for it was only a third. It is a balancing act where we have a social responsibility for a lot of the other elements of the game in Wales; if it was a pure business then you'd be tempted to cut a lot of the branches and concentrate on the top of the tree and the grassroots that feed it, but we're not a pure business, we have that responsibility.

"Still, we made a massive effort to prioritise certain things Gary wanted to bring in and we were able to do it – and a big reason for that was the World Cup draw. It was a difficult group and we obviously hadn't started well, but pulling England out of the hat gave us that extra bit of money from TV revenue and other spin-offs that we needed to make it happen."

England would be Speed's first competitive game in charge, some three months away in the March, but he had other things to establish first before getting caught up in the hype of a Millennium clash with the old enemy.

The immediate talk was of the return of former players in time for that game – Speed remaining open to recalls for Giggs and, somewhat surprisingly, Savage – but before he made the calls to them and his existing squad, the new man in charge had other people to speak to.

One of the first was Raymond Verheijen, or 'Dutch Ray' as he had already been dubbed in the media having first arrived onto the Welsh football agenda for his fitness work with Craig Bellamy at Manchester City and, perhaps more specifically in terms of his profile, his outspoken and typical honesty on social media.

Speed met Verheijen less than a month into his tenure as he sought to craft a backroom team beyond the more traditional No.2 and first-team coaches. He had been recommended by a man already hand-picked by Speed, Damian Roden, who was to become the national team's new head of performance. Speed had been a huge advocate of the benefits of sports science, a role Roden carried out at Bolton under Sam Allardyce where Speed had enjoyed a successful top-flight twilight, including a last crack at Europe. Roden had been involved with Welsh football for some time, lecturing on the FAW's coach education scheme run by its developmental arm, the Welsh Football Trust, and had even been a development officer for the Trust in Flintshire in Speed's native north Wales.

Roden had been head of sports science at Manchester City where he had seen Verheijen's work on 'periodisation'. It was a school of thought that had had a huge impact on Bellamy. The forward's injury problems, that had hindered most of his career, were eased on the Dutchman's approach that training was less about getting fit and more to ready you for matchday. Bellamy had been so won over by the results he personally paid for Verheijen to assist his training when he moved to hometown club Cardiff in 2010.

But Verheijen was more than a fitness man, boasting an impressive international experience to show for it, coaching alongside legendary Dutch manager Guus Hiddink, in the 2002 World Cup with South Korea and Euro 2008 with Russia, as well as the Dutch national team in Euro 2000 with Frank Rijkaard, and four years later with Dick Advocaat.

Verheijen saw the same potential with Speed and the talented squad of players in need of stewardship as he had done with the South Koreans that had reached the semi-finals in 2002 and with Russia six years later in the Euros, knowing full well that the man he would be working with had the same emphasis on preparation and its role in success as he did.

Speed, by that time, had already identified player withdrawal as key – the same issue that had eventually wrestled a submission from Toshack. If he could ensure that he'd have his best players on the pitch then Wales already had a better chance. He wanted Verheijen to help create a competitive environment within the set-up, one that had recently been missing and had deteriorated to a point players were being praised simply for turning up for international duty, rather than what they were achieving in terms of results.

A nod to the fact that Verheijen's role would stretch far beyond training and towards tactics was illustrated by the fact he was named as Speed's assistant in February 2011, yet there was another pivotal appointment that was needed to be made.

Osian Roberts had already been gradually growing a reputation in the game before Speed surprised some by bringing the former Porthmadog Town manager in as coach. For those outside Welsh football, his name wouldn't have registered, but Roberts had already been making waves after climbing the coaching ladder following a playing career where the Northern League and Bangor City was as good as it got.

In 2007, his grassroots coaching credentials had seen him

appointed the Welsh Football Trust's technical director, the man responsible for nourishing talent at junior level and up to Under-16 – a role he remains in.

As part of that remit, he had also helped establish the FAW's coach education course where managers of the future studied for the UEFA badges required to manage at almost any level in the modern game. It saw him travel Europe, learning from the best in the business, before mentoring the next generation with Roberto Martinez, Tony Pulis and Garry Monk just some to take to the Premier League having spent time under his tutelage. That, in recent years, playing legends such as Patrick Vieira, Thierry Henry, David Ginola and, most latterly, Craig Bellamy have all passed through his doors says much about the esteem he and his work is held in. Speed had been another.

"Through no particular reason other than give young players some good opportunities and inspiration, I always felt it was good for players to give something back," says Roberts of the time. "When we'd play with the Under-16s in Derby, Robert Earnshaw would come in and do a session, Carl Robinson did some too – and then there was Gary.

"He was an obvious future manager coming through the programme and he was the one keen on coming down and working with some of the elite young players. He was playing at Sheffield United at the time, but he'd drive down to do a session, drive back the same day and never ask for a penny, not even for fuel; he just loved doing it.

"Being on the course and working closely together, he saw what we had been putting in place at a junior level. Obviously, he saw elements of my work and I guess he thought I could help him given that he was still relatively inexperienced. I think he wanted people who would support him, of course, but who would also challenge him to make sure what he was doing was right.

"It wasn't long after he was appointed that we had a meeting and he asked me to be a part of things going forward. He wasn't exactly sure how it was all going to work at that stage, but he definitely wanted me there and I definitely wanted to be involved. He said 'I want you to ask the right questions of me' and he knew from working together as part of his coach education that I would be prepared to do that."

There were questions from some in the FAW over the appointments, but Speed stuck to his guns in an early show of strength and had his support from Ford and the table-banging Pritchard. It seemed that, between them, the man who needed the power to make the changes to improve the set-up was seeing it shift his way.

Speed was not going to waste it. He had been waiting long enough.

"I used to tease him that he'd end up being my boss," laughs David Cotterill. "I was at Sheffield United with him and we used to share a car from Manchester to the training ground, and there was never any doubt he'd not only be a manager, but he'd be Wales manager. You could tell he wanted it too, though I don't know if anyone expected it at the time.

"When other lads asked about him, I had no hesitation in telling them what he was like and you could just tell straight away the impact he would have. Aside from people knowing what a good player he was and that he was one of those guys that no-one in football would say a bad word about, he had that ability to stand in a dressing room and have instant respect so everyone would listen what he had to say.

"I'd get a lift back from games with him and even if the manager at the time had said I'd played well, it was what Gary said that I took more notice of. He was just a great leader and I'd seen the professionalism and standards he set himself first-hand, so I knew what was coming with Wales."

Speed had been concerned from what he had heard about the side's preparations, or perceived lack of it. If he had achieved his first goal – surrounding himself with strong characters and telling them he was not looking for 'yes men' – the next was to use that partnership as he sought to get things right off the pitch. The remote chance of qualification after three straight defeats had given him the leeway to leave the playing focus to evolve at a slower rate.

"We put together a plan of what we wanted to do over the camps we had left before the next campaign," explains Roberts. "It was stepped progress of six phases and it was a conscious decision that we would build slowly and have clear objectives about each camp. We wanted to develop a style of play and, because we were already out of the campaign, we knew he had the time.

"If it had been the case that we needed results straight away, we might have taken a different approach, but we knew we had 13 games over 18 months before the World Cup qualifiers started and we needed to use that time. If we hadn't, we would have been going into it doing the same things but expecting different results. It would have been madness."

The problem for Speed, once the initial glossy euphoria of his appointment died away, was that few on the outside could appreciate the mining for a new mentality being done beneath the surface. The new era kicked off with a 3-0 defeat to the Republic of Ireland in Dublin in the ill-fated Nations Cup – a short-lived and poorly-attended attempt to revive the old Home Nations Championship without England.

"I remember Gary going up to one journalist on the way back from Dublin and asking him why he was so miserable," recalls Roberts. "He was trying to tell him not to worry about the results for now, that it would take time but we would get it right. And we were getting it right. It was just a slow process that needed to run its course, but Gary couldn't believe how negative things were around the national team."

It was perhaps symptomatic of a growing feeling of pessimism that the potential of this side which had been clung to would never be realised, that this would be another glorious failure without even the qualifying challenge to show for it.

"He knew he had to take it, that it was down to us to change this feeling and people's perceptions," adds Roberts. "It wasn't a case of having his eyes closed about it. We'd spoken a few times and we knew that it could come to it and we could lose 4-0 to England at home. I said to him 'Are you as manager prepared to take that hit?' – and of course he was. He knew we had to do something different. He was prepared to shoulder all that as long as he knew where we were heading – and he was confident the changes we were putting in place would make sure it was along the right path."

Joining him would be Craig Bellamy. A close friend and a former teammate, Bellamy had been contemplating hanging up his international boots. The muscle injuries that accompanied the long-time issues with his knees – having required major surgery earlier in his career – had seen him carefully managed on his loan switch to Cardiff and he had not been part of the squad for the two qualifiers under the caretaker charge of Flynn. It was on his mind when Speed called him immediately after taking the job yet, knowing he shared his own passion when it came to his country's team and cause, his mate turned manager would have known he had a chance of convincing him to stay. Like Speed himself, Bellamy had that ability to have a dressing room's ear and if he would embrace the changes Speed wanted then it would have a compulsive drip effect on the rest of the squad. If Bellamy bought into it, others would easily follow.

Although the highly respected forward asked to relinquish the captain's armband he had kept for three years, Speed's promise of bringing in the best backroom preparation, which both knew was badly needed, immediately had Bellamy signed up to the cause.

Speed was as good as his word and got to work.

"Gary had been a fan of sports science for a good few years so he brought us right up to speed," says Chris Gunter. "Things changed from one extreme to the other; it was unrecognisable."

He wasn't alone in noticing the difference.

"It was a total revamp," adds Gabbidon, another who had been persuaded to return to the fold after his own injuries and indifference had seen him call it quits. "In terms of what we were doing in the build-up to games it was back to Mark Hughes and times ten. Even in those first few camps it was probably the most forward-thinking set-up I had ever been involved in. It was clear he had gone to the FAW and said he wanted things done right, that he wanted x, y and z in place and he had got them.

"From saying I was surprised at not having energy drinks in those early days under Tosh, there was now everything you could imagine. The minute you woke up you'd have urine tests and saliva tests to check dehydration so you could be properly prepared. We had all the things we had been accustomed to in the Premier League and then some. We wanted for nothing."

What Wales wanted was a win. Speed had previously spoken of his heart breaking while seeing the side having to perform in front of a quarter-full Millennium crowd, but the arrival of England meant that a sell-out was set to greet his new side in a first home – and first competitive – fixture of his reign.

It would not be the only first. All had awaited his choice of a new captain but few, if any, had predicted Speed's naming of Ramsey. Indeed, when he announced it with a smile at a press conference to confirm his squad a week before the game, he was asked to repeat it to be sure.

Not that it was an unwelcome choice; Ramsey, along with Gareth Bale, had been the pin-up idol of the golden generation and one of the greatest reasons why hope remained that this clutch of Toshack-capped players would still repay the faith placed in them. Those who questioned the wisdom of making him skipper at the age of 20 were not taking into account the steel that lay behind the quiet, sometimes shy, figure. It had surprised Arsene Wenger, Ramsey's manager at Arsenal, believing it was too much pressure for the player to handle. The England game would be his first international since November 2009 and the injury that had raised so many doubts over his playing future and whether he could still be the player that so many were excitedly predicting and willing him to be.

Yet where others saw weakness, Speed saw strength, believing the mental toughness displayed by a comeback was all the evidence he needed.

"When I stopped worrying what others might think, it was a no-brainer," said Speed as he selected a captain not just for England, not just for then, but what he saw as for the life of the team. Perhaps he imagined Ramsey standing in a hotel room years later, accepting an armband and asking Speed what took him so long.

Indeed, it was hard not to think that Speed saw a little of himself in Ramsey, a player who could be a figurehead for his generation and the embodiment of a new Wales. A new hope.

"I was rooming with Rambo so I'd known before it went public," says Chris Gunter, the full-back who had come through the Cardiff City academy like Ramsey and had remained close pals as the pair joined North London rivals within a season of each other. "I remember thinking at the time there wasn't one outstanding candidate so, to me at least, so it wasn't a complete surprise Gary thought the way he did. It was clear it was something he thought Aaron could grow into. Speedo thought he was going to be captain three or four years down the line so why not give him that experience now and grow with the team?

"It's not like it is with a club where the captain is someone you might go and see every day for something and has to organise a lot, a link between the staff and manager. We all knew what was happening in camp, we had all been there long enough by then and it was all laid out for you. I think the only thing he had to get used to was the rule that no-one leaves the dining room after eating together until he does. There was hardly anything on top of what he did normally; it was a different kind of responsibility, more so when it came to the pitch – and you could have no doubts about Rambo when it came to that.

"He is the same type of guy he was when he was 12; he has never been one charging around the room, ranting and raving, he was never going to be that type of captain firing people up, so no-one was expecting it. He was going to be a captain and lead by the way he performed on the pitch – and this was a guy we all knew had that in him.

"We were still a young squad and, because of what he was doing at his club, no-one thought he was too young to carry it off. After all, this was a guy performing in the Champions League.

"I think it symbolised something: a fresh start, a young captain for a young manager. It made a statement of what we were about and how we were going to do things."

The decision had Bellamy's backing – a long-time and firm fan of Ramsey, his talent and his temperament – and had even formed part of those initial discussions as Speed persuaded him to remain in Welsh red. Speed had already made his choice but his most senior player had had the same thought.

Ramsey would also be able to lean on Bellamy's leadership while defenders James Collins and Ashley Williams – the other contenders for the captaincy that Speed spoke to before naming Ramsey – meant this was not a side short of lieutenants.

They would, though, be without Gareth Bale who was injured in training, meaning Speed had to fight off talk about Tottenham's upset during the build-up to the derby qualifier, just as Ramsey had to manoeuvre his way through reliving the tale of his injuries and his feelings towards Ryan Shawcross, the Stoke defender whose challenge had done the damage.

"He knew it was coming," says Gunter. "We'd chat in training leading up to the captain's press conference the day before the game wondering what was going to be asked so we'd come up with some potential answers together. But Rambo's a clever guy and even if he wasn't fussed about all that side, he was fine with it."

The expected inquest at the press conference failed to open old wounds. Covering the resulting operation scars on Ramsey's leg was a tattoo of angels and Caerphilly Castle, the striking monument of his hometown and an indicator of his native pride.

It was another character trait shared with Speed. Born in Mancot but, as Chester-born father Roger would sometimes say, "the only Welshman in our family" Speed had an incredible loyalty and sense of belonging to his country. At one point of his playing career, he would even switch his car stereo to play Tom Jones as he crossed the border onto *The Green, Green Grass of Home*.

If he did not fall into the 'Welsh trap' of claiming that a victory over England would represent a career high point – that position saved for qualification, he maintained – he did see the opportunity to, as he put it, "reignite the spark in Welsh football". He was eager to use the platform to show there was again reason to have pride in the national team and coupled that with a chance to increase the sense of connection in his camp.

Ian Gwyn Hughes, the former BBC commentator who had been appointed the FAW's director of communications, was asked to explain the lyrics of the national anthem to the team – some of whom were Anglos and whose first exposure to the proud tune would have come while picking up age-grade caps.

"Gary then had the idea of bringing in the Miss Wales at the time to teach some of the boys," adds Roberts, Courtenay Hamilton having been a classically-trained opera singer. "He handed out sheets, one with the Welsh lyrics and another with them spelt out phonetically and we all stood as a group, arms around each other, and sung it together. It was all light-hearted – some were struggling more than most – but it got the message across. This was us, we were in it together and he had managed to stress how important it was that we had that connection with the Welsh public. It was a big statement but he managed to do it with everyone smiling."

Speed was keen on ensuring there was an enjoyment to things with Wales again, knowing how vital it was to have players wanting to turn up. Speed had rarely missed games during his 14 years as an international, even having to be told by Terry Yorath to stay away and enjoy the title celebrations with Leeds as he attempted to report for a friendly with Austria just a few days after Howard Wilkinson's side won the championship in 1992. But that was Speed. He knew he couldn't expect such obvious commitment without working for it, but had to do it with a balance of providing the right environment for serious work, as well as the enjoyment so that the notion of Wales camps being a chore could be ended.

Trying to tighten up the perceived looseness of the previous management, Speed was strict in laying out what he expected but the players sensed he was trying to treat them like adults, playing on their increasing responsibility that they found at club level. Yet it was done with egalitarianism, camps becoming dry with staff opting out of alcohol with meals to show the players they were all making sacrifices together.

He thought deeply about balancing the firm and the fun. He would arrange entertainment for each camp as a way of integrating the group, with one camp seeing a magician performing over dinner. The next had a comedian. Wales had been the butt of jokes for some time but there was a seriousness that underpinned Speed's idea.

"We wanted them to enjoy spending time together," says Roberts. "We'd arrange something in the early part of the week because we knew the camps could be intense with the new ideas and things we were putting in place for them to take on board, so it was a way of making sure they could still have a laugh together at the same time. We wanted them to be passionate about playing but Gary knew the importance to them to, first of all, just enjoy turning up and being part of things.

"We had been aware that we wanted to be fairly strict early on because there was a sense things had got a little loose and we knew we had to quickly put a structure in place for the camps.

"We had banned golf when we were staying at the Vale hotel to keep a focus on what we were doing and because it wasn't great physically in the build-up to a match.

"But I remember Craig [Bellamy] coming up to us once and asking if he could play a round because if he wasn't able to go and switch off that he'd be bursting at the seams come the Thursday and be spent psychologically. Gary thought about it and realised Craig had a point, that the week was too long, and told him to go off an enjoy nine holes – though using a buggy. It showed that, although he wanted to bring a shift in mentality and a greater focus, he was young enough to appreciate what it could be like for the players, and that he was prepared to listen to them. He wanted their input."

Speed wanted players to come out of their shells. He introduced former squash champion Adrian Davies as team operations manager, effectively a players' liaison role, to try and encourage a light-hearted feel to things. He quickly became part of the scene around the camp and introduced quizzes and a game called 'Show Off' where players would have to take it in turns to stand up and effectively brag about themselves, be it their career appearances or their GCSE results. If the rest of the squad enjoyed what they heard, the applause would end the suffering – if not it would go on. They wanted a club feel to things, more of a closeness which can be hard to develop with so few games in a year. Before one match they organised a barbecue where families were invited along to enhance the sense of community among the group.

It was only a touch of lightness but it was on the basis that Speed wanted his squad to be more vocal and to interact more. There was a sense that they had shied away under Toshack but Speed wanted his players to take a responsibility and to become part of the process.

It is why, when he found meetings were not seeing players' speaking up, he broke them down into unit meetings where the smaller groups, be it defenders, attackers, and so on, would feel more at ease to discuss and talk, before the squad would regroup and put their findings together.

But he was very much the leader, the one pointing the way forward with the new ideas and new methods he and his new staff were very quickly introducing.

If the changes he was bringing were necessary, they were not insignificant in either their importance or their numbers.

"The first couple of camps were almost like a shell shock," says Gabbidon. "From not feeling like we were doing much in the build-up to games, now we were taking a lot of information on board. Mentally it was very different and it tired you to start with, trying to cope with such a change in pace. Before, it had been something to eat, perhaps one meeting, and then back to the rooms to occupy yourself. Now it was meeting after meeting, the schedule jam-packed because he wanted to try and cram a lot in. It was meticulous."

Immediately the staff size increased, almost quadrupling. Analysis was immediately increased, with staff moving over from the Trust to give detailed feedback. Not just on the opposition as a whole now, but the individuals who players would be marking and, perhaps more importantly, each and every training session filmed and edited so players could see the progress that was now expected of them. Players were provided with computer tablets where they could see and track their own performances and view key information about the man they were expected to come up against in a few days' time.

"It was brilliant," admits Gunter. "We all felt it straight away and knew it was what we needed. Things rarely stand still in football and the growing sense that you had to look for those small extra percentages and it was what we had been seeing at our clubs.

"We had started to gain the experience we needed with Wales but there was a feeling that when we came away on international duty we were missing what we were getting week-in, week-out and what we were doing began to feel a little out-of-date.

"Before, when we'd have video sessions, the footage wouldn't be edited so you'd watch the whole of the half rather than the pertinent parts. Even when the ball went out of play or stopped for an injury we'd all be sat there watching it, even the anthems before the game.

"Footballers being footballers, you tend to find if it goes on for longer than 25 minutes then a lot would lose focus on why you were watching it in the first place and what you were supposed to be gaining from it.

"Camps can be long and it takes a lot of work to keep things sharp and focussed, and as the campaigns had been going on, it felt it was all getting dragged into a cycle we were going to struggle to get out of. We'd definitely benefited from what had happened before but we did need this change to take the next step."

The extra emphasis on analysis would be needed. The positivity that had emanated out of the camp and into the build-up for the England game – even surviving the late withdrawal of Bale – lasted all of seven minutes. A rash foul from James Collins on Ashley Young gave Frank Lampard the chance to score from the spot, a lead England doubled seven minutes later through Darren Bent and never looked like losing. The sell-out crowd – including many day-trippers lured by star names and the prospect of a derby – fell flat and the distant hope that the fixture could have provided an early catalyst for upward momentum fell with it.

Coupled with a world standing that had now fallen out of the top 100, it provided the excuse for much 'state of the nation' type analysis.

As the Nations Cup played out with an end-of-season defeat to Scotland and a weary first win over Northern Ireland, watched by very few either in Dublin or back home, those looking to kick Welsh football had never found it so easy.

By the July, Wales were 117th in the world, immediately below Haiti with Guatemala and Guyana lording it above them.

Though rankings had hardly been fair on Wales over the years to that point, qualifying wins – where the most points came from in FIFA's calculations – had been few and far between. Toshack had ended with 21 wins from his 53 games in charge, a win ratio of 40%, but many victories had come in friendlies that counted little when it came to the ranking number crunching.

Though the team had remained around the 60-80 mark during Toshack's tenure, the failure to rack up much of a number of results against sides ranked higher than them had begun to take its toll. Protecting the young team from heavy defeats was never going to be reflected.

Even the fact that Wales had improved in that game against England, slowly getting to grips with things in the second-half, those small steps made no impact on the scoreboard and would be lost in the post-match headlines of how far Wales had fallen, because the uncomfortable fact of the matter was that they were statistically Europe's fifth poorest side with Liechtenstein not far behind.

All of a sudden, Toshack's protestations over the pub team description felt even more awkward.

It came at a bad time too. Not aided by a rankings expert informing FIFA that the Faroe Islands had been given an incorrect rankings point total, Wales swapped places with the tiny nation and slid into the bottom pot of seeds for the 2014 World Cup qualifying draw. The proud nation of Charles, Rush and more were read out alongside Kazakhstan, Luxembourg and San Marino. A scan through the names available to Speed were a reminder that Wales were no-one's whipping boys but, regardless, the symbolism of the country's name languishing at such a level represented a very real low point in the national side's history.

Speed, both as proud patriot and manager, was embarrassed. Though he had presided over three losses from his four games, the standing was hardly his fault – but the revival was his responsibility.

He was not perturbed by it. The challenge had not become any greater and both he and his close staff had not only seen enough in their side to know that momentum could soon build, but they had also seen enough, even in defeat to England, to know that they were already inching forward.

"The easiest thing we could have done, 2-0 down against England, would have been to tell them to stop, to stop everything we had told them to do," says Roberts. "We could have got the message out to stop building from the back, don't implement what we had been planning over those first few camps, skip it all and change it and maybe we could get back into the game and nick a draw so we could all cling to that.

"But had we done that, come the final whistle we'd have been nowhere nearer to where we wanted to be. We'd have been just reacting to that one game and we'd lurch from one fixture to the next, staying where we'd always stayed.

"But we didn't, we stuck to the plan. Obviously Gary wanted to win the game but he wanted to carry his plan through. It was the best thing he could have done because if we had scrapped it we would have lost all the players, there and then.

"We had been loading them with information, putting out there how we wanted to go forward and asking them to put their trust in us and the plan we had. If we had thrown it out the first time it had gone wrong they'd have thought 'If they don't believe in it, why are we wasting our time?'

"We had to be strong and be seen to be strong – and Gary was. The fact he stayed believing in what we were doing may not have won us that game, but it made sure the players, even when we lost, kept the same belief as he did.

"We could see that and we knew we had something to work with. This was a proper qualifying game where we had 90 minutes of footage where we could sit down and, first, show them what we had been working on in training, and then compare it to the match itself to highlight where it wasn't being executed."

Speed and his staff showcased how the team had kept their focus on keeping possession but had dropped too deep while doing it, the link between midfield and defence lost and the frontmen isolated. Without Bale's thrust and outlet, Bellamy had been starved and England won the ball in high areas easily without much comeback.

"We could point out to them how they were 15 yards deeper than they should have been compared to what we had worked on in training, and how we couldn't breathe and play out," adds Roberts. "We could show them why we had been doing what we had been in training, and the consequences of what happens when they didn't carry it out. We had that greater understanding from them straight away because the best coaching tool possible is to be able to show just why you are doing what you are doing. The players had trusted us but now they could see it for themselves too."

And there were plenty of them seeing it. While Toshack and Flynn's 'Golden Generation' groundwork had left him with a deeper player pool, Speed was eager to be able to utilise it rather than simply speak about it. Injuries were often unpreventable but he would have known all too well himself from his recent playing days – and from his time as an international – the kind of pressure placed upon stars when it came to the chance to rest knocks and niggles in friendlies or competitive games where qualifying wasn't on the agenda. He spelt out the need to his squad to turn up come what may, but he also sought to gain the trust of the top-flight managers he was, in effect, borrowing players from. He wanted to make sure that his players' commitment would mean something.

Rather than get caught up in rows, Speed's natural charm and respect saw him make the necessary calls to the likes of Arsene Wenger at Ramsey's Arsenal and Harry Redknapp – by then managing Bale at Tottenham – to lay out his plans ahead of an August friendly with Australia just three days before the start of the Premier League campaign, a game he saw as the start of the side's bid for the 2014 World Cup.

It was more than just words. Speed's immediate increased use of the latest sports science had earned some faith from club managers having been at pains to point out that training was now more based around getting players game-ready, as opposed to getting them fit.

A traffic-light system had been introduced; those in need of getting up to match pace in the green category, with those needing to tick along and simply retain a sharpness in red. Player wellness and preparation were key and Speed wanted to make sure the clubs knew it. There was an element of self-interest in his aims, of course. But just as important in Speed's eyes was ensuring Premier League bosses knew that he wanted these players to avoid injury as much as they did – and it would serve him no good, short or long-term, if he abused this new trust.

It would have meant little if it was not embraced by the players themselves, but there was little doubt that they had. Joe Ledley had turned up for the end-of-season games in Ireland despite injury, Bellamy likewise despite missing out on Cardiff's ill-fated bid for the play-offs with a hamstring strain. Neil Taylor brushed aside the disappointment of being suspended for Swansea's Wembley promotion final following a red card in the semi-final by quickly calling and asking to be added to the squad. Come the August, James Collins, Andrew Crofts, David Edwards, Ched Evans and Sam Vokes all reported to camp even though they would not be able to feature. It seems they could see things were starting to move forward – and none of them wanted to be left behind.

"It was a big plus for us, a real message from the players that they understood what we were trying to do and where we were trying to go with it," says Roberts. "Players like David Edwards, who had a real problem with his back, still came into camp so when we went through things, he understood the game plan and it wasn't a case of playing catch-up when he was fit. It helped us make sure we could have a continuity even when there were injuries, which is always going to be the case.

"But as much as a player wants to do that, clubs aren't going to allow it if they think they won't be looked after properly. We had improved the sports science and medical side of things, and efforts like that showed that we were already getting a benefit from it."

It was a victory of sorts for Speed, a first sign that the player withdrawal problem which had blighted Wales for so long – be it through luck or lack of belief in methods – might not be such a telling factor going forward.

What Speed now needed was a victory on the pitch but, against an Australian side almost 100 places higher in the rankings and who had beaten Germany earlier in the season, it did not come.

It felt like a setback and, judging by his harshest words since coming into the job, it appeared Speed sensed the same. Players spoke of letting their manager down, that they weren't able to showcase the strides they said were being made. Indeed, it was only in the final 15 minutes, when Darcy Blake reduced the Cardiff City Stadium deficit to the 2-1 final scoreline, Wales found any attacking purpose to go with their possession.

The players were there – Bale making his first start of the new era and Bellamy the other side of a three-pronged attack – but Speed and his staff now sensed the need for a tweak in tactics.

"We had started so slowly in that game," recalls Roberts. "And it was something we needed to see because after that we changed things slightly. We had a plan and we weren't moving away from it, but it would have been foolish not to review and reflect on it.

"That's what we did. It dawned on us that when we started slowly, we struggled to get any tempo in our game. We sat down and talked it through and decided we needed to move away from starting a game by building from the back. We needed to go more direct early on to get us higher up the pitch, to get the crowd going and that tempo high where Gareth and Craig could be involved more.

"We thought that it would get everybody into the rhythm we needed and then we could switch back, to playing out from the back so when we did it we could do it with a purpose.

"The game had been disappointing but Australia were a very organised side who had been together a long time, so it was two teams in two completely different stages – and because of that we learned so much. We felt we were ready for the next step."

Pressure was certainly building for them to take it. Impatience from those ignoring some of the signs of greater sharpness and promise would build towards the Montenegro home fixture the following month. The group's lowest seeds, Montenegro had surprised by challenging England at the top of the group. Still, the narrative had been set that Wales needed to win to stop the Speed reign – just five matches old – being dragged into the same kind of gnashing of teeth that had accompanied Toshack's final days.

There were suggestions the rookie boss would be forced into a review of his backroom team were Wales to lose. Yet Speed's supporters within the association's hierarchy backed the manager by supporting some out-of-the-box thinking from him in the build-up.

Speed hadn't been alone in wondering quite what had gone wrong in the game against Australia. Training had been particularly impressive with players not holding back from displaying an edge, despite the concerns of their clubs no doubt ringing in their ears so close to the domestic season's start. Perhaps it would be unfair to call it a final throw of the dice, but Speed was keen to symbolise a fresh start; that things were now going to be different. He had tried everything else and his plan was to change the scenery. He was granted the request to switch hotels to the luxury of the Celtic Manor on the outskirts of Newport – the setting for golf's Ryder Cup less than a year earlier – despite the FAW's contract with the Vale Hotel where the team would still have to train. There had been no complaints regarding the Vale where the side had been based for a decade, but Speed just wanted to do something different, to give a feel of newness and to physically leave past disappointments behind. It would cost the FAW £15,000 just to do so.

It brought grumbles from plenty at the association but it also brought the desired result. The 2-1 victory was not only a first three points of the hitherto winless campaign, but it was a major point proved: that the steps being taken were leading somewhere.

The players who were asked to step up did so, belief and a desire to win – for both their manager and their country – shining through from the moment Steve Morison opened the scoring before Ramsey had made it two.

The display – one of the biggest upsets in FIFA ranking terms with a competitive victory for a side 98 places below their opponents – had backed up some pretty high praise from Speed beforehand. He had claimed that the team had the potential to be better than any of the Wales sides he had played in – and it was now down to a matter of making the players believe it. Even though a crowd of just 8,000 would witness it first-hand against Montenegro, supporters could ignore the fact such words had been heard all before; they were now seeing the evidence for themselves.

"I had started to feel embarrassed coming out in front of the media and supporters every game and telling people it would come and that things were better – but without the win to back it up," said Ashley Williams following the victory, one that included a decent rearguard action after Stefan Jovetić had threatened a comeback with Montenegro's goal 19 minutes from time.

"You can talk all you want but we knew people were getting tired of us saying the same things. We felt we owed a performance and a result to everyone.

"There was a feeling we had to stand up and be counted and every one of us did that. I think you can say boys turned to men with that performance."

The latter point would have resonated with Speed who was keen for his team to become ruthless winners, previously describing them as "ideal son-in-laws". Given the former midfielder had a career that blended an ability to be tough as teak in a tackle alongside his polished passing game, he was perhaps asking them to follow his lead.

They undoubtedly looked ready to; the win – the first qualifying victory at home in three years – not so much providing relief, as previous triumphs had, but providing faith that a run of results could and would follow.

Even defeat to England at Wembley a few days later could not quell the growing feeling that a corner had been turned. The confidence that Speed had seen in training was now flowing out on the field of play. It came even after the loss of Craig Bellamy through suspension, a yellow card at Cardiff City Stadium costing the veteran what he might have imagined as a last chance to play at Wembley.

"We battered them," smiles Roberts, giving an indication of how a performance can sometimes provide as much satisfaction as a result, Ashley Young's 35th minute goal and Robert Earnshaw's late miss denying Wales the draw that was the least their endeavours deserved. "I have a passion for coaching and tactics and that side of the game and it was a highlight for me being able to look over to the England bench to see Fabio Capello and Stuart Pearce; they just didn't have a clue of how to stop us. They had millions of pounds' worth of talent on that pitch and we had a young side trying to pave their way – and we played them off the park. It was a great night from that perspective."

It could have been even better. Ramsey's free-kick with 14 minutes to go was met by Darcy Blake and knocked down to Robert Earnshaw, unmarked at the far post, who somehow scooped the ball over the bar. Speed had been off his seat, covering his mouth, aghast at the chance slipping away.

Yet he felt the bigger opportunity was even firmer in his and his side's grasp as he sat around with staff at the team's hotel base on the outskirts of London. Even a natural-born winner could take positives from a loss, as the music-lover took requests from those around him to play from his iPod collection. Despite defeat, Speed was content.

The side had listened and carried out instructions to the letter – allowing England to have possession in their own half then pressing hard, taking good care of the ball themselves and utilising Ashley Williams' ability to hit a scything diagonal pass to release Bale to stretch and switch play when needed.

He had also made a strong statement in his selection. Blake had long been regarded a player of potential but had suffered for his versatility somewhat, playing in different positions at the back and even in midfield at Cardiff, without being able to nail down a role and often finding himself out of his club's starting XI. Here he had kept James Collins out of the team as Speed rewarded the performances during Collins' suspension, the more established player having made a string of costly errors in previous games. It was a message that not only was Speed prepared to make big calls, ones that he would have had to answer to had it gone wrong, but that this team would be one of players who could perform to the standards he demanded and not what had gone on before. Blake, 22 at the time, repaid him with a marking job on Wayne Rooney that many more seasoned, stellar players would have struggled with. Inexperienced he may have been, but Speed was showing the confidence that suggested he had belief in himself as much as he did his side.

"He was very focussed on what he wanted to achieve," says Roberts. "He was prepared to make brave decisions because they were the right decisions, made simply on who would be best in that situation. He was definitely growing as a manager with every game."

It showed. There wasn't so much a swagger about Speed come the following month's visit of Switzerland but there was an air of authority about him, one of relaxed confidence that fed into even the journalists during the media sessions in the hotel where the team were based, let alone the players who were camped there for the back-to-back finale to the group.

Even the loss of Damien Roden – released by the FAW over a messy contractual dispute that Speed had hoped to overcome but knew was a battle he had little chance of winning this time – did not impact on the smiling but stern sense of what lay ahead. He teased reporters about his team selection as he sipped a coffee outside the press conference room, telling them when they got hot or cold over the right names and comparing predicted Swiss line-ups. This was a man who appeared in control of his destiny, fuelled by the faith in a side now completely convinced they could go places under his and his staff's charge. He even enjoyed the fact that Switzerland were complaining about playing the game in Swansea and the extra travelling their officials and squad would have to endure, knowing full well that "little old Wales" had been shunted to various outposts of foreign countries when they had gone away over the years. He had never looked more comfortable as an international manager.

With such an assured aura overflowing from the top, Wales' display against the Swiss came as little surprise to those who had been in his company before the Liberty Stadium clash.

Managed by the hugely-experienced Ottmar Hitzfeld – a double Champions League winner – Switzerland had no answer to a Wales display that was better than most could recall. The Swiss had been unbeaten in nine before the fixture and still in with a chance of joining England in qualifying, yet they had been clearly second-best in Swansea even prior to Reto Ziegler's 55th-minute red card for a lunge on Chris Gunter, with Wales deserving to be ahead long before Ramsey's 60th-minute penalty was followed by Bale's 71st-minute second.

With Switzerland ranked 18th in the world going into the game, it was the first time Wales had recorded back-to-back home wins over top-ranking nations since Speed's wide-eyed international playing days when Enzo Scifo's Belgium and reigning world champions Germany were beaten by a 1991 side containing the then 21-year-old midfielder.

Granted, Ramsey's scruffy penalty and Bale's race onto Steve Morison's pass behind the Swiss defence and calm slotted finish are unlikely to live as long in the consciousness as Ian Rush's stab past Bodo Illgner at the National Stadium, yet those who walked out into the Swansea air that night couldn't help but feel that new significant memories would be created soon enough.

The introduction of Joe Allen as a starter seemed to make a difference, the Pembrokeshire playmaker having not only overcome worries of whether he was able to step up to the Premier League with Swansea, but now looking a natural fit at the highest level with his anticipation and awareness of the passes around him. Reunited in a side with the drive and cutting edge of Ramsey – having been successfully paired in that Under-21 Flynn win over Sweden four years earlier – the three-man midfield looked to have the balance that brought even more out of a young side enjoying the football they were playing.

The players felt they were close to getting it right too, going into the final group game with the kind of delightful optimism and excitement that usually accompanies the start of a campaign. It made sense; as far as they were concerned, it was the start of something.

Regardless of whether the improvements off-the-field aided Speed or it being a case of some of the injury luck that had avoided others benefiting the new manager, when a fully-fit squad headed to Bulgaria three days later he could name an unchanged side for the first time in eight years. For a theoretically meaningless game, it appeared to mean much as the buzz of a climb up the rankings and attacking the bid for Brazil began to infect all. It only increased as Wales savoured a 1-0 win in trying circumstances, Bale ignoring the heavy pitch to cut inside and fire the only goal.

Bale's form itself was reason enough for the Rio dreams that spread like wildfire in Sofia – the increasingly influential and explosive talent made it two goals in two games having not scored for a year prior to the Switzerland match.

But it was the all-round effort and understanding of their jobs in the team that underpinned the feverish feel-good factor Speed's side imposed on the Welsh public from afar. Indeed, even with the likes of Sylvester Stallone and Bruce Willis staying in the city as they filmed scenes for their latest action blockbuster, the only top-billing stars that concerned those back home were the ones writing their own script – with the hope of a Hollywood-ending to come.

All the excuses were there for it not being the case, of it being a game too far. Speed had noted the issues regarding the surface – Bulgaria seemed to have let the grass grow long – and the bizarre sight of a largely-empty Vasil Levski Stadium could have easily have had an effect on a still inexperienced side. It was only when the team arrived in the Bulgarian capital that the news of a boycott from the home fans over the running of the local FA and national team had spread. Any doubts of whether they would carry out their threat were washed away as the 46,000-capacity venue contained little more than the odd suited official and steward – and the 650 travelling Welsh faithful.

It felt all a little bit surreal but the revival looked genuine and the fact was that Wales had ended the campaign with their first back-to-back competitive wins in six years and first successive clean sheets in more than three years.

Furthermore, they had done it away from home too where a victory over a higher-ranked side on the road had eluded them since that Toshack highlight of a Slovakia win four years previously. Sixth seeds they would remain going into the World Cup – where they had drawn a difficult group containing Croatia, Belgium, Serbia, Scotland and Macedonia – but, despite having not collected a point before the penultimate month, only a final-night Switzerland win over Montenegro stopped the side finishing third.

Players were now talking about their regret at having to return to their clubs rather than the eye-rolling that sometimes accompanied international duty, with duty being a key phrase when such genuine hope wasn't as obvious. For once there was little envy of those figuring in the November European Championship play-offs while Wales welcomed Norway to Cardiff for a final friendly of the year. The excitement of the qualifying climax for a major finals would ramp up without Wales, but Speed's dressing room was collectively convinced they would taste it themselves soon enough.

It was a mindset only strengthened by the way Norway were swept aside through Wales' heady mix of pace and possession on the platform of an increasingly sound defence. Granted, the one goal Wales conceded in the 4-1 win was a collection of mistakes, but by the time Erik Huseklepp did score for the visitors the red-shirted supremacy had already been glaringly obvious after Bale and Bellamy had smashed them into a two-goal lead before a Sam Vokes double in the final two minutes wrapped it all up nicely. It was a refreshing criticism of the side that the only concern from Speed was a touch of complacency in such comfort, but overall he struggled to contain the optimism about the team, like the rest of those watching.

"I couldn't have got in this side," he maintained as he discussed the fifth win of his ten matches in charge. It prompted denials from the standing huddle of reporters who remembered Speed in his playing pomp, but the proud manager who fitted the suit jacket bearing the FAW crest so well, was satisfied with what he had said. "Honestly, there is so much quality and speed, I would have struggled to have got a look-in."

It's a struggle to agree, but even if it was the case, Gary Speed had stamped his presence right through the side regardless. His playing days attitude that had gone before him was being replicated by those he now oversaw. He admitted some surprise at how quickly progression had come after those slow, faltering steps of less than 12 months earlier, but stressed that it was all about how the players had bought into it with a vigour and verve.

"We've thrown a lot at them and they haven't moaned, they've taken it on board and they're reaping the rewards," he added. "Hopefully they can take confidence from what they are doing and realise just how good there are. If they believe that, we can improve even more."

Craig Bellamy believed. He has since described it as the best Welsh side he had ever been part of, that he came off that Cardiff City Stadium pitch after that game adamant that the qualification he and the country had longed for was possible with these players, with this manager. The feeling on that November evening was that anything was possible. Wales believed. The future was theirs.

6

Tragedy & Tension

"Every day we'd all ask 'why?' with no-one having an answer.
That's the thing, no-one will" – Neil Taylor

Sunday, November 27, 2011.

It was a day that began as an unspectacular one yet, by the end of it, the date had indelibly marked itself upon Welsh football. Upon football as a whole.

Not in the way great results are remembered, not in the way most fans of a certain age know without second checking that it was June 5, 1991, that Germany were beaten at the National Stadium. Not in a way anyone could ever have darkly imagined when the calendar first turned over that morning.

And yet it had already happened, the date's fate had already been irreversibly set.

Few were to know. Certainly, as the day's football agenda turned to Swansea's Liberty Stadium there was understandably zero appreciation of what was to follow and how the coming hours and days, weeks, months and years would be shaped by the words no-one could ever be prepared for.

For all the belief and optimism laid in place by Wales in the weeks leading up to that particular Sunday, the national team was not on anyone's lips as the day geared towards the early afternoon Premier League fixture between Swansea City and Aston Villa.

The win over Norway had been 15 days earlier and attention had quickly turned to club matters. The fixtures for the World Cup campaign had been arranged, agreed and announced earlier in the week after Gary Speed led a delegation to Brussels for the necessary

III

meetings to plot out the schedule for Group A of the 2014 World Cup qualifiers, and all had been already analysed and discussed in fullness; there is only so much to say about the order in which ten games can fall.

Not even the appearance of Speed on the previous day's *Football Focus* had given much reason to start taking attention away from domestic football narratives. Relaxed, charming, insightful, Speed had seemingly been himself on the BBC programme without giving the Sunday sports desks any need to rip up back page plans. In many ways, there was a wish he would have done, that there was something more significant in what he said, the way he acted, something to cling to. But no-one was to know that then.

The press room at the Liberty had been its usual self, the previous day's Premier League incidents debated loudly among laughter as is standard fare on any given match day. From the door on one side of the room, a member of Swansea's backroom staff poked their head in carrying an expression that mixed concern and confusion. They were looking for a familiar face, looking for assurance as they whispered to one individual that there had been some awful things been mentioned by some around the players' tunnel, almost pleading for confirmation that they could report back that all was well with the world. It wasn't but the blank looks received in return saw them vanish back behind the door, leaving the room as they found it: oblivious.

It was around 10.30 am, more than two hours before kick-off where Wales internationals Ashley Williams, Joe Allen and Neil Taylor would line up for the hosts and James Collins was due to wear the claret and blue of the visitors.

Then the texts came, ones that felt unreal to read, that prompted one or two to rush out of the room for a better signal and a return call to ask what on earth the senders were on about. The messages had made no sense, like nothing would that day. They seemed to be a series of unrelated words. Journalists usually thrive on wanting to know, to be able to have the one conversation to break news, hoping as they hear the ringtone that the story will be on the end of the pick-up. Not this time. Every dial was done with the prayers that the whispers could be silenced. They were not. Each check call brought with it a sickening realisation that there was a tragic truth lying behind it all.

Some knew that truth already. Jonathan Ford had received his call

90 minutes earlier, an unknown number ringing at his family home on the outskirts of Cardiff to deliver a message that would devastate the chief executive in the same way it would shake each and every person hearing it for the first time. Ford was told, by a member of the Cheshire Constabulary, that the body of a man had been found at his home. Gary Speed was dead.

It transpired Louise, Speed's wife, had found her husband on the steps leading towards the garage of their mansion home. He was hanged, seemingly having taken his own life.

The FAW had been charged with making the announcement but, even without the fateful formal statement that would be delivered around midday, the news no-one wanted was in the air. The journalists' hurried walks to and from laptops and conversations with disbelieving desks were being punctuated with grim glances of a nightmare knowledge, of empathy that this would be one of the most difficult days they were to experience in covering sport because, frankly, football didn't matter right then.

Kevin Ratcliffe was ushered from his seat in the press room, glassy eyed as he was told of what had happened to the boy who once delivered his newspaper to him on a Saturday morning while dreaming of growing up to star for Everton and Wales, as he eventually did. John Hartson, that man who sang duets of Stereophonics songs with Gary in a Swansea pub before beating Italy and shared many more unforgettable international nights, walked into the press room then, upon hearing the terrible news, immediately turned around to head home to be with loved ones rather than try and undertake a pointless exercise in media duty.

Then, at 12.16 in the afternoon on Sunday, November 27 2011, the simultaneous pings of a dozen or so email alerts provided the darkest news in black and white.

Dear All,

Please note the very sad news below:

The Football Association of Wales are sad to announce the death of the national team manager Gary Speed. We extend our sympathies and condolences to the family. We ask that everyone respects the family's privacy at this very sad time.

Thank you.

It still seemed untrue, the tributes that immediately flowed seeming more like ones for players' retirements than this, that there was more to write and say rather than the awful full stop that had been placed by what had happened.

Broadcasters stumbled over words, Nigel Adderly's voice creaking and cracking as he interrupted some inane talk in the studio to tell BBC's Radio 5 Live and the listening world. Around the ground the usual smiles of supporters' excited matchday anticipation disappeared one by one as the news hit, like a devastating domino. Speed had no connection with Swansea as a club apart from its nationality, yet the live televised nature of the fixture, football's first port of call that Sunday, meant the Liberty felt like the centre of the football world as the shock ate into the air.

But no-one was thinking about the game. This was not a day for football.

The assumption was that the players would feel the same, that the news that had sent so many into a daze of disbelief would render those who knew him on either side unable to carry on.

It was said wheels were already in motion, that a postponement was not possible, though only the Premier League and the broadcasters – perhaps more so than Swansea as a club – could say why the game went ahead when no-one really wanted it to. People wanted to contemplate not celebrate at that moment.

The warm-ups were about to take place when Williams was pulled out of the dressing room by James Collins. On the Villa side was Shay Given, the former Newcastle goalkeeper and close friend of Speed, who had received the call first and in turn told his teammates and manager, Alex McLeish, before the teamtalks. Blood ran cold in the changing rooms. Such was Speed's status in the game, everyone felt they knew him and seemed to be affected.

Swansea's manager, Brendan Rodgers, spoke afterwards about wanting to play in tribute of a true football man and his words were hazily reiterated by the likes of Williams after the final whistle, though it seemed more as if they were trying to convince themselves.

Williams had stood without expression as the teams lined up before the game, arm in arm as Kev Johns, Swansea's matchday announcer and club chaplain, began to speak. He did not need to ask for quiet as his words carried through a stadium deafening in its silence.

"In the great tradition of the great game of football, I'd ask you now to stand and remember Gary Speed with a minute's silence."

Only the crowd didn't, managing to only last a few seconds before the claps of one slowly turned into the applause of thousands. 'One Gary Speed' rang out through the ground, tears falling then as they would do for hours and days, weeks and months. Joe Allen stood head bowed, Rodgers later admitting his worry over the mature youngster he described as a deep thinker. Given was broken, running back to his goal trying to wipe tears from his eyes. The Republic of Ireland international made an important save in the predictable goalless draw that followed, though few could recall it when what was taking place on the field seem so insignificant. Never has a point felt so pointless.

"We had been asked if we were okay to play, though it seemed the game was going to be on at that stage anyway whatever we would have said," recalls Neil Taylor of a day he and so many would rather forget but are understandably unable to. "To be honest, I think we said yes at the time because it hadn't sunk in. None of it seemed real. It was just words.

"We didn't have time to process it, to start thinking too deeply about it because you're already in game mode at that point, it had all come so close to kick-off. I don't know if it would have been different if we'd played later in the day but we're footballers, out on the pitch is where you get your release, where instinct kicks in and you don't think of anything else. It was probably the best place for us.

"But I can't say it was a normal game, that we could forget it all completely. Nothing happened, it was never going to. All I can remember out there was the eerie atmosphere, nothing like you'd normally experience in a Premier League game."

Swansea's players made their way home, catching up with the messages between Speed's squad that had gone around since that morning. For all the notion that there is a divide between footballers and the public, of us and them, the helplessness and the stomach-churning sadness felt that day was felt by all.

The awful news had reached them in different ways. Bellamy, the closest of any to Speed, refused to believe the calls coming his way until Liverpool manager Kenny Dalglish told him before their game with Manchester City, ignoring his pleas to play through the pain and sending him home.

It began with guesswork, players hoping calls would reveal the worst as rumours in the same way reporters had been, ending in that same grief that was now being felt by the nation and the game as a whole.

"He was a legend," says David Cotterill, another badly affected by what had transpired. "Everyone looked up to him, not just to him as a manager but because of who he was, the person he was. We all felt like that about him. He was more than a manager, certainly to me.

"I had been driving home from Swansea having been told I wasn't playing and I rung my wife at the time to tell her I was on my way back and she mentioned something had happened. Andy King was on the phone, Jack Collison, everyone trying to work it out but not really knowing. My wife had become friendly with Gary's family when we were at Sheffield and by the time I was home she told me it was all true. It had started to spread. It was on the TV. I just sat there for hours staring at the screen. None of us wanted to believe it."

They had no option. The tributes poured out, the words of Aaron Ramsey – Speed's captain, the player that had symbolised his era and seemed made from the same mould – formed the black-framed front page of a mourning *Western Mail*. "I am devastated. The world has lost a great football manager, but even more sadly a great man. He will be missed by all."

And he was. Death affects all in all walks of life but the outpouring of emotion around Speed's death was of a level and depth that few had experienced before. It said something of his standing in the game but also of the vulnerability of life. At 42, this was before his time, but it was the why it had happened that appeared to take a grip on so many. Speed was an idol, a hero, someone who so many had looked up to. Heroes aren't supposed to die. The uncomfortable, dark thought crossing many minds was if Gary Speed was so susceptible, then is anyone truly immune to such bleak weaknesses?

While the grief was shared, it was obviously more acute with those who properly knew him, those who had been close.

"It was only the day after that it really started for me," says Taylor. "I remember going home the night it happened and still not fully believing it or accepting it. People were saying it but it wasn't computing. Perhaps it was because it was so difficult to comprehend, to understand why it needed to happen or why it did happen.

Everybody has lost somebody and everyone grieves but, and I don't know why, this felt different.

"It's difficult to use a word to explain what I went through, what we all went through, and then at the same time you felt a little bit guilty because if we were going through it, what was his family going through?

"That's what I couldn't shake. I'd known his lads – Ed and Tommy – from my time at Wrexham where Eddie was in the younger youth sides and I was constantly thinking about what they must have been feeling. I hadn't long become a father myself and it would just keep on going through my head."

Players dealt with it in different ways. Bellamy did eventually get his chance to play through it, starting for Liverpool in a League Cup game against Chelsea a few days later and putting all his emotion into a performance he later described as worthy of his friend's memory.

Taylor was among those who visited the FAW's headquarters on the outskirts of Cardiff Bay. On the journey from Swansea he clutched a Wales shirt with words of dedication written in black marker across its front. He wrapped it around the post outside the red-brick building in what had become a makeshift, impromptu memorial in the same way they had formed elsewhere in the country where Speed had made his mark. Flowers lay at the feet of the statue of Billy Bremner at Leeds' Elland Road, beneath Sir Bobby Robson's image at Newcastle's St James' Park, at Goodison Park the home of the former midfielder's beloved Everton. In Wales, where the emotion was arguably that much rawer, Taylor's shirt took its place next to scarves of supporters. The togetherness Speed had sought in his side, the connection between team and nation, was tragically never more illustrated than in those sober hours.

It was felt in the media, perhaps none more so and none more poignantly highlighted by Sky Sports' Bryn Law. Bryn, from Wrexham, had a closer relationship with Speed than anyone else in the pack that followed the national team, stemming from their north Wales background and coinciding times covering and playing for Leeds. He had wanted to pay his own tribute by covering the following day from Elland Road, the emotion eventually taking its toll as he told his own personal story of how a returned call on that Sunday never came. His tears stood for many others who covered Speed's Wales, who had spent the previous day blocking off their own feelings to produce the words to do just tribute, only for the barriers to eventually break.

It was part of Speed's charm that he made all feel as if they knew him even when they didn't.

Which was all so painfully obvious by the circumstances of his death. The fact he had gone was perhaps not the toughest thing to accept, it was the why.

When the inquest into his death was held, it provided no real closure for anyone on that subject. There had been no telling, public signs of depression. A narrative verdict was given, the details of how it happened seeming to be irrelevant and intrusive to the last hours of a man who had been both private and obvious in the love of his family.

It was the 'why' that overshadowed, from the family funeral to the mass tributes held in his name at every ground in the country, but most emotionally at Welsh grounds and at former clubs such as the heart-breaking *Cwm Rhondda* sung at St James' before their December game with Swansea. "Seeing Roger with Gary's lads on the pitch, even a fortnight later, that was perhaps the toughest time for me," adds Taylor.

Most had spent that time still coming to terms with it all. Videos of that last TV appearance were pored over, looking for clues that perhaps were never there. Speed's mother said at the inquest that his smile in front of the camera never reached his eyes, father Roger saying that he could see something troubling his son when looking back over that last high-profile appearance.

Last interviews were reflected upon. There had been smiles when he walked out of the press conference after that win over Norway, but others suggested a quietness that did not sit right.

He had spent part of that November camp going through plans for the next campaign with a clutch of senior players, asking for input as to when to play the fixtures ahead of that Brussels meeting. In keeping with his reign, the smallest details were on the table in front of them, from the temperatures in different countries at different times of years, the closeness of Champions League fixtures that may affect teams with more elite level players, the available hotels, whether to fly directly home after the game, every potential variable. In the two-hour meeting, the talk was only of the future.

Some have said there were one or two comments during his trip to Brussels that were out of character, but perhaps only in hindsight do they mean anything or even if it is simply a case of trying to find answers and understanding were there were none. Where there still are none.

"Every day in training we'd talk about it, all asking each other 'why?' with no-one having answer," says Taylor. "That's the thing, no-one will. Of all the people, Gary was probably the last person I would think would do something like that, he was that big a personality. I couldn't comprehend it and I think that's what took so long to come to terms with."

It was reflected in the words in the book of remembrance housed in the FAW offices. As supporters were invited in to pen their condolences and tributes, they would have been among staff who had been hit as hard as anyone. Ford addressed the solemn FAW office workers and football administrators the morning after the day before, explaining the day's events, wanting to share with those who had shared Speed's company. Tearful as they acknowledged Ford's sentiments and calls to stay strong when looking towards the future, while also remembering the raw, recent past, they had seen first hand Speed's leadership and likeability, his effortless way of setting standards with a disarming 'one of us' way rather than demands. He would join in on charity runs, was part of the 'birthday club' chipping in for cakes and cards, part of the office meals and drinks when time allowed. The drinks were always on Speed.

The FAW was and is a small organisation in comparison to its rivals and yet Speed used it to his advantage, refusing to be restricted or embarrassed and only wanting it to be the best it could be, just as he had done with his team.

"He was one of the staff," says Ian Davis, the association's commercial and marketing head who had arrived just a few months prior to Speed's own appointment. "He was always immaculate and could command respect but he had that natural charisma that would bring out the best in people, that made you feel you had to give that little bit extra. He involved himself fully in the business, asking people their thoughts just to make them feel part of things, to feel special, if you want. People wanted to please him and he was good for us as an association as a whole. He was that figurehead for the association and as much as his focus is always on the first team, on producing a winning team which could help everything else, he knew the importance of being successful off the field. He helped bring people together."

The question no-one wanted to ask was who would do that now?

It would be wrong to suggest there were not moments of almost selfishness amidst the sadness of the time. Anyone connected with Welsh football, punters, players, pundits alike, would have all had that unspoken question come up even in the immediate aftermath of the tragedy. Who now? What now for the team Speed had put in place, the dreams he had dared everyone to embrace? What next?

Few would articulate the uncomfortable necessity that the future and Speed's successor had to be considered and considered quickly, but the elephant in the room couldn't be ignored forever.

Even though the subject was strictly off the agenda of the full FAW council meeting that sat in Cardiff just three days after Speed's death, Ford and other senior officials knew that a difficult process would have to be undertaken sooner rather than later.

"We did come together, we did cry together, but then we had to turn to each other and ask 'Right, how do we do this?'," reflects Ford. "There were no precedents to follow, no previous examples of how to handle such a situation. There is no crisis manual to turn to for a national team manager taking his own life. The only thing we could do, which we always said from the start, was to do what we felt was right. Not so much what the head was telling us but the heart."

Ford refused to set a timeline but there was a keenness to try and have someone in position by the time the team next met as plans for a memorial match were set in place for late February, the visit of Costa Rica – the team Speed had first pulled on the beloved red of his country against – satisfying supporter demands to pay tribute on a full, fitting stage.

"One of the problems we had was that it was such an extremely sensitive situation," recalls Ford. "When Tosh left we didn't need to advertise the job – the press tends to do that for us – and you quickly have people coming forward and registering their interest.

"After Gary died, people would have known we would eventually need to fill his position, but it wasn't a case of my phone ringing.

People understood that this was different and we had to go around the process differently."

Ford quietly went about letting certain figures know that if they were interested there could be conversations to be had. He had already made a point of staying in touch with previous potential candidates because of the unpredictability of football, though it is more than safe to assume this was not the kind of circumstances he would have envisioned.

One of those was Ryan Giggs. It would have been the easy choice and it is thought the FAW had been led to believe there was a greater chance of bringing the Old Trafford icon into the fold, that one year on he would be more open to taking first steps into management having begun to combine coaching and playing at Manchester United. There were even suggestions of a part-time role, his ability to command respect and to harness his profile to pull people together being enough to overlook the fact that Speed's work had very much underlined the full-time nature of the post.

Regardless, Giggs, 38 at the time, was soon offered a new playing contract by Sir Alex Ferguson who clearly saw his managerial path being along Sir Matt Busby Way.

There were suggestions Giggs wasn't as clear cut a favourite choice with all of the FAW decision-makers, but by Christmas it was clear other options would have to be explored.

Quite who they would target had now become the main discourse around Welsh football, with opinions flowing fast and firmly, including those of the players. As the year turned, the name of Chris Coleman, Speed's friend who had been his main rival for the job little more than a year previously, became increasingly linked with the job. It prompted apprehension, not so much over Coleman himself, who had by now publicly declared an interest, but by any changes to the set-up that his arrival could spark.

At that stage, though fast-becoming a senior player, Gareth Bale had not been one for strong comments and yet he had spoken about how it would be "ridiculous" to make sweeping changes, that Osian Roberts and Raymond Verheijen needed to remain as part of the coaching team, and his hope that the FAW "would see sense".

Verheijen was not an employee of the FAW and even before Speed's death had used social media to question whether the association was prepared to continue to fuel ambition as part of the team's continued rise. Wales had reached 48th in the FIFA rankings by December and, after the rise of 69 places, were honoured by FIFA as their yearly 'Best Movers' the week after the loss of their manager. Unafraid of speaking out on Twitter, Verheijen continued his confrontational stance by writing: "Hopefully the board will respect Gary's wish so Osian Roberts and I can lead the team to Brazil.

"There is no need for a new manager with new ideas. Our success was based on Gary's clear structure. Everybody knows what to do for mission Brazil 2014."

With the messages coming just 48 hours after Speed's funeral, the nature of the tweets and their timings were frowned upon by many. Verheijen later explained that he was simply responding to a build-up of inquiries he had deliberately ignored before the funeral and that, despite the views of some, he was not effectively applying for the job.

In a candid interview with the *Western Mail*, Verheijen claimed his intention was "to make clear that all we wanted was to be able to continue to protect Gary's legacy" adding that a new manager with new ideas and new people brought with it a danger that Speed's work would "fade away".

He continued: "If that was to happen and things went in a different direction it would be like turning their back on what Gary did."

There were plenty outside the camp doubting the significance and influence of Verheijen's role in Speed's Wales. Perhaps some were based on his sometimes abrasive personality or his primarily fitness background, but 'Dutch Ray' undoubtedly played his part, contributing both to the tactics and the new environment that had been created in the space of a year. Though technically a theorist, he soon won over any doubting players in the squad and the harsh honesty of his personality blended well with what others in the coaching set-up offered, resulting in an almost 'good-cop, bad-cop' feel to the management.

"He was quite full-on," admits Gabbidon. "A few of us weren't sure of him to begin with. We had only heard about his background. There were one or two – like Bellas – who knew him and it surprised some of us how involved he was, but it didn't take long for us to see he knew what he was talking about. Gary obviously had respect from us the minute he walked in because he'd been such a great player – it was one of the reasons I didn't hesitate to come back when he called – but we were probably unsure of Ray to start with.

"He quickly gained a respect though because he really did have his own thoughts and wasn't afraid to make his philosophy clear. A lot of the lads quickly bought into what he was saying and I remember even after the first meeting a few of us saying we liked what we'd heard from him, what he was thinking, the way he saw things. You could tell he was a real student of the game, doing things we had never done before, really innovative stuff and it complemented what others were bringing.

"And he had a real sternness to him too. If we weren't doing things right, even simple things like five-yard passes being a little bit off or not quite quick enough, we'd know about it. It was very, very different to what a lot of the lads had seen before, especially with Wales."

The pair quickly became an unlikely duo despite not having known each other before Speed reached out to him to fill the role he needed. There had clearly been a working respect developing, even if there was more than one suggestion from the camp that perhaps the pair would never be best friends if it was not for their shared football aims. Nevertheless, for the doubts of Verheijen's significance even while he was sharing a dug-out with Speed, the fact the latter saw fit to have him so close said much about his value.

"He was driving things as much as Speedo was," adds Gabbidon. "He was taking sessions, involved in how we were going to play. I don't know whether he was involved in picking the team but he was very much involved in the tactical aspect of things."

Still, it was clear who the manager was. Speed would still very much take the lead, unafraid of being firm in front of others should Verheijen overstep things. Yet the partnership worked, with Speed's wish for strong characters and to be challenged clearly there.

"They didn't seem like mates, but they complemented each other perfectly" says Taylor. "I think it just showed that Speedo wanted the best possible people for the job because it definitely worked for us."

It was perhaps natural that players who had seen the benefit of Verheijen's involvement would become so protective of the way things had worked and so eager then to put such views across.

Verheijen's own words around a situation still so sensitive were thought to have riled the FAW, though the association remained silent on the increasingly public tension of those next steps, ones thrust even further into the frontline media by Aaron Ramsey. As Speed's captain, his heir-apparent in the Wales midfield in many ways, there was always the feeling Ramsey had been affected more than most by what had happened, certainly of that Golden Generation that Speed had done so much to polish. Strong-minded even at the age of 21, it wasn't a particular surprise that Ramsey would be unafraid of speaking up for himself and – as Bale had previously suggested – what was claimed to be the rest of the squad. Yet it was unusual to hear Ramsey speaking on Radio 5 Live's flagship breakfast show – not the usual outlet for such sporting matters, particularly Welsh ones – as he repeated the claim that there was no appetite for change. He went further, backing some calls for a 'figurehead' manager that Verheijen had mentioned, one to work alongside Roberts and the Dutchman with Ian Rush a name that was now cropping up to fill such a role.

The sentiments were understandable, the message a consistent one: the things Speed had put in place needed to remain. Ramsey didn't stop there, expressing frustration and disappointment he and other players had not been consulted by the FAW over the process, something the association denied.

It prompted – mostly social media – claims that Ramsey had been badly advised about speaking up, that he had been put up to do it and that it was an attempt to force the FAW into a corner. Ramsey replied by tweeting the contrary and standing by his comments.

It was threatening to turn ugly but the FAW carried on regardless and the notion of a 'figurehead' had been quickly dismissed by those charged with making the decision, and while they were aware of the foolishness of ripping up what had gone before, the man they were appointing was a manager. When Chris Coleman resigned at Larissa over financial issues in timing he called coincidental, he was the Wales manager in waiting.

A friend of Speed, a former room-mate even from their days in the squads of Mike Smith and Bobby Gould, Coleman had long been talked of as a future Wales manager, even if his star had waned somewhat after an initial impressive impact in his career at Fulham.

"We stuck to that notion of going with our heart and we didn't think there could be a better person than Chris in those circumstances," says Ford. "Who better than a personal friend of Gary who had gone through a similar experience to us? Of course, in an ideal business world you'd be completely neutral, but there is something about being Welsh that allows you to tap into another level of passion and commitment and then also to have an empathy with what we and Welsh football as a whole were going through. So it was very natural to think of him having been part of the process a year earlier when we'd appointed Gary. Not much time had passed so we knew what he was about and – and I'm not just saying this – he had been very close the first time around.

"We had done what we had felt was right and it was testament to Chris' understanding of the situation that the way he handled things was pitch perfect."

Coleman was unveiled as manager on January 19, 2012, where he prepared to face the media and persuade them that he was the right choice to be sat where Speed had been just 13 months ago. The job of managing your country is always perceived as an honour, but the feeling was the work that had been done beforehand and the stage of the team's development meant it was more so than ever,

Coleman no doubt knew it and knew the players would need to be won over just the same, hence spending the previous 24 hours telephoning key players to inform them of his appointment. Players he spoke to tell of an awkward conversation, one where the desire to carry on where Speed had left off was obvious, but so were the conflicting emotions coming through. The excitement at reaching a personal high was clashing with the circumstances of how he had arrived there.

"That was genuine," says Ford. "We could sense it ourselves. It was understandable."

And perhaps an early indication of the struggles the man would face to keep alive the new hope that still flickered even after Welsh football's darkest day when, in Gary Speed, it suffered its greatest loss.

Coleman didn't shy away from his own confusion of feelings when he was presented to the media, admitting he had questioned whether he was capable of taking on a challenge where the potential of success was overshadowed and almost outweighed by the circumstances that had been faced and were to be faced. He must have sensed that he was not the man people wanted to see in charge if only because that man was no longer with us.

"We were friends, we used to room together," says Coleman of the North Walian he would play against in schoolboy matches as a ten year old, even trialling at Manchester City together a few years later. They eventually became teammates at Wales youth and then senior level, both sharing a passion for playing the guitar and bringing life and laughter to the camp. "I had only spoken to him a couple of weeks earlier; we didn't have to speak often but when we did it was like old times straight away.

"And then I was sat in my office in Larissa before a game on that Sunday. I'd just given the team talk and I was having a cup of tea before the match. The phone kept going and I was wondering what was going on because nobody calls me on a match day because they know I never answer. A text came through from Lee Clark who I'd known at Fulham, asking if I was all right, that he was devastated at the news. I asked him what he was on about and he replied that Speedie had hanged himself. 'Speedie?' I thought, he must have meant David Speedie, the old Coventry and Liverpool player. I never twigged once he would be speaking about Gary. He was the last person.

"I texted him back, 'Speedie?' and he said 'Gary' and I rang him straight away. As I did, my coach came in telling me we had to see the referees. I snapped that he had to do it instead, the phone connected and I said 'What the fuck has happened?'"

The answer was as blunt and incomprehensible as relayed to everyone else on that day.

"I sat in my office thinking...well, not sure what to think. There were no tears, just this numbness," he adds. "All I knew was that I couldn't take charge of this game. I had to in the end, but I never made a decision in the game, not a substitution, I didn't talk in the changing room.

"Afterwards I rang everybody. A few days later I rang my father, asking the same question as everybody else. Why has this happened? Why would he do it? I couldn't believe it. I still can't believe it. I still have no idea what happened. It leaves you a bit angry in a way."

Leaving Larissa because of legal and financial minefields, it didn't take long for the call to come and anger to be replaced by a far different feeling.

"I thought I could do it, it was a job I had wanted and Speeds knew that," says Coleman. "When it had come up after Tosh, he had phoned me up, saying 'You've got to go for it big fella'. I asked him if he fancied it but he'd said not really, that he'd only been a manager for five games, saying 'I can't do that job yet, not now'. I spoke to him about Sparky going into it as his first job and, obviously in the end, he went for it.

"It had come down to me and him, and when he got it he rang me up and asked me where I was. I told him I was in my house and he said: 'I'm in this big leather chair in my new office. It would have suited you just fine', laughing at me. The fucker!

"But that was me and Speeds. I thought I could go in there and do it, my confidence, ego, whatever had said the same to me when I took over Fulham when some were telling me I wasn't ready.

"And then when it came....I remember the first press conference and not knowing what to say. It was so raw – it had only just happened – I felt I had gone behind his back. I felt I was stabbing him in the back because I was sat in his seat, where he should have been.

"I remember walking in to the room with all the journalists and cameras and it hitting me when I saw everyone, trying to compose myself because I didn't know what to do. Normally when I'm nervous in those situations I can bluff my way through it, but I was all over the place.

"I was trying to talk but to this day I couldn't tell you what I said. I could feel what had happened and the impact being with everybody in the room and there I was, sat there trying to take his job on so soon. It was horrendous. I knew it would be difficult but right then I knew I'd been naïve, that it was going to be harder than I had ever thought. It was awful."

Yet he would not be allowed to wait nor dwell on the situation. Regardless of the fact the game with Costa Rica was little more than a month away, the immediate questions surrounded the make-up of his backroom staff. In particular, with Coleman's fellow former Wales defender Kit Symons in place to be appointed as his assistant, players were still left wondering whether there would be room for 'Dutch Ray'.

Ford, speaking at the time, made it clear that he had not enjoyed what he saw as attempts to make a difficult process even harder and his use of words showed just what he thought of some of the suggestions.

127

"We have explored every avenue, every scenario possible," Ford said at the press conference.

"We have taken on board the thoughts and views of the backroom staff, the players and the supporters. All along we believe that we have been respectful and dignified and had no wish to be involved in a public debate on the appointment of Gary's successor.

"Gary was the manager of Welsh football and of course we want to continue his legacy. "He was not a figurehead, he was the manager and that is why we have decided on the appointment of Chris Coleman to build on the excellent foundations put in place by Gary."

And he would do so with Osian Roberts.

"I didn't know Chris and I was in the same position as a few others, not really knowing how he would do things," says Roberts. "I still had my main role with the Trust and I'd had no input to the appointment so I was the same as others in thinking what was going to happen.

"The players were in a place where they wanted it to continue as it had done, as you'd expect because we'd been doing so well.

"Of course, when Chris came in there was a question mark for all of us because 99% of the time a new manager brings new staff with him. If it had happened, as much as I would have been disappointed, I would have accepted it because that's the industry.

"But he contacted me and we agreed to meet. He completely understood the situation and was very aware of that, but the most important thing for me is when we started talking about the game and how he saw it. The kind of football I believed in was the football he believed in.

"He told me he had spent some time in his career having to play football that went away from those beliefs but had made him successful, and trying to go back to his beliefs was why he had gone abroad, to re-educate himself in a way. He had wanted to get back on the grass, get back to coaching and to develop that side of his management.

"And then he said that what he had seen with Gary was brilliant and that he wanted it to continue. He said, like Gary had done, he wanted people to challenge him and I told him that's how I worked. From there he asked me if I would be happy to stay and, of course, I told him that's what I wanted. And then he asked me about Raymond."

The Verheijen issue stayed on the agenda. Coleman had come across very much as a hands-on manager and while the intelligent but unassuming character of Roberts seemed a good fit, Coleman and Verheijen appeared to be two alphas unable to co-exist let alone co-manage.

Yet the pair did meet, speaking at length in London after which Verheijen tweeted that talks had been positive while both spoke of meeting again. They never did.

"It seemed it was going to work, but clearly it didn't," says Roberts. "I've never really asked why.

"Raymond had been good for us, he was very much part of forming the environment we had. I hadn't known him before we had started but it became clear we shared a similar outlook on things. Quite often we'd be sat around the dinner table and I'd notice something that wasn't right by the standards we wanted or expected. Raymond would nudge me, 'Did you see that?' kind of thing, so we were on the same page in that respect and we got on very, very well.

"At the same time we disagreed a lot as a coaching team about what we wanted to do, but that was good, it was healthy conflict. We needed that for what we had wanted to do and it helped make sure we had a good clarity of the messages we wanted to put out. I know the players had enjoyed their time with him but, for whatever reason, he wasn't carrying on. All I'd heard was that they had been expecting him at a meeting at the FAW but he didn't turn up. Quite why I don't know."

Verheijen had been expected to take joint charge of the team alongside Roberts for the Costa Rica match, with Coleman making the right decision to take a back seat where possible, even if the media duties and therefore the focus fell on the new manager in a first match that wasn't really a first match.

As it transpired, it was Roberts alone who led the team, with Verheijen having tweeted his intention to resign five days before the game, cryptically citing "political and destructive games" that he had grown tired of.

"Raymond was an academic, someone who would think ahead of others and his work on periodisation was fundamental at the time," explains Ford. "If you look back to that time, it seemed to me the players had had their conversations and the pitch was that we think 'we're onto a good thing' and the best way was to continue and work with somebody who can help us do that. I'm sure there was an element of self-preservation but I've no doubt there was a belief that it was actually the best way forward.

"We'd appointed Chris and were happy with that decision and how we had gone about it, as well as the way he could build and take us forward. When I was due to have a meeting with Raymond I approached it with that potential of a working relationship in mind. When it came to it, my impression was it had been more about Raymond being manager. That was never going to be the case.

"He was an interesting character and he had given the set-up a balance, but to me it seemed Gary had grown more confident in what he was doing and personally I have my doubts whether he would have still been part of things if Gary was still here. They obviously worked well together but I don't know whether it had run its course. Regardless, we were quite prepared to move forward as we did."

The tensions remained in the build-up to the memorial match, Verheijen expressing his disappointment that Adrian Davies wouldn't be retained following his match-by-match role under Speed.

But all the background noise quickly fell silent when it came to February 29. Three months on from that most difficult of days, Welsh football was to have its chance to pay its respects.

"It was the first time everybody had been together since it happened," says Roberts of the preparations for a game where he would take charge of his country but could take no joy from it. His concern was for the players, of doing it in a manner that would befit his close friend's name and be approved by Speed's family who were attending the game. "It wasn't a football game, it was a coming together for everyone in Welsh football for Gary, that's what it was about. The football was secondary."

What was of primary focus was the players and their mindset as they walked into the St David's Hotel for the first time since the Norway game, knowing full well that the smiling figure that had thanked them, shaken their hands and renewed belief in a future together would not be there.

After breakfast on the Monday, two days before the game and a time normally reserved for team meetings on tactics and their plans for that morning's training, Roberts called all players and staff into one of the conference rooms. The man who admits to thriving from the study of coaching knew he did not have any textbook to follow in that moment but could only speak from the heart. He spoke of the need to press on, to finish the work that had been started, but above all he spoke of the manager, colleague, friend, person they all had lost.

"It wasn't something to brush under the carpet," reflects Roberts. "I guess we had two choices: to do nothing, to try and just carry on and hope the players had dealt with it themselves already, or acknowledge the situation for what it was and – the most important thing – pay our respects together. It wasn't really a choice because we felt we had a responsibility to do it for the players and for the staff. We had to deal with it. We knew this awful thing was there and that we had to confront it and get it out in the open so everybody feels it.

"They would have all gone through it at the time, we all did, but the players were in different groups. They were at their clubs, with their families and no doubt they would have all grieved and perhaps some of them had been starting to put it towards the back of their minds.

"But inevitably that week and the game and all that was going with it was going to open wounds. Just getting together was going to do that because it was in this group where we had known him, where we had been together. Whether we had done something that week or not it still would have opened wounds because we were in the same hotel, doing the same things, yet one person would have been missing.

"We had to talk about it, we wanted them to talk about it – I could never have had the heart to have gone in there in that first meeting and gone 'Right, Costa Rica, this is how they set-up'. Of course not. Something significant had happened and we needed to make sure we paid our respects and then make sure we gave everyone the best possible support in our environment."

Psychiatrists were on hand if players felt the need, while Sky had set up a camera in one of the nearby rooms where players were given the chance to put their tributes on camera. Some took up the opportunity, some wanted to but feared breaking down, others preferred to stay away. Before the meeting ended, a video montage of Speed was played in front of them all as they stood, arm in arm, watching together.

"It felt it was the right thing, a way of coming together and celebrating the man we knew," Roberts adds. "It was important for all of us so hopefully we could get through that week, get through the game and then hopefully move on."

The game indeed was secondary. The occasion was handled well by the FAW, fans singing Speed's name from the moment they entered Cardiff City Stadium, holding up a mosaic during the emotional anthems, spelling out 'Gary' in the red, white and green of the country that loved him. 'Can't Take My Eyes Off You' has never sounded quite the same as it did that night.

The applause for his name began before the referee's whistle to signal the minute's tribute and lasted long after the second whistle. In his suit, the injured Aaron Ramsey walked alongside the captain for the night, Craig Bellamy, and Speed's sons, Ed and Tommy. Eddie had already spoken in front of hundreds in one of the hospitality suites before the game, many of whom were Speed's friends and former teammates of club and country, but it was his speech following the game that made the biggest impression that night. Speed's father, Roger, had already addressed the players before the game but, at full-time, Speed's 14-year-old son had asked whether he could say a few words in the dressing room. It fell silent as he spoke, putting his obvious hurt to one side to show the kind of courage that all could associate with his father. When he finished he walked around the room, shaking each player by the hand and thanking them. Most just wanted to thank him.

That they had lost the game concerned no-one in truth. Joel Campbell, the Arsenal forward then on loan at Lorient in France's *Ligue 1*, had scored after seven minutes and while Steve Morison hit the bar and Bellamy came close, it was of little surprise that the winning tribute was not possible after a week that had drained so many, where every conversation had asked emotional questions of a team that were going through something no other has had to suffer.

"Of course we wanted to win the game but, as I say, it was about getting through it," says Roberts. "I had been worried about making sure the game was going along with the wishes of the family, as the FAW had been, and while a result would have been great, my biggest regret would have been if by the end of the night, Roger, Carol, Louise and the kids would have liked to have done something differently or they hadn't been able to speak when they wanted to.

"We did try and focus on the match when it came but it wasn't possible. There were times things weren't right on the pitch but you had to forego that side of you because you knew why it wasn't right, the human side had to take over from the coach.

"Ash came in at half-time saying he couldn't move his legs, he couldn't run, they were dead – and this is a player who never misses a game, someone full of energy and he couldn't move. How could I have stood on the touchline screaming for him to push on when we both knew he wasn't doing what he normally would? I could have never have done that because we knew why: the psychological blow of it all had affected them so much physically too. They were only being human in being affected by it. We had to accept it and it didn't matter. We just had to get them through the game."

After a moving night, it was time to move on and for Coleman to step up. Doing it, though, proved more difficult than most could have imagined.

7

Struggles, Shackles, Salvation

"They don't realise where we are, they don't understand
what we are going through" – Osian Roberts

Chris Coleman sat alone. Figuratively and literally, the lights were out and the ceiling was caving in. The qualifying campaign was just 180 minutes old but, even amid the darkness of the manager's dressing room, the obvious was painfully clear. There would be no World Cup for Wales.

The sounds from the players' changing room on the lower floor of the shambolic, crumbling clubhouse were non-existent but the noise would have been deafening for Coleman.

Moments earlier, as the final whistle sounded in Serbia, he had strode past the stone stand-alone away terrace that looked down upon the touchline. Those who had endured the awkward trip to Novi Sad, the Danube-banked city close to the Croatian border, penned in by authorities all afternoon and without even basic toilet facilities, had not been shy on making their angry frustration clear.

The Wales boss had kept his head bowed as the boos and the abuse rained down. He may still have been a novice in international management, his tenure eight months and four games old, but would have known what was coming well before Miralem Sulejmani struck the sixth goal a minute from time. All the hopes and dreams, all the talk of 'Rio for Speedo', had turned into a nightmare in the humid September skies a long way from home. The belief that had taken so long to build up had been ripped from Welsh football, the brutal manner in which it had been taken away leaving doubts of whether it could return. Sitting alone in that darkened room, Coleman doubted it too.

"The stadium was awful with the changing rooms part of what was like a clubhouse," he reflects on the 6-1 defeat, Wales' third heaviest since the Second World War. The score hurt on its own but just as painful was the embarrassing evidence that, two games into the campaign, qualification seemed beyond this team already. "Where the staff had to get changed there were no lights and the ceiling was hanging down. I remember sitting there after the final whistle and the atmosphere was something that I've never witnessed. I was crushed."

So were Wales. Not since that horrendous hallmark of Bobby Gould's era, the 7-1 beating in Eindhoven, had the national team suffered so badly in defeat. The sense of the 'bad old days' was inescapable, made all the more worse by the fact that the promise of good times had been so close and so recent. It was difficult to comprehend just how it had gone wrong so quickly. The only major difference from the burgeoning period of less than 12 months ago had been the manager. There was no surprise, then, where the spotlight of scrutiny fell.

Coleman had been a popular figure as a player, both in terms of teammates and with fans. A talented centre-back who could blend ball-playing with the more traditional toughness of old school defending, he was one of those perhaps unfortunate to have not been born into better Wales teams.

He had grown up not too far from Swansea's Vetch Field, raised in one of the tougher parts of the city that made the club's notorious North Bank what it was. Coleman was soon playing in front of it, making his debut for his – then – lowly hometown team at the age of 17.

By 21 he found his way to top-flight football with Crystal Palace, earning enough appreciation in his four years there to be later voted into the Eagles' team of the century and to tempt Blackburn Rovers, reigning champions at the time, to pay close to £3m to take him to Ewood Park.

At his peak, though, Wales had dipped during the times of Gould and Mike Smith. He had been an age-grade and Under-21 teammate of Gary Speed, yet was not a regular player in the Terry Yorath side that had come closest than most to the World Cup and, by the time Mark Hughes was trying to steer Speed and others to the Euros, Coleman's career had taken a new direction. Not by choice.

Late at night on January 2, 2001 and sat behind the wheel of his Jaguar, the kind of sports car that came with the wages and status of his captaincy at Fulham, Coleman was driving through the leafy lanes of Surrey close to the house of Mohamed Al-Fayed, the Harrods owner who was helping bank-roll the Craven Cottage club to the Premier League with Coleman's £2m arrival four years earlier part of that aspiration. While the club would realise their ambition eight months later, Coleman would not be part of it. As he lost control of the car, it ploughed through an iron fence and into a field before wrapping itself around a tree.

The first emergency services were concerned Coleman's trapped foot would have to be amputated on the scene, and while such an extreme option was avoided as he was cut out of the wreckage, the damage and the pain the crash had caused was obvious.

"I thought a tree had gone into my leg," Coleman says of the immediate fall-out from the accident. "It was actually my bone sticking through my trousers, but I couldn't work out what had happened."

Still only 30, there was more a concern if he would ever walk again let alone play again. The right leg was completely shattered, both the fibula and tibia smashed, muscle and flesh torn away. He underwent five operations in the space of one week including a steel rod being inserted alongside his shin and pins placed into his ankle. Damage to the veins and arteries that was causing internal bleeding around the injury was repaired by skilful surgeons who took skin and muscle from under his left arm and effectively plumbed it into his leg.

Incredibly, Coleman did play again, though his reserve outing for Fulham 14 months after the accident only served to show he would be unable to reach the levels he was once at. His cameo from the bench in the friendly win over Germany that May, receiving a standing ovation as he replaced goalscorer Robert Earnshaw, would be his last moment as a Wales player. But by then he had long known it had been coming.

"It was torture," he says of a period in his life that was devastating in one way, and yet defining in another. "One of the things that kept me going was the desperation to get back on the pitch in some sort of capacity. But even then I knew, deep down.

"I had been improving and improving but it got to a stage where it just plateaued and I knew it was not going to get any better. From that moment, I knew I would have to make a decision because I wasn't going to be able to play football again.

"I can remember clearly the day it really sank in, before anyone told me I'd have to quit or there was any decision. I had been at training, in a double session. It was about four in the afternoon and I was driving home. There were kids everywhere on the pavements walking home from school and I'm sat behind the wheel not being able to stop tears rolling down my face because I knew that was it. Football was all I'd known and it was gone. Genuinely, it wasn't about money or anything like that, it was just that all I'd known was the dressing room and the Saturday afternoon. I didn't know anything else and didn't know what to do now. I was gone."

Coleman was fortunate others had already made plans for him. Jean Tigana, Fulham's French manager, had laid out a pathway for his former captain to begin coaching the club's school-age talents, working his way up quickly towards the first team before he could eventually take control of the side and allow Tigana to move upstairs into a director of football role. Before the year was out, Tigana was fired and Coleman found his calling.

"Jean gave me the confidence to go into the other side of it," he says. "I thought I may have stayed in the game, perhaps been a coach, but he believed in me to become a manager. As it happened, with five games of the season to go, Mohamed Al-Fayed asked me to replace him instead.

"I wasn't sure at the time; Andy Melville was captain by then, one of my best mates who I'd known since I was ten years old and now I was supposed to be his manager. I was worried about coming out of the dressing room where I had been popular, and then to tell people whether they are playing or not. That was tough to come to terms with but after those five games, that was it it was what I wanted to do.

"It's funny how things work out because, if not for the accident, which was a really hard time for me and my family, then I wouldn't have been able to have done what I've done. Going through that, that stress and some pretty dark times where I didn't know which way to turn, it gave me a little steel, it hardened me.

"I wouldn't say it was depression, but there were periods where it was quite dark and it lasted a while because I had been fighting for so long to try and get fit and battling with the doubts and fears.

"But once you go through an experience like that and learn to be comfortable with things, the next time you face adversity you can think to yourself: 'I'm okay with this, I've gone through worse, I can handle it'. It toughened me up for what was coming and, as hard as it was for me and others around me, out of something so bad came something really good. Had I kept playing, gone on until I was 35 or 36, would have I gone down the same path? I don't know because it was the crash that led me in this direction. Perhaps it's fate."

Coleman's first success was immediately steering Fulham away from their fate of relegation by securing safety as the top-flight's youngest manager, continuing to impress by leading a side, containing stars such as Edwin van der Sar, Louis Saha and Steed Malbranque in their prime, to a series of mid-table finishes. When they were sold and Fulham subsequently struggled, Coleman was sacked. Three months after leaving in April 2007, he followed the path trod by John Toshack in taking over at Real Sociedad only to resign within a season. His spell back in British football at Coventry failed to bring a return to the early success that had seen him named a natural option to become a future manager of his country, financial issues and scrapes with survival eventually seeing him sacked in May 2010. By the time Wales came calling, he had headed to Greek football with Larissa. He was an illustration of how fickle football can be, of how the flavour of the month can soon become unpalatable.

He arrived in the Wales job with more of a reputation of being a bread-and-butter manager rather than the innovative, insightful type that Speed had been. His claims that he had been attempting to play a more patient passing game akin to what had been instilled at former club Swansea – and, in turn, Wales – were little more than soundbites that failed to appease the cynical ear. With next to no-one able to verify whether his Greek odyssey had indeed seen evidence of such a philosophy, he had been out of sight, out of mind, with the overarching worry that he was out of touch.

A friendly against Mexico in the vast surroundings of New Jersey's MetLife Stadium – home of both the NFL's New York Jets and New York Giants – had brought defeat but it had not brought too much concern. At the end of a long season, the plan had been more about getting players away from it all and the emotional rollercoaster of the previous 12 months, with the energy-sapping heat and the standard of opposition seeing the loss in his first true match in charge largely ignored. Or at least until it was followed up by a comfortable win for Bosnia in Llanelli less than a month before the World Cup campaign began against Belgium at home.

The Bosnia fixture had been hand-picked by Speed, a true test against an emerging European force which was hoped to ready the side in terms of confidence for the opener against the quality-assured Belgians. Wales failed the examination. At Parc y Scarlets, they were brushed aside 2-0 with the game turning more into a typical start of the season affair where the impending domestic campaign managed to overshadow things, even in the sun of the August evening.

Disjointed, rusty, lacking in the kind of confidence and flow that had screamed out of those autumnal benchmarks set under Speed a year earlier, pessimism was descending. In what became his trademark honesty, Coleman did not shy away from criticising and spelling out where the team stood.

"We can be better, we need to be better," he said after the game. "If not, it won't be good enough. If we're not better than that we'll be going nowhere."

It was true but the circumstances in which Coleman had found himself in a position to criticise only underlined the difficulties he and the side as a whole faced.

Coleman was wearing the blazer with the FAW badge but there was a feeling from some that it wasn't yet his team to criticise, not yet his right to find fault in players who had been successful under the man before him. Whereas a manager – quite rightly – pointing out areas in need of improvement should be seen as a sign of strength, now it was giving off a sense of tension.

It did not get any easier. In what was meant to be the chance to explode into the World Cup qualifiers against Belgium, the big stage Wales could finally step up to and provide the kind of momentum needed to carry them through the campaign, the optimism imploded.

In front of 20,000 at Cardiff City Stadium – including a sizeable and noisy contingent from Belgium who unfurled a banner reading "Gary Speed. Respect" to much applause – Wales had started brightly enough, only for the game to be taken away from them within 25 minutes when James Collins, out of position and trying to cover a Belgian counter-attack, lunged in on Guillaume Gillet on the halfway line. His red card undermined Wales' 'contain and counter' game that had suggested there might be the merest of hopes of a result, Vincent Kompany going on to head the visitors into a half-time lead. There were glimmers of attacking invention, mostly in the shape of Gareth Bale, but in truth it was easy for Belgium even before Jan Vertonghen cracked home a late free-kick.

The night that was supposed to have sparked Wales into World Cup life had been a cascade of calamities, starting before camp as the withdrawals returned – the serious ankle break suffered by Neil Taylor a week previously the worst of the lot – and included the late loss of the side's most consistent and capable passer in Joe Allen, who succumbed to a virus before kick-off and saw Ashley Williams shuffle uncomfortably into midfield.

The disappointment, one that was natural after so much hope had been placed on the significance and symbolism of this one game – perhaps unrealistically – at the start of a campaign that was supposed to be different, meant the same tired excuses from Coleman felt out of place.

The defence of Collins' decision to challenge how and where he did, the blaming of the referee, all jarred, as did Coleman's talk of needing 'to earn the right to play'. Tension was all too evident.

Suddenly the words of Verheijen – who, over the summer, had predicted a qualifying disaster – seemed ominous, even if plenty had been willing to overlook and give the benefit of the doubt.

Yet those doubts were everywhere as that shrill of the final whistle signalled full-time in Serbia. For the first time, Coleman heard the calls for his head.

"Sat there, I had doubts whether I was capable of doing it. I can't lie, those doubts were there," he says of that night in Novi Sad. "It's different to doing a domestic job. It's a job I wanted to do but I found myself asking if I'd come in at the wrong time? Could I do it?

"Right then was the lowest I've ever been. I've been at clubs and I've been in tough situations, where you lose a game or you have a bad run of games, but we didn't just lose in Serbia, we embarrassed ourselves and when you do that in international football you embarrass the country – and that's another ball game. I'd never felt that before."

Serbia were a side of talent, of toughness who made their presence felt with some heavy early challenges, but they were also a team who had failed to score in five of their previous six outings. Here they looked like they could score at will, Wales descending into clueless chaos the moment Aleksandar Kolarov scored from an early free-kick. Coleman did have the first goal of his tenure to cling to, when Bale drilled home a set-piece of his own, but the manager's description of it being men against boys didn't do it justice. Embarrassing wasn't the word.

"It was one of the toughest nights I'd ever had with Wales," says Gunter of a match which, with eight games remaining, hadn't made qualification impossible but it had made that unconquered mountain seem as unscalable as it ever had been. "I hadn't been too disheartened by the Belgium game because it changed after the sending off and no-one can say they could really know how it would have panned out if that hadn't have happened.

"But Serbia was different. Things were really low after that, one of the worst moments we'd gone through. It seemed everything was against us, everything they hit went in. I remember one deflection looping over Boaz Myhill at the end and thinking nothing was going to go for us.

"We flew straight back after the game and I got to my parents' house in Newport about five in the morning. I think I managed an hour's sleep and got up before anyone else and drove back to my club because I didn't want to face anyone, I didn't want to speak about it. You never like losing for your country but as a group we were embarrassed."

Coleman didn't have the option. As he sat in his darkened contemplation, efforts were being made to round up the travelling Welsh media to board the waiting bus to take them to Belgrade airport where they were set to fly back to Cardiff with the squad. With Coleman yet to show for the standard, compulsory press conference, there was no chance of anyone budging from the small room. Questions were in need of answering. Coleman eventually took his seat, humiliated and humbled, but perhaps more concerned with the questions he was asking of himself.

"When I got home I spoke to my wife, who was my girlfriend at the time, and I spoke to Kit Symons and went through it all," recalls Coleman. "After a few nights, when you have more of a chance to think, I went round to Ian Gwyn Hughes' house for dinner. We sat down, had a glass of wine and a chat. It was tough, but it was needed.

"It helped me decide I'd have been a bit of a coward if I'd have walked away. If this was going to be a fight, my father had always said to me: 'If you're going to lose, you've at least got to be walking forward throwing punches, not on your hands and knees crawling away getting kicked in the backside'.

"But it still hurt. Winning for your country is great, but losing in that manner when you are the manager, you are responsible, that was something new to me. I'd never experienced that."

Yet he wasn't alone in going through testing new experiences. While the appointment of Coleman and the new campaign had forced most on the outside to draw a line on what had gone before, inside the camp the effect was still being felt more than anyone could appreciate.

"Everything about that night in Serbia was horrible," recalls Osian Roberts. "The pitch was horrendous, the environment was hostile, the dressing rooms were scandalous; it was just uncomfortable for us from the start. You have to try and overcome those things but it was obvious it carried on into the game. We were nervy and we were under some early pressure against a good side and we couldn't ride out that storm. They were bad goals to concede but we could see from the sidelines that it wasn't just that which was the problem: everything was wrong. We were not balanced, we weren't right physically or mentally. We were outside our comfort zone and you could see it.

"We were still quite inexperienced going into a lion's den but the big thing was that the psychological aspect of what had happened was still there. People were underestimating the impact of what happened with Gary had on us – and I still don't think people fully appreciate it. It was huge, for the players, coaches, masseurs, everyone. It had been a massive blow and we just couldn't shake it off. It was there everywhere we turned and it didn't matter what you said because we were in an environment where we were supposed to carry on, where everything was the same, everything was structured the same because it had been working – and yet one key person was missing. Everybody knew it, everybody felt it and everybody knew it was time to move on – and yet we just couldn't. It was impossible. It was there.

"You could put it to the back of your mind as people do, section it off, but it would always come to the fore when we got together.

"And in Serbia, and the horrible atmosphere at the end, just summarised where we were and the feeling that everything was against us. We had walked off being booed by the fans – getting it from club fans isn't great but when it's your own countrymen: I couldn't think of anything worse at the time. We deserved it – we had just lost 6-1 – but there was a part of me looking up and thinking: 'they don't realise it where we are, they don't understand what we are going through'. Everything we had gone through, and were going through, and now we were getting this as well.

"The dressing room was silent, stunned, no-one said a word and right then it felt a very small group who were going through this psychological hell, getting hammered by the media, hammered by at least some of the fans. It was just us and only we could do something about it because no-one else will help us."

Perhaps it needed to happen. Several have spoken about the night being a turning point, certainly for Coleman and how he approached things. He had been asked to explain events by the FAW on his return, although a change in management – something openly being discussed by fans – was not on the cards. Coleman knew such an agenda was not far away if he simply waited and hoped for the issues embedded in his team to disappear.

"Maybe we didn't deserve that compassion we felt we needed," reflects Roberts. "Maybe if we had got it, if we had been given that sympathy, it would have gone on longer, that we would have kept on feeling sorry for ourselves and not finding it in us to do something about it.

"We had been trying. I remember after the game against Bosnia, Craig Bellamy spoke to the rest of the group in the dressing room, saying 'Listen lads, I know we've been affected badly, I know we're hurting, but we have got to get over this. I don't know how, but somehow we've got to get going again'."

Bellamy struggled himself, admitting later his absence from the squad over the next year was because of exactly that.

"He couldn't handle it; a lot of them couldn't handle it," says Roberts "He wasn't alone. Everyone tried to deal with it in different ways. We had tried with the Costa Rica game to get it out of those who were struggling to deal with it, to get them to talk to each other and not suppress it and almost deny this awful thing had happened. We hoped it would help the process but it took longer than we thought – and it still is taking its toll on people. Despite the greatest will in the world of everyone, we couldn't shake it off. Nothing worked.

"Maybe it was going to take what happened in Serbia, the game and everything else, for us to take that forward step because we knew in that dressing room we had hit rock bottom. No-one wants to get there but sometimes you have to in order to climb back. It's not nice, but in a way it was what we needed."

The players had been willing to put their hands up to try and take responsibility for what had gone on in Novi Sad and yet all guns were pointed at Coleman. It seemed to galvanise the group, perhaps serving to bring the squad closer to the manager who they knew had done his best in an almost impossible situation.

"It was very difficult for him because of the circumstances," says Gunter. "He had gone about things the right way, he had been sensitive to everything and listened to some of the players and the staff in keeping things the same.

"We had our system – a 4-3-3 of sorts – and we knew the way we were going to play. The manager wasn't going to come in and change it because, if he had, people would have been wondering straight away why you would go away from the things that had put the team on such a good run.

"But at the same time, when things started to go against us, you could sense he wasn't really believing in what he was coaching and some of the things we were doing. Perhaps he didn't really feel like it was his team at the time, that it had been taken from somebody else. It was a delicate situation and it was going to take time."

But Coleman couldn't wait. He had promised not to try and be Gary Speed when he took over the job, but neither was he being himself. In an attempt to try and be all things to all people, Coleman was failing to meet the expectations of anyone. Himself included.

While there was a clamour to keep things the same, the attempt to do so was sending things spiralling the other way and not only was the feel-good factor slipping away, so was the sense of this golden opportunity provided by the golden generation he had inherited. Change was needed.

"He was damned if he did, damned if he didn't at that point," says Roberts. "Looking back now, it was quite an educational piece of work in terms of management and adaptation. It was his first time in international football as a manager which many struggle with on its own, and it did take him a while to get comfortable in that different environment, where you haven't got that day-to-day element of things or the amount of games to feel your way in. It took him a while to understand what his role should be.

"We wanted everything to continue as it was but, in terms of the coaching team, I was one of the only links left and perhaps he relied a lot on me – but I was the voice of the past. What we perhaps needed was for him to take more ownership, make a stand and show this was about the future.

"I remember being in Warsaw in a conference with Kit and Cookie and when we sat down he told us he felt he was going to have to do things differently, that he knew he couldn't continue as we had been and time was against him.

"But that's when good leaders come to the fore, that's when you see the measure of a man. He had to make some brave decisions – the right ones, not just for the sake of it, but brave ones all the same. He had been treading on eggshells, trying to do things the right way and it probably had to continue like that for a while because of the situation. But then that bombshell in Serbia allowed him to draw a line, first and foremost to get a response. It was his chance to do something to enable everybody to snap out of things and move on."

In his mind there was much to do. The fine-tuned foundations would remain the same, the work done to bring the Welsh set-up kicking and screaming into the modern Premier League era would not only stay the same but be built upon, yet Coleman saw need to bring greater organisation and resilience to a defence from which the natural passing and pace game of others in his squad could flourish. The biggest change though, the biggest statement that the team had to be now considered *his* team, was to appoint his captain. As it leaked ahead of the squad announcement for the games with Scotland and Croatia in October 2012, the news that Aaron Ramsey – the player almost anointed by Speed to carry his vision of a new Wales onto the pitch – had been told by Coleman to hand in his armband was controversial, dividing opinion. It seems the decision had the same impact inside the camp as out of it.

"I sat down with a few of them, Kit, Osh and Ryland Morgans

(Wales' head of performance) and told them what I was doing," Coleman recalls. "I'd already made it clear to them I didn't want them to nod along with me and wait until afterwards when I went out of the room to say what they would have done, but to say it there and then and we'll discuss it. We'd done that a few times but when I said I was changing the captain a few of them said 'Easy, hang on'. They could see the issues."

There had been fears that the relationship between Ramsey and Coleman wasn't, at that time, as it should have been between captain and manager, let alone at the level enjoyed by Speed and his skipper. It was natural to some extent and another example of the aftershock of the tragic events the team had to deal with.

Coleman's public courting of Ryan Shawcross did little to alleviate the public's sensing of an unease between the pair, whether imagined or not. A centre-back of value, if not one who fitted into the way many wanted Wales to play, Shawcross, the man whose challenge had robbed Ramsey of a year of his career, qualified for Wales through his schooling and there had been a tease of interest from the Stoke centre-back that Coleman was keen to investigate. Ramsey was willing to stand by his manager if he was called up, but made it clear both to Coleman and in the media that he wasn't about to start pretending to be friends with his apparent foe. In the end – and to the relief of those worried about the impact on the dressing room – Shawcross opted to stick with England, leaving the question whether the debate had been necessary in the first place. Taking the captaincy away from Ramsey, of which he was so obviously proud, would only heighten speculation that Coleman was driving a wedge between himself and such a key player.

And yet there was a sense it was needed. Ramsey had struggled for form with Wales and, more than most, had suffered a night to forget in Novi Sad. While he never used the captaincy as an excuse and teammates talked of him being the same man whether with the armband or not, his performance in Serbia appeared to betray the pressure of responsibility he felt. He seemed so desperate to stop what was happening, he was trying it all and failing the harder he did so.

"I think you could see it weighing on him in that game," says Coleman. "He almost wanted to take the corners and head them in himself. I knew he was a top player – he still is a top player – and the team needed him at his best, but I didn't think the captaincy was helping him. I had my reasons and some staff agreed with me that we needed to take that pressure off him, but some were worried we could lose him. I knew deep down that was a worry but I had to gamble because of where we were.

"I wanted to speak to him in person so I travelled to Arsenal's training ground, sat down with him and he was brilliant with it all which was huge for me, for us. He was always going to be disappointed – who wouldn't want to be captain of their country? – but he told me he had actually spoken to his father and said he might not be ready for it. I told him to forget about it all, to concentrate on being Aaron Ramsey. I know I could have lost him but I needed to do it."

Ashley Williams was the player who Coleman felt he needed in his place. The Swansea City centre-back was already captaining at club level and had been established as a senior figure in the squad even before Coleman's appointment. With some sections of the fanbase – presumably from a Cardiff City-supporting section – focusing in on Coleman's Swansea roots as an avenue for their frustration, turning to an idol of the Liberty at the expense of a former Bluebird was hardly going to help on that front, though it was not a mindset worth pandering to and Coleman seemed to be only further hardened in his stance that he was doing the right thing.

Yet, while his public presence was one of fighting determination, the move undoubtedly heightened the pressure on his shoulders against Scotland which, just two games into the campaign, had the feel of a must-win game. Jonathan Ford made utterances in support of his manager, that the changes were endorsed, but his backing was delivered with a heavy hand that made it clear mistakes had to be learned from and – crucially – the first qualifying points were "a must".

In the end, Coleman could cradle all three on offer in the Cardiff rain against Scotland. James Morrison's first-half goal had undone a good start from Wales in the downpour at Cardiff City Stadium, a nothing effort caused by a simple flick that underlined the work needed to be done at the back. Steve Fletcher, who had set up the first, was denied a second by the linesman's flag and for all the efforts, it seemed Coleman's fate was to become the first Wales manager to lose

147

his first five games in charge, with many openly wondering whether he would get the opportunity to take charge of a sixth.

Gareth Bale replaced the question mark with a full stop, or at least a comma. With ten minutes remaining, the then Tottenham star took it upon himself to win the game.

He had been irresistible all night, ignoring the close attention handed to him by fellow celtic opposition, and, in those finals stages, drove into the Scottish area to tempt Shaun Maloney into the challenge that provided a destiny-swinging penalty. The claims of the travelling contingent were that of a dive, or at least making most of the contact, though it fell on deaf ears to those who remembered it was 35 years to the night of Joe Jordan's infamous Anfield intervention.

Not content with firing home the penalty, Bale saved his best for last when he picked the ball up with two minutes to go. He was on the white of his own half's centre-circle when his ran began, only to be stopped by the cynical body check of Charlie Adam, a player who had previously left his physical mark on the forward. He loitered around the free-kick, demanded the ball once more and set off, running at and past Adam before unleashing a shot of such venom that Allan McGregor would have had little chance to stop it even if had not been destined for the opposite top corner. Bale had taken the mantle of being a match-winner to a new level.

His celebrations were iconic, surrounded by teammates as he roared. Coleman's too, letting his feelings of raw relief known as he punched the air around his dug-out, unmoved by the rain soaking through his suit. He had witnessed one of the great Wales goals, one of the great individual performances. He had witnessed his own acquittal.

"I knew what it meant," he says. "When you want something for a long time, have it in your grasp but then feel it slipping away, you scramble, you do anything to claw it back, you put everything you have into keeping it. That game was like that for me. I knew I couldn't lose both games and that – with no disrespect – we had more chance of getting the win against Scotland at home than Croatia away.

"It had been decent enough, an open game, and then they got the goal but as soon as Gareth won the penalty I knew it, I had that feeling in my gut.

"But the way he won it.... When he was on the move I thought

John Toshack made no apologies for what he saw as the way forward for Wales, and appointing Brian Flynn as youth chief played a huge part in the vision.

A 16-year-old Gareth Bale trains with Ryan Giggs in 2006, the man he'd replace as Wales' great hope. One week on from this session in Bilbao, Bale would become Wales' youngest international.

Shattered Wales boss   questions future

BELL'S HELL: Wales captain Craig Bellamy looks dejected after the 3-1 defeat at the hands of Cyprus yesterday

PICTURE: DAVID RAWCLIFFE

IS THIS THE END FOR TOSHACK?

JOHN Toshack walked out of the GSP stadium in Nicosia after raising doubts over his future as Wales boss.

Toshack refused to answer questions on the dire display in Cyprus where Wales turned a

By CHRIS WATHAN
IN CYPRUS

1-0 lead into a dismal defeat after conceding three goals in 21 minutes.

But he threw up questions on his role as Wales boss when he admitted: "I will have to have a long hard look at myself and what I am doing here. After

what I have seen in this match I am obviously doing something wrong."

Toshack has never been under any pressure from Welsh FA bosses who believe the side is heading in the right direction.

But after his admission they might now start

scrutinising the progression of his team more closely.

Captain Craig Bellamy admitted there had been an inquest into the pitiful performance inside the locked doors of the Wales dressing room, but refused to jump to his coach's defence.

"I've said before it is not for me to say whether we are heading in the right direction," said Bellamy.

"I'm just a player and I need to concentrate on playing – it is up to the people in charge to comment on things like that."

■ REPORT, REACTION: SEE SPORT PULLOUT

The push for youth failed to bring much obvious early progress a hapless 3-1 defeat in Cyprus saw Toshack question his own future before turning his frustration on players following a dressing room inquest.

SPORTWALES
sport@mediawales.co.uk   Mon   ober 2007

Toshack crisis talks with his Welsh stars

My players are spoilt – Tosh

Bryn Terfel leads the singing of the anthem against Liechtenstein in 2008 but the growing apathy at even the start of a qualifying campaign meant there were few in the stands to join in.

Shorn of senior stars, an end-of-season qualifier in Azerbaijan in 2009 saw Wales' youngsters step up. Pictured taking a break from training in Baku are (left-right) Simon Church, Ashley Williams, Shaun MacDonald, Aaron Ramsey, Chris Gunter, Owain Tudur Jones, Joe Allen and Andy King. All bar one played in the Euro 2016 campaign seven years later.

Fading qualification hopes were ruined when Finland's Jari Litmanen 'stood Wales still' in March 2009 to leave Toshack facing serious questions as patience ran out and pressure grew.

The response was to build the side around the teens and twenty-somethings with a midfield masterclass from Aaron Ramsey – shown here celebrating with Bale and fellow goalscorer Simon Church – in a November 2009 win over Scotland. "I felt after that we could really do something," said Toshack. What followed was a blow from which he never really recovered.

The old and the new: Toshack shares a joke with his successor Gary Speed at a Swansea City game following his appointment in December 2010.

Speed surprised many by appointing a 20-year-old Ramsey as the captain for his revolution, but there was a clear bond between the pair from the start.

Speed demanded all players stood together to sing the anthem, bringing in a soprano to teach the team together and posting lyrics around the hotel. It was an example of the small details he believed would soon add up.

For all the new hope, Wales had sunk to their lowest place in the Fifa rankings. A win over Montenegro in September 2011 was the overdue reward for the efforts to shake Wales into life.

Speed and right-hand men, Osian Roberts and Raymond Verheijen,
address the squad in Sofia the night before the final Euro 2012
qualifier in October 2011 having beaten Switzerland a few days earlier.

A surreal experience but a genuine revival. The win – in a stadium
bizarrely boycotted by home fans – gave more belief than ever that
Speed's young side were on the brink of something special.

Craig Bellamy – who had been unable to say no to good friend Speed's pleas to return to the Wales fold – leaves the field in the closing moments of the impressive 4-1 friendly win over Norway in November 2011, admitting later he was convinced qualification was around the corner but unaware of the devastating blow to come.

Ramsey hands over the armband to Ashley Williams – the player he would see take the captaincy full-time later on. Speed had found his leaders and they would be needed like never before.

Western Mail

Monday, 28 November 2011
PAPUR CENEDLAETHOL CYMRU
NATIONAL NEWSPAPER OF WALES
◆ 60p
WalesOnline.co.uk

The world has lost a great football manager but even more sadly a great man

– Captain Aaron Ramsey leads the tributes to Wales manager Gary Speed, found hanged at his home yesterday

GARY SPEED
1969-2011

FOOTBALL IN MOURNING AS TRIBUTES POUR IN
Pages 2-7

THE GREATEST AMBASSADOR WE'VE HAD –
SPORTS EDITOR
Back Page

HIS WALES PLAYERS SPEAK OF THEIR HEARTACHE
Sport pullout

The headlines no-one wanted to write on the news no-one wanted to hear.

"I was sat in his seat, where he should have been."
Flanked by FAW chief executive Jonathan Ford (left) and president Phil
Pritchard (right), Chris Coleman struggles to hide his inner turmoil as
he is unveiled as friend Speed's successor in January 2012.

Speed's side listen intently to the words of his father, Roger, as he
speaks before the memorial game with Costa Rica at Cardiff City
Stadium flanked by Gary's sons, Ed and Tommy,

A stern-faced Ramsey leads Wales out of the Novi Sad clubhouse and into one of their lowest points on the pitch. A still shell-shocked side were about to suffer at the hands of Serbia in September 2012.

The 6-1 defeat left Coleman – minus his suit jacket – questioning his decision to take the job and plenty questioning how long he would keep it.

Having come through the ranks together since they were teenagers, the 'no stars - one team' ethos was embedded; even when it came to table tennis.

Not for the last time, Bale would save Wales – and Coleman – in a brilliant matchwinning display against Scotland in October 2012, the emotion as obvious as the Cardiff rain.

Hal-Robson Kanu rises highest in Hampden to score amid the snow in March 2013, cementing cult status and creating a classic Welsh football image.

Bellamy walks away after insisting captain Ramsey takes the penalty to seal a October 2013 win over Macedonia. It could have been a fitting final goal for Bellamy in his final home game before international retirement, but he smiled later "Fairytale endings? Life isn't like that." Ramsey missed the penalty.

Chris Gunter @Chrisgunter16 · 3 Sep 2014
Walesssssss. @aaronramsey @joe16led

↺ 390 ♥ 612

Gareth Bale ✓
@GarethBale11   ⚙ Following

On route to Andorra with the welsh boys
@joe16led and Jonny. Can't wait to start our
#EURO2016 campaign #BigGame

RETWEETS LIKES
1,823   3,069

**The closeness of the side that grew up together is showcased on
social media in the lead up to the Euro 2016 qualifying campaign in
September 2014.**

**With the mountains looking down upon them, Wales' players warm up
for training and get a first look at the plastic pitch that would cause so
much worry against Andorra.**

"One player can't qualify for Euro 2016 – but what Gareth can be is Wales' leader. It doesn't matter who they play in the qualifiers, when Gareth is on the field they always have a match-winner." No-one was arguing with Zinedine Zidane's verdict in Andorra as Bale first levelled and then scored a stunning late (retaken) free-kick winner to avoid embarrassment and kick-start the momentum Wales needed.

"This is our home and you're not taking points off us. This is our land."
Joe Ledley spells out the new determination shown in the goalless
draw against Bosnia in October 2014.

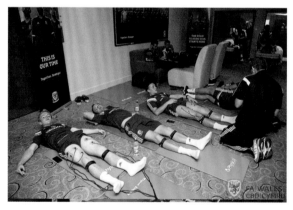

How to spend your Saturday night in Cardiff Bay. Jonny Williams,
Andy King and James Chester are among those undergoing recovery
treatment at the team's St David's hotel base before the game with
Cyprus a few days later. Joe Ledley and Chris Gunter wear their
compression boots and Gareth Bale receives a massage with the FAW's
#TogetherStronger messages surrounding them.

"It had been a hard few years for me. Not many had realised what I had gone through but it was with Wales in mind that helped me through it. That goal was an incredible moment for me after all that." David Cotterill comes off the bench to curl Wales into a 1-0 lead over Cyprus.

Soaring support was not let down in terms of result or attitude as Robson-Kanu's goal ensured an unbeaten start.

The Brussels braves and the Brussels raves. A important rearguard effort is celebrated by a Zombie Nation in the away end as a 0-0 draw with favourites Belgium keeps belief building.

 Chris Gunter @Chrisgunter16 · 16 Nov 2014

To you lot and the fans who travelled without a ticket;thank you. Stay safe and have a 🍺or 10.. Cymru

↩   ↻ 346   ♥ 520   •••

In the country where Wales last took a major step towards a major finals in 1958, Chris Coleman's class of 2016 produce the style in Israel to go top of the group with a convincing victory.

Gareth Bale
@GarethBale11

What a performance from the lads!

RETWEETS 5,551   LIKES 8,745

The crowd and team stand as one to sing of the land of their fathers, the days of apathy long gone.

The rest of the stadium froze, but Bale was just ice-cold as he punished Belgium as part of a tireless team display that no-one there will forget.

The fans and their team celebrated the famous Wales victory against the Belgians, the top team in Europe according to FIFA rankings.

Gareth Bale @
@GarethBale11

Following

Not going to forget tonight!

RETWEETS   LIKES
3,733   6,782

2:43 p m · 12 Jun 2015

Chris Gunter @Chrisgunter16 14 Jun 2015

Never experienced anything like this before...not a better anthem in world football..

Wales 1-0 Belgium | Welsh national anthem
Wales fans singing the national anthem at Cardiff city stadium vs Belgium.
youtube.com

70   105   •••

The Wales on Sunday rams home the significance of the win – and the prospect of what could follow – as the win over the star-studded Belgians propels Wales into the top ten football nations in the world in time for that summer's World Cup qualifying draw. So long the butt of jokes, Welsh football was laughing last and hard.

The expressions from Ashley Williams (far left) and David Edwards (second from right) say it all as Wales face up to the heat of qualifying pressure in the late summer sun of Nicosia.

The picture that sums up a qualification campaign. Bale celebrates the winner over Cyprus to the delight of a team that all know takes Wales to within a whisker of their dream.

October 10 2015: Bosnia 2 Wales 0 . The greatest defeat in Welsh football history.

"That moment....to see the look on their faces, you can't buy it, that feeling, not just for myself but for them, for us all. To see some of them crying with joy is something I will just never forget." Coleman savours the moment with fans in Zenica.

Wales' national newspaper marks the historic moment as a squad and country celebrate as one.

Gareth Bale's Tweet says it all.

 Gareth Bale @GarethBale11 · 10 Oct 2015
We've done it!!!!! #euro2016 #TogetherStronger

↩   🔁 7.2K   ♥ 9.9K   •••

Chris Gunter watches the celebrating fans as he contemplates the journey they'd all been on.

Kit man Dai Griffiths strums the guitar as the squad sit together and reflect on their achievement in their Zenica hotel. The togetherness displayed in one, perfect moment.

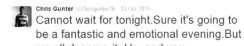

Chris Gunter @Chrisgunter16 13 Oct 2015

Cannot wait for tonight.Sure it's going to
be a fantastic and emotional evening.But
we all deserve it. Us, and you.

113   203   ...

**Chris Gunter sets the tone for the homecoming party against Andorra,
sparked fully when Aaron Ramsey scores the opening goal.**

The comfortable 2-0 victory over Andorra complete, the qualification party gets going.

Only days after his impromptu performance on the pitch in Zenica, Joe Ledley needs no persuading to encore his celebratory dance as the players enjoy the party atmosphere. The FAW won praise for their 'Diolch' T-shirts, worn by the players in the after match festivities: another example of a small but important detail, got right.

The decades of failure and heartbreak had finally come to an end. The golden generation had delivered.

he was going to keep going but he let fly and I was right behind it. I couldn't have had a better view of the ball and I watched it all the way in. That feeling was incredible."

Bale had bought Coleman time, even if it led to obvious accusations about not being able to rely on such brilliance every game. Indeed, Bale was unable to provide the goal as the lone attacking threat in Croatia a few days later when an Ashley Williams mistake helped the heavily-fancied hosts to a 2-0 win.

Still, if qualification wasn't on the agenda, improvement was. An emerging Austrian team were dispatched in a 2-1 win in Swansea where signs that the team was being built, not so much around Bale but making the most of his strengths, were furthered as he scored one and provided another. The lowly crowd, with only around 8,000 present for the February friendly fixture, did ask the question whether the Welsh public understood how good a talent they had in their backyard and whether Coleman's side and steps forward were in receipt of a public vote of confidence. Where they did not, Bellamy did, returning to the squad and admitting that he would willingly pay to watch this team in action.

The following month saw the best indication yet that, at last, the sense of direction lost with Speed had returned. Scotland were again the team Wales stepped on to inch forward, proving something valuable to themselves in the process.

Bale's performances – and goals – had understandably been the focus in the build-up, both a perceived strength and weakness of the side in that if you stopped Bale then you stopped Wales. In March snowstorms, it appeared the Wales camp believed it themselves as they feared heading to Hampden without him. Carrying an ankle problem, it was actually a virus he had picked up that had prevented him from training and led to the decision to fly him to Scotland separately from the rest of the team. He travelled to Glasgow on a private flight and was kept in isolation.

He played, booed mercilessly every time he touched the ball, but was clearly below fitness and unable to grab the game by the neck as he had done in Cardiff after Grant Hanley's goal had given new manager Gordon Strachan a first-half Hampden lead in his first game in charge. As Bale's number was held up to be replaced by Jonny Williams, staff on the Scottish bench were said to be seen high-fiving each other. Within 45 minutes, and the glorious natural enthusiasm of Williams' game part of it, Wales had reason to celebrate themselves as the superb Ramsey held his finger to his lips to mark the silence of the boos that had transferred from Bale to the rest of the side.

It had been Ramsey, at his playmaking best, who had levelled when he smashed a penalty in off the crossbar after Robert Snodgrass earned a second yellow card in fouling Gunter, before Hal Robson-Kanu leapt to head home Andy King's lofted delivery. The image of Robson-Kanu floating in the manner of the best Wales No. 9s, Hartson – Charles, Davies, Toshack, *et al* – surrounded by the snowflakes that speckled the night sky is one that will live long in the memory.

"I remember after about 35 minutes thinking this was one of the best team performances I'd played in for either club or country," says Gunter. "We'd already put some decent performances in during that time but couldn't quite get the results or push on in games.

"But that night, even though we had to come back again, we'd done so well to control the game. If you think about it, the derby nature of the game, away from home in poor conditions and with the crowd against us, and where we had been as a side, it was pretty unbelievable.

"We could have buckled there, especially having played well and then conceded to a set-play right before half-time, but I remember Bellas speaking at half-time and telling us to forget the score and that, whatever happens, this was how we were going to play moving forward. It didn't matter if we didn't come back, this is what we were going to do because it will take us somewhere.

"Getting the win only added to it and it did feel like we'd taken a big step that night. It felt we had settled again and that the manager had settled into it more; it was more his way, he was coming into himself.

"People had a perception of him on the outside that they were sticking to, but so many of the boys just thought 'What a top man' and it was starting to show that we were playing for him.

"It was those games where you felt he was getting his head around things and he had put a lot of work in to make that happen.

"You could see things starting to turn, doing things more his way. I remember him saying that he was prepared to fail doing that, but at least he was going to fail on his terms – yet the way he was growing into things and how we were adapting to him made you think that if we could just get that little bit of a run together we would be okay.

"It was genuinely upsetting when we were losing games because so many of us wanted to do well for him as well as the side. It felt unfair he was getting the criticism when it was the team as a whole, and he got that from how he dealt with us as players. If you had a problem or needed to speak to him, you could, he was there. We felt we could trust him and you don't always get that with managers. At that time it was a big step for us as a side in being able to move forward."

Even defeat to Croatia four days later did not stop the sense that the team were back on track. A Bale penalty had given Wales the chance of victory with some impressive football played in Swansea, though the demands of the back-to-back games without Ramsey – sent off in the dying seconds in Glasgow – eventually allowed Dejan Lovren to level and then ex-Arsenal man Eduardo to win it in the final few minutes.

There were still questions about the team selection, about the balance of the side and whether they could create enough without relying so heavily on Bale – something raised again during a fairly forgettable scoreless August friendly with the Republic of Ireland that brought to an end a bizarre record of having gone six years without a draw – but in the main there was the sense there was something to work with and that Coleman was doing just that.

With four qualifying games remaining before the focus firmly turned to the European Championship campaign, there was a case to claim that Wales looked capable of rising to the challenge.

And while Coleman was still to convince many, he had at least convinced some that the toughest part of things had been dealt with, those emotional and mental obstacles he had to help the side overcome. Most importantly, he had convinced himself.

"I thought I was getting there by then, but I'd be lying if I said there hadn't been real doubts right the way through," Coleman says. "Not at the start though; before I walked through the door I thought I could do it, I could have a crack at it and have a real go of taking it on. After a bit of time I realised I'd got it totally wrong, I should never have taken it at this time. The circumstances were too much. Had Gary left or got the sack, fine, but the emotion attached to it was too much.

"I was having to adjust to a new way of working, everyone had to adjust to me and then, on top of that, we had to adjust to it with this awful thing hanging over us – and I definitely underestimated that. I underestimated how it would affect them and how it would affect what I was trying to do.

"Looking back, I had tried to be strong with the players early on, trying to make my mark and perhaps I pushed too hard where I should have thought that sooner or later it would come, that I had to wait for it a little and we just needed to help each other out.

"I tried to do things but I felt at times it wouldn't have mattered what I said. They weren't ready to come with me – and I totally understand why, even more so now with hindsight, because I just don't think anyone realised the effect it had on them. Me too, if I'm honest. I gauged it wrongly. I was too full-on.

"I just thought I'd get their heads into the game, that once it came to the matches they'll get on with it, things would kick on and it would work itself out. But it couldn't happen that way.

"I know that now but, then, in my head, I had to qualify, I had to get it right from the start. The thing was everyone was expecting us to qualify but when you looked at the group realistically you can see how hard it would be; we'd been on a roll at the end of the previous campaign, finishing so strong, the optimism was huge – and then wallop.

"I brought a lot of it on myself, the criticism. I was so desperate to succeed and I was still hurting because he was my mate. I felt I shouldn't be doing the job, guilty almost. It affected me and what I was doing, so I'd invited that criticism.

"And then, when it wasn't working, when I wasn't being honest with the way I was doing it, I felt worse. It was a terrible time for me in that first year or so and even after that it took a time.

"Then, as we got to the end of the next campaign, because we had shown that bit of improvement, I thought I'd be able to have another crack at it – but then I put myself back in it."

From which he almost never recovered. Wales did not so much take a backwards step in Skopje as a team, but the farce that accompanied defeat to Macedonia felt like a leap back to the embarrassment associated with Bobby Gould's time in charge.

Most arriving at the Philip II Arena for the standard training and press conference held by visiting teams 24 hours before a qualifier had only Bale on their minds, his recent world record move to Real Madrid and doubts over his fitness meaning anything said on whether he would play or not was easy and entirely justifiable copy.

Stood waiting to enter the ground, a sweeping, impressive enough venue inside but surrounded by enough rubble to resemble a building site outside, word slowly spread that it would be Kit Symons facing the media rather than Coleman. Having not, on this occasion, travelled with the team, journalists were not to know that neither had the manager. Experiencing what was initially spun as "passport issues", Coleman remained in Cardiff. It transpired, after it was eventually squeezed out of those in FAW suits, the issues were simply that he had lost said passport and, while the squad flew to Skopje and undertook training at the stadium, the manager was heading to Newport's passport office for new headshots and approval before a convoluted flight to the former Yugoslav republic.

Jonathan Ford, arriving after a tetchy press conference where Symons had to try and uneasily laugh off the incident, did his best to protest that "it wasn't a story", though he knew he was fighting a losing battle and someone else's fight at that. It was a story. The reaction, when ringing back to the newsdesks with the news, confirmed the same first thoughts of the press pack at the stadium and back pages were cleared. When the coverage was questioned, the easiest reply was to ask what would have been the scenario in the London redtops had it been the England manager rather than the Wales manager who made this mistake?

On top of that, while in reality the training the night before a game is little more than a stretch out after travelling and getting a feel for the stadium, Wales now had the world's most costliest player in their ranks; what had been parochial stories before were now global fodder.

The irony was that the fall-out had kept journalists penned in the press conference room while the team trained, unable to see the concerns over the pitch and Bale clearly showing issues over the foot injury that had delayed the start to his season after the prolonged £85m transfer from Tottenham to Madrid. Coleman named him on the bench when he made his belated arrival, the idea being to worry Macedonia that he could be brought on at any stage and perhaps alter their thinking when, in reality, he was never fit to play. As Wales went down 2-1, the reports were filed and questions readied unaware of

153

the ploy. Even when revealed, Coleman's protestations of mindgames didn't go down particularly well.

It had been bad timing for Coleman. He had entered discussions over his contract yet the claims of how close the two parties were over an agreement differed. It would not have furthered the manager's case as FAW council members strolled around the sunny, if strange, streets of Skopje where the faux fountains and statues saw plenty of Wales fans either shaking their head or rolling their eyes when the word of the lost passport spread.

If the humour of singing 'Everywhere You Go, You Always Take Your Passport With You' to the tune of Crowded House was of typical away terrace charm, it was wrong to say there had not been anger from a section too. It was a feeling boiling up in Coleman as he spoke after the game.

He had defended his position over Bale, but when it came to the passport, the interchange was incendiary.

The old defender was in battle mode when he was asked if he had anything to say on passports.

"No, but you have obviously. You write it. We are building a good little team here but you won't write about that. You won't write that the last six or eight games have been very positive. That's up to you. You make out of it what you want to but, do you know, if I was sitting here when we'd won, you wouldn't be making so much out of it. But you will because we've lost, but that's up to you."

All said with the same eyes that would have stared down plenty of strikers in his time. He had a point too; had Wales won the matter would have been brought up but with a lighter touch than the punch in the gut the headlines would deliver him the next morning. Yet they hadn't won, despite impressing for large parts and looking set for an optimism and belief-building victory that – on the back of the March points and performances – could have helped the team gain the same momentum that had done so much create real hope in Speed's final games.

With more of the injuries that had nibbled away at attempts to field a settled side through the campaign, there seemed more of a balance and there was something of an injustice when David Vaughan's foul on the veteran Macedonian playmaker Goran Pandev saw a deflected free-kick slotted home by Ivan Tričkovski.

But Wales were in control of the game by the time Ramsey – excellent all night despite the treatment being handed out by the hosts – converted a penalty he won himself before half-time, only for injury to Jonny Williams to push the game back in the hosts' favour. Coleman's introduction of Andrew Crofts to steel it out unbalanced things before Aleksandar Trajkovski's goal ten minutes from time mathematically put Wales out of the World Cup. No-one had planned to go to Rio – whether you had a passport or not – but the bigger concern was that it had been assumed Wales had moved past this point, that they could win winnable games and tough out results.

In reality it was a blip, but it was done after a blunder not befitting an international manager.

"There were words," admits Ford, of those events. "Look, we've all misplaced wallets or passports or whatever, it's just when you're in the position of national team manager you do it with a megaphone. Still, it should have been avoided – and we told him that."

Coleman probably did not need telling, but the sideshow was not stopping there.

With a defensive crisis centred around Ashley Williams' suspension, Wales succumbed again to Serbia. Compared to the six in Novi Sad, Wales only conceded three in Cardiff, but the meek and mistake-ridden nature of the display left the national team bottom of the group and Coleman listening to an angry section of support calling for his head. Serbia second time around had proven no greater comfort for the manager.

"I have to take the responsibility; I was taking pats on the back before and when results don't come I have to take the criticism and take it on the chin," he said after the game. "I won't blame the supporters for being annoyed and angry – the very least they want is a performance and they never got it. I take responsibility for that."

Refusing to bury his frustration, Coleman made the most of the platform with the media after the game to reveal how James Collins had turned down a call-up. Within 24 hours Collins had issued his own statement denying it, the row rumbling on until the following month with FAW officials wanting to know what had gone on as the unsavoury war of words continued in public.

Coleman was not for turning, taking a stance and slamming the door shut on Collins. The former Cardiff City centre-back had been left out of the initial squad but then was said to have twice snubbed the chance to cover injuries and absentees.

Regardless of who was right or wrong, the fall-out placed question marks over the then West Ham defender's future, but within a month, face-to-face meetings – held in the public bar, as Coleman joked, to stop it 'kicking off' – had allowed them to thrash a way forward. Collins was even selected to start against Macedonia, who were brushed aside at home as they should have been away.

Ramsey shone that night though the tributes were for Craig Bellamy – provider of the goal for Simon Church – who had confirmed it would be his final home game as a Wales international.

There would be one more outing, though perhaps he could have been forgiven for being fearful heading to Brussels with a side stripped to the bone by injuries to face Belgium who had romped to qualification.

A case of so close, so far for the player who made 78 appearances in both good times and bad and would now have to watch on as Premier League peers in the Belgian side celebrated the end of their 12-year exile from a major finals, an absence from the main stage that had tormented their fans but was hardly comparable to Wales' apparent life sentence. "Fairytale endings? Life isn't like that," said Bellamy with a knowing smile before the game at the King Baudouin Stadium. "You read a story to your daughter, but sometimes at the end you would be doing her justice by saying 'the prince does die'."

It wasn't quite fairytale stuff, but Bellamy could have been proud of his last stand as he clutched the bottle of Cognac – handed to him as a gift by old Manchester City teammate and Belgium captain Vincent Kompany – following the 1-1 draw where a weakened Wales had battled and stood toe-to-toe before Aaron Ramsey cancelled out Kevin de Bruyne's opener in the final two minutes. It was a suggestion of a touch of maturity in the team, of a tick in the experience box of getting a result at a full-house away from home against a side of stars.

"It's easy to do when you have nothing to play for," said Bellamy of the result, having been in those end-of-campaign, false promise performances in the past.

"That's when we've usually done quite well because the reins are off, the pressure's off and it's easy to play football then. It's not so easy when the pressure's on and you need to get big results to try and qualify. It's vital for us because this generation is a good one, it's not one we've seen down the years. A lot of them had the potential we saw a few years ago, but a lot of them have come to the fore now and we can build on that. This is an opportunity for us, it really is."

With some speculation still surrounding the last details of Coleman's contract to be finalised, Bellamy's name had cropped up as a potential managerial candidate. Bellamy had made no public play for the role but the idea wasn't being dismissed out of hand by some at the FAW either. Yet, as he said in Brussels, Bellamy expected Coleman to want to keep the opportunity he had. It was what many players wanted with several, somewhat suprisingly, speaking publicly about their desires to stick with the manager and giving further indication that the squad were with him.

"Deep down I knew that the next campaign could be different, that with time we could go again," Coleman says now, eventually signing a two-year extension after flirting with the vacancy at Crystal Palace. "We had been going along nicely before Macedonia and Serbia. The performance in Macedonia wasn't actually that bad but I had put myself in that situation, I had brought it on myself again and, to be honest, I was angry that I'd done that. That's why I was ready to go back and fore in the press conference afterwards.

"I messed up but, at the same time, I knew they'd stay with me until the end of the campaign and if we could finish well we could move on.

"And I knew that I'd be ready this time, ready to step it up again – and I knew the players were ready too. I knew what I wanted to do and I was confident again. I had said to myself that I couldn't give a toss what others thought, that I had to go for it in that next campaign. And we did."

And when you had the world's most expensive player – and one of your nation's greatest ever – there was good reason for such an attitude.

8

The £85 Million Man

"It will be a tragedy if he never gets to play in a World Cup or European Championships. He is one of the top five players in the world – for him not to be there is just wrong" – Zinedine Zidane

Only a handful more than 150 people live in the village of Colney, four miles to the rural west of Norwich. Two of the dozen or so people stood on the touchline of Norwich City's training ground had driven the best part of 300 miles to watch this game. While the couple knew the importance of the early afternoon Under-18s game on the career prospects of their son, they, like those 150 or so inhabitants, could not have realised the full significance of what would take place in Colney village that day.

It was January 22, 2005, and Frank and Debbie Bale had been made aware that Southampton's coaches were concerned with the development of their 15-year-old son, Gareth.

The talent first spotted by a Saints scout when, six years earlier, Gareth had turned out for a local boys team in a tournament in Newport, had never been questioned.

Neither had his attitude, the desire to earn a first academy scholarship, one that would see him remain with the club in his late teens, seeing him practice and practice on a left-foot delivery that the world would get to know – and both fear and love – soon enough.

It was nothing new. Bale had long been encouraged to challenge his own ability, his technique so good while at school he would be ordered to play one-touch and banned from his preferred foot to strengthen his right, as well as – presumably – to level the playing field.

Southampton knew they had something special in the young left-back who, at 14, was running the 100 metres in 11.4 seconds while also excelling at middle-distance running, and who had excited scouts and staff after initially joining the club's satellite academy in Bath, going on to make the regular trips from south Wales to the south coast as he survived the cuts of youth hopefuls, year on year.

Yet football's ruthless side doesn't simply stop at senior level but perhaps even hardens as it drips down the age grades. Regardless of how much hope there was for him to succeed, the coldness of the sport had placed question marks whether a 15-year-old who had struggled with pains in his back associated with growth spurts could physically cope with the demands that would only increase. His injury problems, and a resulting lack of games, had prevented proper evaluation of his chances of making it. And so came Colney and a final 90 minutes to earn faith and a future.

There have been reports that Bale's Southampton won the game 5-1 against their Norwich counterparts – managed by one-time Wales caretaker boss and future Under-21 assistant to Brian Flynn, David Williams – yet records suggest the score has been embellished over the years. It is of little surprise because Bale's composed, assured performance in that village of 150 has had ramifications for a nation of more than 3 million. Whether it was 2-1 or not, with Theo Walcott scoring and future England teammate Adam Lallana in midfield, there is no confusion over Bale doing enough that January day to reassure the Southampton officials that they would come to regret any decision to doubt the young hopeful.

Before the following season was out, in April 2006, Bale had made his first senior appearance for Southampton in a 2-0 win over Millwall at St Mary's. A fortnight later he played again, starting in a 2-0 win over Leicester. Already Brian Flynn was purring about this "Rolls Royce of a player", handing him his Under-21 debut alongside Chris Gunter and David Edwards against Cyprus.

It would be wrong to say that the interested afternoon observers that day walked out of Port Talbot's Victoria Road convinced they had seen the nation's future talisman; shunted around from left-back to left-wing, it was clear that this was a player of real potential, but there were yet the headlines proclaiming that Flynn had found the next Ryan Giggs in the way the Manchester United man had once been labelled the next George Best. His debut is mentioned almost as an afterthought in reports of the game at the time. Indeed, when he shyly spoke to reporters in what could well have been his first interview, the fascination was more about his former youth team roommate Walcott whose star had risen considerably faster with a £9m move to Arsenal already secured and a surprise place in England's squad for that summer's World Cup confirmed. It is safe to assume the journalists in question have not hung up the clippings from that first article that revealed how Walcott would borrow Bale's aftershave for dates with future wife Melanie Slade.

As ever, Flynn's eye was the one to trust and his excited descriptions of Bale's style and speed had long been relayed to John Toshack.

"He would tell me constantly: 'I've seen someone at Southampton, from Cardiff, and you've got to see him'. He would go on and on about him," says Toshack. "When we got him in training with the others we could see what the fuss was about. When we saw what he could do that was that."

Within hours of those headlines, Bale had been called into the senior squad for Wales' end-of-season games with the Basque Country XI in Bilbao and Trinidad & Tobago in Graz.

Having got the taste for international life just 180 minutes into his senior football career, Bale was scheduled to jet back to the UK to play for Flynn's Under-21s in their qualifier, appearing as a second-half substitute against Estonia at Wrexham's Racecourse. Yet, in a fitting narrative, when Giggs withdrew with injury, Bale returned to Toshack's squad. At 16 years and 315 days, Bale's appearance against the World Cup-bound Soca Warriors made him Wales' youngest international, a feat he seemingly wasn't content with as he provided the ball for Robert Earnshaw's winner for good measure.

It didn't come with the same fanfare as Giggs' debut in Nuremberg had done 15 years ago; it was a low-profile game away from the eyes of most, and perhaps the number of new boys Toshack had reached out to, even at that stage of his tenure, lessened the impact.

Yet those who were there, those who could see those flashes, were sure that Wales had something special.

"I'd played against him in a pre-season game when I was at Bristol City when he had just turned 16," says David Cotterill, who also played in that May game in front of a few thousand in Graz. "We actually shared the same agent at the time and he'd told me beforehand I'd be playing against this kid and I should look out for him. I remember having the better of him in the first-half but then, because he was a machine then as he is now, he just kept going and he came out on top. I said to myself then this kid is going to be good.

"The boys all knew too when he came away with us for the first time. We'd have shooting practice and you could already see his left foot was a joke. He wasn't as fast as he became later but, like I say, he was a machine, a freak almost with the things he could do with the ball."

It became increasingly obvious over the next 12 months, a first start for Wales coming in the 'away' friendly at Tottenham's White Hart Lane and the first thrusts down the left-flank of a ground that would soon rise as one whenever he picked up the ball.

Bale had not reached double figures in appearances outside age-grade football at that point yet, no-one was questioning why Toshack trusted him against the iconic yellow shirts worn that night by Ronaldinho and Kaka. Though the South American giants predictably triumphed and Bale was simply getting used to the demands of international football rather than delivering on the demands to be made of him, there was enough to which to attach hope and excitement. Indeed, Brazil's Inter Milan right-back may well wish that night had been the last time he faced his Cardiff-born opponent.

The seeds of his high-profile humiliation – where the chant of 'Taxi for Maicon' rang through the November North London air in 2010 after a Bale blitz helped Spurs beat the holders in a Champions League group clash – were sown in that Wales-Brazil friendly. The then Tottenham boss Martin Jol was watching and, having already been previously impressed while seeing Bale in a reserve game a year earlier, immediately understood Toshack's desire to throw a 17-year-old into the international environment.

By the end of the season, in May 2007 – and after Bale had teased Wales' fans of his potential further when he swung that free-kick in against Slovakia, the ray of sunny hope in among the deluge of visitors' goals – Jol had persuaded Tottenham directors to part with £5m up front and a potential further £5m to sign a player whose club football experience had been limited to the Championship. Most importantly, with Manchester United also showing an interest, Jol persuaded those who had been stood on the touchline in Colney.

"I promised his mum I would play him," Jol said a few years later. "That's why he came to Tottenham. There was another choice for him, but I knew he was good enough to play and he would get better by playing because he is a fantastic, fantastic player, one of the best talents on the left flank in Europe.

"Maybe a lot was expected of him at such a young age but it depends what you want from him.

"Attacking-wise he is a big talent but that isn't the only thing. He has a few things he has to improve on, as all youngsters do, but they only come from experience."

Jol was speaking in the summer of 2009 when manager of Ajax, sharing the same perplextion as those in Wales who seemed to be seeing a different Bale to the one struggling at Tottenham following the Dutchman's departure. Injury, including a damaged ankle that needed two operations, hampered his progress under his successor at Spurs, Spaniard Juande Ramos.

Then, regardless of his growing promise when flying down international flanks with Wales – with a performance away in Russia of particular note, regardless of his failure to convert an early penalty one of his attacking surges had won – it seemed he could not force his way in under Harry Redknapp.

Nottingham Forest were among those monitoring a situation that now seems surreal. Bale had unfairly been mocked because of an anomaly of a statistic that showed he had failed to win a single game as a Premier League player, one that had lasted 24 outings over two years and had – according to Redknapp – a seemingly superstitious Sir Alex Ferguson admitting he would struggle to pick him because of the 'bad omen' potentially affecting others.

"Was there a time in that period when I thought twice about picking him? Yes, I'd be a liar if I said that it wasn't a consideration," Redknapp said that season. "There are times when you think about things like that. We're all superstitious, I'm very superstitious anyway – I'll wear the same suit when we're winning and chuck it when we lose, things like that.

"And you think 'this doesn't seem right, it doesn't seem possible for this to happen'. But we got it out of the way and since then he hasn't looked back."

The so-called curse – which said more about Bale's lack of game time and Tottenham's struggles for consistency at the time than the then 20-year-old – was lifted when he appeared as a September substitute with Spurs 4-0 up at home against Burnley. Tottenham added one more with Redknapp admitting he simply played Bale to break the hoodoo, as he called it, claiming it had affected the youngster.

Bale didn't seem to agree, even if it looked to annoy him when it was brought up, and it is more likely that his lack of game time was of greater frustration. Redknapp spoke of teasing Bale about him being preoccupied with his hair – something the player accepted was a correct kick up the backside – and claiming he needed to be toughened up.

Physically, that was always likely to come, but mentally Bale was ready. Redknapp had, by that point, no plans to move him forward and saw his future as a left-back – yet also saw the Cameroon international Benoît Assou-Ekotto as first pick. Nottingham Forest, Birmingham and Burnley were all monitoring the situation and may well have made their move, but senior figures at Spurs were keen to ensure that he was going nowhere.

Instead, Bale bided his time until Assou-Ekotto was scheduled to play in the Africa Cup of Nations and, even while it was a hip injury that removed the barrier to a starting place, Bale seized his moment. In a manner similar to the way he would burn past markers from then on, he did not look back.

Inevitably he crept further up the pitch until the obvious could not be ignored any longer and he became a No. 3-wearing winger. Goals and wins over Arsenal and Chelsea followed, as did a four-year contract and the chance to play Champions League football, the supposed Jonah from Wales by now laughing loudest. The Bale that had been seen by those west of the Severn was now being seen by the rest of the football world, the San Siro the stage for his European breakthrough as he scored a hat-trick against Inter Milan after his side had been four goals down within the first 35 minutes. There was a similarity of power and precision to each of his goals, the Internazionale stars simply unable to stop him as he began to stretch his increasingly-muscular legs and firing across Júlio César. Come their trip to White Hart Lane, the calls for a cab for Maicon, even without Bale scoring, illustrated this was now a player of consistency as well as class.

Coupled with Gary Speed's arrival in the national post and Aaron Ramsey's return from injury, it all added to this unshakable Welsh optimism that Bale's brilliance could be the difference. Even as the struggles threatened to swamp Chris Coleman in the first year of his reign, the virtuoso display against Scotland at home showed his developing ability to take on the match-winning responsibility that was so clear at Tottenham as he picked up both the PFA's Player of the Year award and Young Player of the year award for 2012/2013, as well as the Football Writers' annual honour. With Cristano Ronaldo the only other player to have collected all three in a single campaign, perhaps it was inevitable Real Madrid would come calling.

The speculation had dragged on through most of the 2013 summer, Bale's absence through Spurs' pre-season with a foot injury only adding to the dramatic narrative of a world record transfer. It had not died as Coleman welcomed his squad into camp for an August friendly with the Republic of Ireland, reporters from the Spanish media matching the numbers from these isles as he trained at Dragon Park, the association's and Welsh Football Trust's new development training centre. Not fit enough to play, he was put through his paces in an individual session all the same, with Coleman joking he assumed he had turned up at the wrong venue such were the numbers of paparazzi. They presumably were the same ones who had tried to doorstep the Galactico in waiting at the St David's – Wales' new plush hotel base in Cardiff Bay – only to get a smiling 'no comment'. Regardless of the fairly forgettable 0-0 draw, never before has a game seen more focus on a man sat in the stands than those on the pitch.

Wales enjoyed the circus, embracing this new level of profile that the team were being dragged into because of their superstar. Surpassing any of the almost 'boy band' levels of adulation seen when the Ryan Giggs factor was at its peak with Wales, inevitably the worries were of whether his move would soon see Bale put Real before Red Dragons.

Yet there was a case of starting as you mean to go on. After protracted negotiations, Bale was signed and symbolically presented to the Bernabéu, close to both the transfer deadline and Wales' squad gathering for the game in Macedonia.

The assumption was Bale would remain in Madrid, and yet he was soon aboard a private flight to meet with the rest of the squad. He had changed clubs, he had moved to a whole new level of status as the £85m man, and yet it was the same Gareth.

Coleman's relationship with Real manager Carlo Ancelotti helped. Travelling to Madrid to ensure open communication, Coleman's trump card was Ancelotti's assistant Paul Clement, the Englishman who had worked with the Italian at Chelsea but, crucially, had also served in the Fulham set-up during Coleman's time at Craven Cottage. Still, it was the player himself who was driving his determination over international availability and, in turn, driving the team forward after the turning points of Coleman's first campaign.

The November friendly with Finland showed a growing level of appetite from the now overseas star before the benefits of his European experience shone stunningly through in the March warm-up with Iceland. As the *Western Mail* report put it "One man cannot make a team. But he can make a team believe" and his growing stature and unplayable nature was already clearly rubbing off on those around him, providing goals for James Collins and Sam Vokes while saving the best for himself: a charging run down the left that the shoves out of touch by his Icelandic marker could not stop as he curved off the pitch and back again to bear down on goal. When he performed the trick a few weeks later in the Copa del Rey final against Barcelona, it marked his crowning by the Spanish press as 'The Prince of Wales'.

If his teammates knew they had something special, so did the Football Association of Wales as a whole. They had seen him proudly display the Welsh flag, *Y Ddraig Goch*, having scored the decisive goal for Real in their Lisbon Champions League final win over city-rivals Atlético, leaping highest to head home in extra time before *Los Merengues* went on to triumph 4-1. He celebrated draped in the colours of his nation, just as Aaron Ramsey had done after scoring the winning goal in Arsenal's FA Cup victory over Hull a week earlier.

Enshrined in history for helping the Bernabéu club to *La Décima* – their long-awaited tenth European title – it made perfect sense for the FAW to put Bale at the heart of their bid to stage games for the pan-continental 2020 European Championships at the Millennium Stadium.

Huge amounts of work had gone into the dossier, overcoming previous issues over hotel space in Cardiff and airport links with Jonathan Ford bringing on board Alan Hamer, the former Glamorgan cricket executive who had helped the county secure the Ashes Test between England and Australia a few years earlier. Still, it was Bale's backing and iconic heart celebration that glossed the package and gave bid promoters just cause to shake hands and press Wales' case with UEFA officials at that Lisbon final.

Although the FAW opted against the hard sell, UEFA's decision to host the European Super Cup final between Real and Europa League winners Sevilla at Cardiff City Stadium was the perfect stage for them to showcase Cardiff's attractiveness, Bale's homecoming played out on a grand scale. Wales' bid would lose out to Scotland in the eventual 2020 vote, but the work done had already laid huge groundwork for the subsequent awarding of the 2017 Champions League final, a sign of how the one superstar player had helped increase Wales' football profile.

And Wales was never far from his mind. In the mixed zone area – where reporters queue and huddle to grab words from players – after the 2-0 Super Cup win where Ronaldo scored both goals but was quick to acknowledge the role of his Welsh teammate in the side's recent success as well as his own personal form, Bale was understandably swarmed by reporters seeking his feelings on playing for the biggest club in the world in his own backyard. Yet, despite the best attempts of security staff to whisk him away to the waiting team bus, he stopped the moment Wales' Euro 2016 qualifying opener with Andorra was mentioned. Still clutching his winners' medal, his country's call was clearly ringing loudly even with the victory songs of his club side still fresh in the Cardiff night as he spoke of the desire to emulate Real's European success in the red of Wales. His was more than hope, the excitement building towards a campaign that contained genuine opportunity for history.

On top of the extra final places on offer of the expanded tournament – the top two from each of the nine groups qualifying automatically, as well as the third-placed teams going into a play-off – the February draw in Nice had given even greater hope that a Bale-inspired Wales could successfully scale their mountain this time around.

Bosnia, from pot one, were a team to be wary of yet did not carry the same threat of a 'super power', a side you could all but guarantee would qualify and a side Wales perennially seemed paired with in so many previous campaigns. Wales knew all about the quality of

Belgium, their position as second seeds misplaced, but Israel as third seeds were the ones to overcome first and foremost and, despite previous issues in Nicosia, Cyprus as fourth seeds were surely there to be beaten. Lastly were Andorra, minnows who had yet to pick up a European Championship qualifying point. In a change from previous years where Wales would have to fight their corner in a fixtures meetings with other associations, a drawn-out process where association power regarding broadcasting revenue was often flexed, the arrangement of fixtures was computerised and so, having failed to see momentum build in recent campaigns, Coleman's side were to be given their chance to get up and running early with a trip to the minute landlocked nation in the Pyrenees.

Bale did not speak for himself but for the side as he enthused about the September start to proceedings. Without him in Amsterdam – as well as Ramsey and Ashley Williams among others – Wales had impressed despite a friendly defeat to the Netherlands, prepared to stick to their guns against quality opposition in Louis van Gaal's side who would go on from the 2-0 win to finish third at the summer World Cup in Brazil. It was a sign that Bale had helped lift an entire squad even without his presence, that the belief that they could achieve was spreading even to debutants such as Fulham's George Williams, who marked his first appearance from the bench with a slaloming run that had the hallmarks of Archie Gemmill's effort against the Oranje in 1978. Williams was eventually stopped in his tracks but there was a sense Wales, as a team, were ready to ride the challenges.

Coleman too, was studiously approaching the group and ready to build further on plans of getting the most out of Bale by unashamedly looking towards his talented talisman, wanting him to springboard off a platform provided by an organised defence and a possession-and-press midfield.

Coleman had leapt upon a sense of now or never, and the authority with which he delivered the positive side of that message had an effect on a team seemingly steeled and prepared for what lied in store.

"I think we could all see it had been difficult for Chris coming in at first," says Danny Gabbidon, whose impressive performance amid injuries to others in the friendly with the Netherlands had rolled back the years and earned him both a return move to Cardiff City as well as a late call-up to the squad to travel to Andorra la Vella. "You could see at the start of the previous campaign he almost hadn't wanted to get too involved and was worried if he had started to change things too early he could have really upset things. It was difficult to impose himself on us and it showed because although we were playing the same way, we were not getting the results.

"When I came back in things were different. There had been pressure and that uncertainty whether he was still going to be in the job, but it was clearer than ever he wanted to be himself and be better.

"That first meeting before Andorra you could sense a difference again. I don't want to say things were more professional because we hadn't been lacking on that, but it did feel that things were more geared to succeeding in that campaign, that this was about delivering right there and then and, because of that, we all felt far more as though we were his side.

"First of all I had found him a little shy but now there was this confidence as he told us how many points it would take, what we needed to do, all the performance markers for getting to where we all wanted. He had done his homework and was marking his card – he knew what he wanted to say and we knew what we wanted to do.

"We had this feeling it was make or break for us as a team; we had everything we wanted in terms of the preparation and we knew we had the talent with the likes of Baley. Perhaps the manager felt the last piece was getting his tactics right and it was obvious right from the off he had done a lot of work on that in time for that first game."

It might have all mattered for little. The players had already been aware of the potential pitch problems at the new sports complex where Andorra would stage the September group opener. Bale had even referenced it in that Cardiff City Stadium chat a week or so earlier.

Fact-finding trips had not shed much light on things given the stadium was still being built and, crucially, the artificial surface had not been laid until the final few weeks before the game. Flash floods did not help prior to the official UEFA test to check the speed of the ball's roll little more than a week before the game. The logistical nightmare of rearranging a venue was mooted, but the second test a few days later passed with the ball moving slowly enough to get the green light. It was only when the team arrived for training the night before the game that FAW match officials had their suspicions of how the

Andorran FA had overcome their pitch problem. The simple bounce of a ball brought with it a black upward spray of rubber crumb that suggested, in Welsh minds at least, that they had overcompensated with the material to get the okay, and while time would have perhaps seen it dissipate and disperse, time is not what Wales had with their campaign kicking off in 24 hours.

Regardless, speaking in the team hotel in Barcelona before the three-hour coach journey over the mountains, Coleman had already insisted there could be no excuses. Wonderings of whether it would have been deemed acceptable for the likes of England to play on such a surface were quickly shelved. Whatever the circumstances, whatever the difficulties, this was a game that simply had to be won.

"Before we'd got there we'd all started to hear about what it was going to be like, but we'd already sort of decided between us that there was nothing we could do about it so we couldn't focus on it or get worked up about it," says Chris Gunter. "We were just expected to win and, no matter what, we needed to get the three points. That was the only thing in our minds.

"We still knew it was going to be tough regardless of the pitch. When it's the first game of the group it almost doesn't matter who you are playing. It's the same with your clubs in that first game of a season, everyone has that belief they can start well and even if you're not going to win the group it's a game people target and they wouldn't have been going into it on the back of any defeats, so you have that initial optimism whether you're Andorra, Wales or anyone.

"When we did see the pitch for the first time it was just ridiculous and a lot of us thought that there was just no way it should have been allowed for a European Championship game. But it was, and there was that thing in your mind that said 'if we didn't get the win the pitch may well have been a big reason' but nobody would have cared, it would have just been 'Wales have started poorly'."

Coleman couldn't afford it, not in the isolation of this game against the whipping boys, nor in terms of the group as a whole. A win was a must for himself as much as it was for the momentum so desperately needed to take the team forward. That sense of feeling was of no surprise to anybody; what he had planned, though, was a different matter.

"It was a gamble," admits Coleman on a decision to play with three centre-backs, including traditional left-back Ben Davies in the middle with Gunter and Neil Taylor operating as wing-backs. "It was done with the rest of the campaign in mind and I knew we had to get ready for it. I was prepared that we might not play well but I knew it was just about winning, that as long as we brought the points home it wouldn't have mattered if it was 1-0 or 5-0. We had to go for it there and then."

The switch had been mulled over for some time.

"Things took time to get right and it took time for Chris to get used to international football and what we were up against," says Osian Roberts. "But when he did, he saw that we had to change, that we would have to be different. We couldn't go into the new campaign playing the same 4-2-3-1 and everybody thinking it was going to end up differently. We had to change and that was the right time."

Players weren't sure but the growing confidence and courage of Coleman saw doubts shelved well before the trip. Still, if the win was already an obvious must, the impact of failure was now even greater had his plan backfired.

"I think the players sensed a change in me, I think I was more authoritative with them," Coleman says. "Not in a headmaster's way – I don't speak to them like that – but they could see I was clear in my mind in what we were going to do.

"I'd been bold with them when, perhaps, in the campaign before I wasn't quite there. I'd been too cautious with them, telling them we have to win, when it was too early for that mindset. We had to get there.

"But by Andorra they were ready for me to say which direction we were going in. I think I had more of an authority.

"When I told them we would play three in the back some of them spoke up; we encourage them to do that and they did say they weren't sure, that none of them had played in it. I asked them to trust me and they were brilliant. We worked on it every day going into that game, we studied it together and we were ready for it. They bought into what I was thinking because I think they trusted in me a bit more, they believed in me because by that point I believed in myself.

"If it went wrong, it was on me, but I was prepared for that and the team were ready to trust me. The mood was more together very early on, more belief, you could just sense it. Of course, then they scored and I thought 'Here we go'...."

As did most watching. Andorra, 199th in the world without a Euro win in 41 outings and who had lost their last 44 competitive games, took the lead after six minutes with their first goal since 2010. The long throw was not cleared and the slightest of tugs from Taylor on Ivan Lorenzo was pounced upon by Mitja Žganec, the additional assistant behind the goal who promptly received the thoughts of the 1,500 travelling Welsh contingent in the 3,300 capacity venue. Needing not to be asked twice by Slovenian referee Slavko Vinčić, Ildefons Lima sent Wayne Hennessey the wrong way.

The doubts and dismay of those watching at home and in the stadium seemed to be embodied in the white-shirted Wales players, some mentally crumbling with the same kind of weak resistance displayed in the pitch.

"When we had trained on it the night before we were struggling to move the ball quickly and it was no different when we kicked off," adds Gunter. "None of us had played on a pitch like it. Some of the Swansea boys were used to 3G because they'd trained on it for a year when their training ground was being built, but this was different again with those black crumbs flying up every time the ball reached you. The stuff was everywhere after the game even in the dressing room.

"And then on top of that the goal gave them a lift and something to hang onto. They could sit really deep so we had no space to go into and they had that mentality where they could try and dig in and frustrate us, just cling on. We were struggling but then thankfully Gareth got his goals."

The first came before half-time, glancing Ben Davies' cross home with a header deft in its appearance and expert in its execution. It was presumed the 22nd-minute leveller would see Wales run away with things but frustration and an element of self-pity had gripped too many. Extra urgency and the attempts of a determined Joe Allen in midfield to try and get Wales doing the simple things were being undone by desperation seeing a loss of shape and flow despite the dominance. With ten minutes to go, time was fast running out on Wales, Bale's dream – and Coleman.

"I knew what would have happened," admits Coleman, almost unable to say the unsayable: that he would have been facing the very real prospect of losing of his job. "It would be pretty obvious to anyone. You can't come away from Andorra not winning, you just can't. I couldn't have come out after the game and say, 'Well, it's a point to where we want to go, they are all tough games', no-one would have been listening to me. I wouldn't have been able to say it, we all would have known the score."

But then it happened. For all the changes, for all the improvements and extra details on the journey from tragedy and turmoil to a potential turning point in the history of the national side, the butterfly flapped its wings, the one step came. George Williams had surged forward from the bench, Lima making the foul. The wall formed, the ball struck, the chance gone, then the salvation shrill of the whistle.

"We knew Wales had a strong side and we would need to play with everything," says Gabriel Riera. "We had played well and we thought we were going to get the draw and then it happened. The referee made his decision. Sometimes you have the luck. Wales had it and that moment was a big moment for them. Bale scored, they won the game and they gained a lot of confidence. It was the motivation they needed to go on."

The free-kick was as delightful in its delivery as it was in its importance, although Bale concedes it helped to have been able to test his range first after Riera's indiscretion in the wall.

"I didn't notice him coming out of the wall," Bale told the *Western Mail* 13 months later, picking the moment as one of his highlights of the campaign. "It was a good job I could re-take it because I managed to get my distance right the second time."

He gave the impression as he stood over the ball that second time that he was nerveless, that it was a matter of time and this was it. Indeed, when it was asked in jest in the medical room as he received a massage the day before the game what would happen if Andorra scored first, Bale replied with a smile that he would get the ball until he scored and keep going until he did so again. Perhaps he was only half-joking, his curled effort indication that he could be as good as even his throwaway words.

Pandemonium ensued even before the ball nestled in the net, Bale leading the way in the corner before teammates joined him, others simply celebrating where they stood, such was the relief.

The fans' celebrations could well have been purely based on the dramatic finish, winning in such fashion with a goal to admire and that completed a comeback victory in the final ten minutes. It would not be the first time such circumstances prompted such joy and loss of control as some supporters raced onto the pitch, past sponsorship boards and stewards wearing sandals. Yet the way the team celebrated suggested they knew the wider importance.

"They were two of the most important goals of the whole campaign," believes Gunter. "The equaliser made sure we were level at half-time so we could almost start again without chasing the game too much – and then that free-kick. It was probably bigger than any of the others that followed because it gave us a chance we weren't going to have without it. The negativity was bad enough because we hadn't played well and we had left it late, but you could only imagine what it was going to be like if we had not come away with the win, with everyone saying 'same old Wales' and refusing to think that this was going to be different.

"I'm not sure how much we would have got caught up in that, but I think the fact we came through it was big for us as a team. There had been so many games where we had been up against sides much higher than us in the rankings and we'd play well, perhaps nick a goal, but they'd always find a way to win and pull themselves out of it. This was when we showed that we could do it too, that we could be the other team.

"It was a massive test for us to come through and regardless if we had won 10-1, or 2-1 in the last ten minutes as we did, we came though it and came through it together."

It was that togetherness that screamed through even amidst the individuality of Bale's heroics. While he followed leaping highest to head the leveller with the signature jumping celebration of Real teammate Ronaldo, there was none of the aloofness in his performance that has sometimes been associated with the Portuguese man of scores. Even as the dream threatened to slip away 24 hours after Real Madrid legend and future manager Zinedine Zidane had described the thought of Bale not featuring at a major finals as a tragedy, there was no throwing his arms in the air in frustration but only an added determination to raise himself and bring others along with him.

"Gareth is desperate to play in a major tournament with Wales – he did not want to be sitting at home in the summer while his team-mates were in Brazil," Zidane had said beforehand.

"It will be a tragedy if he never gets to play in a World Cup or European Championships. He is one of the top five players in the world – for him not to be there is just wrong.

"One player can't qualify for Euro 2016 – but what Gareth can be is Wales' leader. It doesn't matter who they play in the qualifiers, when Gareth is on the field they always have a match-winner."

As if Wales needed telling. Or Coleman for that matter.

"He got me out of it," the manager admits. "He did it against Scotland with those goals, buying us the time we needed, and then he did it in Andorra.

"They are the moments that stick out but you always know he can do that, not just because of his talent but because of how he is in the camp. He is our best player and if your best players are not having you as a manager, you're dead in the water.

"But he's with us. When we speak with him and tell him what we're thinking of doing, as long as you talk through the process with him, he's fine.

"He's intelligent, too. He will ask questions and as long as you have answers he is with you.

"And then, when he's in that dressing room with that jersey on, he's fantastic. You could see it before he went to Madrid but he's grown since because he was placed in a situation where you can either deal with it or you can't. He has embraced that, he's seen it as a challenge and it's benefited us because he's not only got better as a player but as the whole package. There's just this huge presence about him."

And yet speak to his teammates, and the paradox is that this much-changed Bale is the same as he's always been.

"He's just one of the lads," says Gabbidon. "When you see this most expensive player in the world I guess you should be a bit in awe but, to us at least, it's just Gareth. It's not as if you can't have a conversation with him or that he looks down his nose at anyone. I wouldn't say he's the same as when he first came into the squad because he was so young, but his personality hasn't changed, he's just become himself. He likes a joke, he likes a prank or two but will be with the rest of us playing on the X-Box or having a coffee and a chat.

"I remember watching the presentation when he signed for Madrid and it was strange to see it in some ways – not that we didn't think he would be good enough but just that it was weird to see this lad we knew being introduced as a Real player and an £85m signing. To be honest, I felt a lot of pride, just so happy for him because he is not only such a fantastic player but a fantastic person too.

"You have seen a bit of change in terms of his profile, the amount of people that will ask for an autograph or a photo – and I've never seen him turn one down – but I don't think he'll ever be fully comfortable with it, but then he shouldn't be such a good player! He takes it all in his stride though and, as much as he's still the same, you can see this growth of aura about him when you get to games."

While there is an intense, 'follow me' maturity to this *Galles Galactico* when it gets to the pitch and those final minutes before fixtures, he remains a big kid at heart.

The landlady at his old lodgings in Southampton has previously spoken of how the polite, well-mannered and well brought-up Bale and Walcott would also be the jokers of the young Saints group, knocking on doors and scarpering. The fun side of Bale, the cheap gags, are still there even with the £85m price tag on his head. There appears to be a comfort in his surroundings, with teammates he has trusted, that he has grown with since their teenage years, that ultimately he can be himself.

"He's still one of the most immature players in the squad," says Gunter with a fondness, the defender having known Bale better than most having also made the move to Tottenham as a teenager. "You can guarantee he's the one messing around, although only at the right times. He's great in that sense, he's relaxed and it relaxes everyone else. That's the kind of atmosphere there is, one where everyone is at ease with each other, there were no pretences.

"If you're not involved in that and see that side of him then you're going to perceive him differently. This is a guy worth millions in different contracts and when you're on the pitch or talking in front of TV cameras then you're not going to be like that, he's not alone in that regard.

"But we'll be on the bus watching him do an interview after a game and then he'll come on board and it's a different person, the one we've known joking around since the Under-21s."

Those who share the team hotel with him suggest that coming away with Wales not only provides a chance to return to Cardiff – Bale having long been known as something a homebird, with Redknapp once remarking that he'd be back over the Severn rather than abroad when he granted his Spurs side time off – but is also an escape from the intensity of Madrid. The fact that, on his first Welsh camp following the record deal, his move was greeted with jokes at his expense and his costly status was instant proof that his teammates were not about to see someone different from the player who had been alongside them for the best part of the last ten years.

"He's a different guy with us to the one everyone else sees but he's no different to the guy we've always known – and we're not different with him," says David Cotterill. "He's always had that giggly side but in public there's perhaps more of an awareness that he's this superstar and people are looking at him. Perhaps he has to project a certain side of him, but there wasn't a difference after he moved from the way he has been in camp."

That constant is a factor in the way Bale performs and approaches Wales camps. In Andorra he set the tone for the rest of the campaign, prepared to do the hard running rather than simply step forward for the showpieces. It has the effect of others looking up and seeing this global name ready to go the extra mile, to chase the lost cause and reminding them that, in turn, it is the least they can do to follow suit. He inspires with attitude as well as ability.

"He knows he's a good player, but the balance comes with the fact he doesn't think he's good enough not to do the other stuff, to just rely on his football ability alone," says Gunter. "The way he approaches games and the build-up to games is what makes him such a good player. It's not just the natural talent he has but how he works on it and then works in games to allow him the opportunities to showcase it. He gives himself a chance to play as well as he does, which is something he's always done from us being kids.

"You could see he was starting to reach another level in that Andorra game on the back of what he had done out in Madrid in his first year, winning the Champions League and playing as well as he had done after all the focus on his move where there were some wondering if he was going to be a success.

"I think most of it was just confidence. He'd always had that in him – when it wasn't a great time for him when we were at Spurs, he didn't doubt himself, he thought he should have been playing and if it didn't work out he'd move somewhere else, do well and go on from there. He's always had that but it was building in him and he seemed to be gaining confidence every game he played.

"But it's not a case of thinking he can do it all. He doesn't see himself as different to anyone else. I've experienced a couple of players in my career where they don't think they should be doing this or that but Gareth is not the same, he's willing to do what it takes as part of a team. He respects us as much as we obviously respect him and that's why it works.

"When you watch a game on TV there's always that player who thinks someone should have done something different and is quick to let them know, and I don't mean in a constructive way. I've never seen that with Gareth – and that's huge for us. He's got the same attitude as guys in the squad from League One or League Two. That's why the team is so together. If you came into the squad and you didn't know, you would never guess which one was the most expensive footballer in the world because he's just one of us."

Of course, there is the acceptance from the rest that as much as he is the same, that he is also different.

"When you look up and see him there you know you've got a chance whoever you are playing," says Jonny Williams. "He's relaxed and a good laugh but then there's also this responsibility as the main man and the younger lads can't help but learn from him. Some of his game is just natural pace and pure ability, but there's so much to learn off him from the work he does technically, things he does in the gym and how he deals with different situations. He'd be huge for any squad."

But it's with Wales where his heart lies, revealing that an early career conversation about investigating the possibility of representing the Three Lions because of an English grandmother lasted all of ten seconds.

"It means so much to him," adds Gabbidon. "Not just because he realises this was such a good opportunity to achieve something, but because he genuinely enjoys coming back to be among his mates, with the banter which he might not get in Madrid. On top of that, there is something special in doing well for your country. I had tasted it under Sparky and you can see Gareth has thrived on the chance to go a step further."

There's a passion in what he does, a genuine sense of pride in his country and what he can do for it. If it is too much to say he prioritises

Wales over his behemoth club, it's certainly not an after-thought that may bring doubts of shaking off cramp or a calf strain on international duty when there may be a Champions League or *El Clasico* fixture fast approaching. It was, fair or not, an accusation Ryan Giggs couldn't always shake off.

Whereas supporters had got used to simply enjoying the fact that Bale had turned up for a squad when club pressure might have suggested otherwise, he himself appeared not content with that being enough. He wanted to do something to be remembered for while with Wales, having already done so with Real. It seemed that night in Andorra that Bale wanted to get to a major finals and was ready to haul others with him when it was needed.

"You can just tell he wants to do things that have never been done before, whether it's qualifying, winning 100 caps, beating Ian Rush's goalscoring record, whatever," says Coleman. "It's not because he's in it for himself, far from it, but things like that inspire him.

"And it's infectious. He's still the same Baley, a big kid sometimes, up to no good in a good way around the dinner table and laughing with the rest of them.

"But then there's the other side when he knows what's needed of him. He knows he's the king and I think he likes it, and enjoys what is needed from him. He doesn't abuse it, but he thrives on it. He knows we can't get where we want to be without him being who he is. I think he likes that feeling and accepts that responsibility. He's not weighed down by it, he's lifted by it."

After Andorra, he was not alone.

9

Belief

"This is our home and you're not taking points off us.
This is our land" – Joe Ledley

There had been times when Wales players would feel conflicting emotions as they stepped out onto the field.

They would look down and see the red, see the badge and shirt worn by their heroes before them and be reminded that this was the pinnacle of their playing days, what they had only fantasised of when on the parks and playgrounds, what had motivated them when making their ways in their burgeoning careers.

Then they would look up and look around. They would see the empty seats, hear the chatter that rose above any chanting and wonder if their feelings for the shirt were reflected by a nation who seemingly didn't believe any more.

Of course there were those who always believed, the hardy few who stuck through thick and thin, supporting Wales not because of success but because of a mixture of duty and almost irrational enjoyment of all that goes with it, picking up as many obscure passport stamps as the side did defeats.

Yet even with supposed crowd pullers such as Gareth Bale and Aaron Ramsey, the globalisation and mass-broadcast of the game on top of apathy around the international team and scepticism of whether this golden generation would ever actually shine meant that it rarely got more than the odd thousand to make their way to watch Wales.

"I'll be honest, it was awful at times," says Joe Ledley. "You'd walk out full of pride and then see a crowd of 4,000 and it felt like being in the Under-21s.

"It was strange. Even when we'd started to do well under Speedo it didn't seem like we could get the kind of crowds you'd expect at international level.

"It was hard. You'd be back at your club and the lads who weren't internationals would go off on their breaks and you'd turn up and it was difficult not to catch yourself thinking 'What am I doing here?' Don't get me wrong, you'd never turn your back on your country but there were times it would be difficult to motivate yourself."

Crowds had dwindled for some time. The Millennium Stadium would rattle with the sad sounds of horns rather than hostile atmosphere or any *hwyl*, John Toshack and players both encouraging the moving of international fixtures to club grounds because the vast venue was seen as more of an inspiration for visiting sides than the hosts. Still, the switch only masked the mass drop off in interest with only the odd visits of England encouraging crowds north of 30,000 and the majority of games increasingly lower than 20,000. It was an ever decreasing circle with the 'floating fans' walking away, put off by the increasing indifference of others. It was a negative spiral of support.

Furthermore, while the money from satellite giants Sky pumped much needed revenue into the FAW coffers that benefited not only the senior side but the wider Welsh game, there was an argument that the move from terrestrial television denied an advertising avenue to the larger public – the sometime supporter if you will – that could generate an interest Welsh rugby enjoyed from being beamed into every household instead of only the odd one.

It cut no ice with those who believed that it was all too easy an excuse, but for whatever reasons it was all a long way from '*I Love You Baby*'. Indeed, it appeared the Welsh public had fallen out of love with their national team.

Ledley had been skipper when, just before that galvanising game of youngsters in Azerbaijan in June 2009, 4,071 turned up at Llanelli's Parc y Scarlets for a friendly with Estonia. For the friendly with Australia as Speed's side stood on the cusp of beginning their upward momentum, just 6,373 made their way to Cardiff City Stadium. A month later for the qualifier with Montenegro and Speed's renewed aim to bring the fans back managed to pull an attendance of just 8,194 – the lowest crowd for a qualifier in the Welsh capital for more

180

than ten years. It seemed to be punishment for not only errors and stumbles while developing as a young side, but also for the failures of those before them.

"When I was with Celtic, I'd bump into people and they'd ask why I was back in Cardiff from Glasgow," says Ledley. "We'd have a game in two days' time or something but people didn't seem to know and a few of us couldn't understand it. That's where it had got to. I think we were all aware of it as much as the FAW were and we did try and help some of the staff by doing things like going to the schools to give out tickets or get our faces in the media, but ultimately we knew as a group the biggest thing we could do to get them back was what we did on the pitch.

"You had to appreciate the difficulties the midweek games meant for those with kids or those having to try and make it down from north Wales when transport made it tough for a lot of people, so we had to look at our ourselves.

"There wasn't one big meeting but there was a sense between all of us that if we wanted to change it then we had to raise it, to give more, to play better, not to give any excuse to have the stadiums half-full again.

"It's what we had all become used to with our clubs, moving up the divisions and playing in packed-out stadiums. When I was at Celtic, the Scotland lads would have games in front of 50,000 at Hampden and they weren't doing much better than us. Ireland were the same. Northern Ireland would have bigger crowds and – without trying to sound disrespectful – we felt we had a better side, better players, but we were the ones with no atmosphere, no big crowds to drive us on when it might get tough in games. We wanted that to change but we needed to change it."

Why it changed that night against Bosnia is a little difficult to fathom. Though the Bale-factor had its own pull, the previous home game – the night of his Iceland wonder-show – had brought in 13,290 which, although creeping up on past attendances, didn't signify a sea change of attitude.

Ticket prices had been slashed as a means of trying to lessen the excuses yet Bosnia, though World Cup finalists earlier that year, were not the kind of star attraction that could command a boost in numbers. Certainly the performance in Andorra was one that only added to the armoury of those looking to snipe at this side and their chances of being different to all those that had gone before.

But, crucially, they had got through it. As Coleman had said beforehand, that was all that mattered and, at the very least, there were some grounds for optimism to swell interest.

It was boosted further by the surprise result of the September openers in Group B. It would have been lost in the wails of humiliation had Bale – and Gabriel Riera – not made their moves in Andorra la Vella, but Cyprus' 2-1 win in Zenica against the Bosnian top seeds had, even at this early stage, blown things open. With Belgium's game in Israel postponed because of the political and security situation in Gaza, there was a chance for Wales to lay down a marker – and the fans felt it.

They did so despite the almost hyperbolic hostility from some which accompanied the Andorra game and its aftermath. There were those who were quick to call for Coleman's head, concerned that this huge opportunity would be wasted under his charge and it was better to avoid delay in what they felt was inevitable. Those closer to the camp, though, could see that the players were firmly with their manager at this point and, if they had bought into the plans for the campaign, so the public had seemingly bought into this young team as they saw signs of a side ready to match their own idealistic beliefs of what playing for Wales means.

Genuine absences because of genuine injuries aside, supporters saw no weak-willed withdrawals and there was a sense that Wales fans believed that it mattered to these players as much as it mattered to many of them. There was no Aaron Ramsey, who had suffered a hamstring injury, no Joe Allen after his failure to recover from a hernia operation, and yet the prospect of success in the back-to-back home games with Bosnia, and Cyprus three days later, had seemingly whetted Welsh appetites.

"We had heard before the game that we were expecting a big crowd," says Ledley. "It was what we had waited nine years for. It was what we had been asking for – and we got it. We saw it as a sign that people saw that we were doing something right, that they felt we could go somewhere. It was a big moment for us and we knew in the build-up that it was almost now or never if we wanted to keep them."

If it was a defining game, Wales were ready for it. Coleman's changes to his system that looked awkward in Andorra had been done with this game in mind, his players fully aware and prepared for what was expected of them.

"There was a feeling we had been building to that moment," says Òsian Roberts. "We wanted the whole campaign to be about the next game, the next challenge in front of us and we certainly weren't talking about Cyprus when we met for Bosnia.

"But at the same time, we had set out what we wanted to achieve in the campaign as a whole, and before it we had set targets together. Not so much just saying 'we want to qualify' because we understood it was a process. Even in the previous campaign and the pressures that were there, we wanted to try and stick to a process and a plan and to adapt which would have been the same if Gary had still been with us; it wouldn't have been a case of getting the team playing the way we wanted and then not evolve. It was about how we improved and setting new aims – and under Chris what we saw as key was being world-class without the ball.

"When we had played Croatia at the Liberty we had played well, but we had gone through the statistics and seen we had conceded 34 crosses and it was inevitable that Eduardo eventually scored from one of them. Regardless of how you play in other aspects, if you do that then the law of averages will go against you so it was a case of what we were going to do about it.

"So we sat down and went through with them what a qualifying team looked like. We benchmarked previous qualifiers: how many crosses do they concede? How many set pieces? Then we looked at the second-placed teams, their averages and how we would go about getting our own numbers down. We looked at where we were in comparison, all together, all shared, and when we set our goals we knew if we met those targets we'd be a qualifying team. It was about the process of getting there because we knew if we could get to those levels and numbers, the results would follow."

It didn't stop with talking about it. Rather than simply maintaining the heightened levels of preparation introduced by Speed, there was a will to build upon it. On top of the standard scouting, team analysts pored over their opponents. As well as analysis of their own training and performances from the often overnight work of analysts Ester

Wills and James Turner, players were issued with individual iPads which were fed with every conceivable detail on the man they were facing that night, their roles at set-pieces, their preferred foot, how many touches they like, a review of their most recent game on top of the general profile, all provided before the crucial final 48 hours before a game so they were not overloaded with information too close to kick-off.

"How they use that information is up to them but each of them go into that dressing room before a game feeling prepared, knowing that they have been given the tools to do the job," explains Roberts. "Physically and mentally they are 100% ready for that kick-off. And when you get that feeling it builds the confidence."

The switch in system did not mean a switch in style. The FAW had, in 2012, launched a strategic review with the aim of not only trying to modernise the association as a whole – an attempt to streamline the decision-making process and move power away from the bloated council system which was backed by forward-thinking new president Trefor Lloyd Hughes – but that laid out a way forward on the field. It had been written in consultation with Gary Speed, the then manager due to provide the voice-over for the glossy promotional video just days after his death; the launch was delayed until after Coleman came into position. It spoke of a 'Welsh Way' of playing based on a consistency of playing style and coaching messages through all levels. It had already been deep-rooted for those who had come through the system, the Welsh Football Trust overseeing moves to small-sided games long before England's move to do the same in 2012, the idea to have young players develop technique by having more touches of the ball. Though it had evolved, the first moves to smaller-sided games came in 1996, from which the likes of Bale, Ramsey and Allen – by now a £15m player with Liverpool – had emerged.

It was why coaches were convinced Emyr Huws – the Manchester City youngster who subsequently moved to the Championship for more game time, but impressively slotted into the side in the build-up friendly with Iceland – and, previously, Ben Davies could make the transition to the demands of the senior side so soon into their top-level careers. The ideals were the same, regardless of what tactics they were asked to employ at their club.

Within that, though, Coleman and Roberts were keen for a tactical adaptability with the willingness to look at modern developments aiding their aims. Roberts had been using coaching software as part of his coach education courses, in particular an application called Globall Coach that former Liverpool manager Rafa Benitez had helped develop. Rather than explaining the aims of how he wanted to set-up on the old fashioned flip-chart, Coleman could now show his players.

"It's basically a tactics screen where you can input all the details and set-ups in moving players around in certain passages of play, but the difference is that it animates it," says Roberts. "It visualises things for the players, not just showing the movements we want them to make but the timing of things, not just what to do but when to do it. It helps make sure that the messages get across, that they are clear on what we are trying to do and make sure they can put it into practice when it matters."

With such clarity came an almost unerring confidence from within the dressing room. Players had long spoken of this team achieving, even if Coleman refused to allow them to accept the golden generation tag until they had done something worthy of the moniker. There was a sense that they had become fed up of talking about it themselves and the development of many key players into truly-established Premier League talents, used to the demands of the top level, had brought a new mentality. No longer was the ready-made excuse of inexperience being bandied around and, as much as there was a focus on getting performances right, what shone through was the fact they now wanted to be winners. They knew what was expected of them.

"I think we all felt we'd reached a point where it was all there for us and that we could only look at ourselves," says Neil Taylor. "We'd all been there in games where you'd wondered whether the match had even been advertised and people didn't realise we had a game on. It was a struggle to believe sometimes, especially when there's Gareth Bale, one of the greatest players in the world, and the atmosphere felt like you were playing for the reserves not for your country.

"But we had sort of come together as players and knew it was down to us if we wanted to do something about it. That was basically winning games or at least showing people watching that we were different and that we deserved the bigger crowds.

"Perhaps we tried to play it down early on but we all knew we had a group of players good enough and it came to a point where we wanted to stand up for ourselves and prove it.

"It was a chance for us that night and there was an expectation on us. Before then it had felt that people were actually expecting us to fail, the 'same old Wales' type of thing. We wanted to put a stop to that."

When it came to it, there was close to a full house, all desperate to put their belief in Wales once more. It came as something of a surprise, a huge surge in sales taking it well past the expected 20,000 crowd and seeing 30,741 arrive at Cardiff City Stadium and FAW officials scrambling for extra stewards. There had been the buzz created by Bale and his Super Cup appearance a few months beforehand while there was a sense that the opposition in front of them after the win in Andorra added to this new found optimism and increase in attendance. Whatever the reasons, it was clear Wales was seeking to place its faith in the national team, wanting to believe. They were not left disappointed.

"It felt different," says Chris Gunter. "You could just sense it in the build-up, that little bit of excitement that hadn't been there for years and years.

"I don't know if we were expecting it because of how things had gone in Andorra. You tend to generally stay away from the newspapers, but even on social media you would pick up on things and that there were a lot still not impressed with what we were doing. It galvanised us a bit and the way the game panned out in Andorra toughened us up. It brought that extra bit of togetherness having come through it.

"We took that into the Bosnia game but the difference was that the crowd really was with us, they were in it with us. They saw the way we started, and had some early chances playing some really good football and it all just built. It was a bit more backs-to-the-wall in the second-half but as we came through it you could just feel that the fans believed in us, that they could see us wanting this so much and we just kept on feeding off each other.

"We just sensed that there was this real wish for us to do well and I think they saw the passion we had and we could feel it in them. The more we dug-in the more they would get behind us and then give us that lift, that belief to keep going."

The crowd had seen over 90 minutes what Wales had only shown in patches before, the team clearly ready to go toe-to-toe with the top-seeded team in the group and refusing to accept their usual fate of glorious failure.

With Bosnia prepared to pay close attention to Wales' most lively players – including Muhamed Bešić who hunted Gareth Bale down whenever he threatened to spark attacking momentum – the team that were once kids were keen to show they had become men.

As Bosnia edged things in midfield as the game wore on, a frustrated kick out from the superb Roma playmaker Miralem Pjanić saw him then goad his counterparts, including Ledley who was delivering his most mature and accomplished performance in a Wales shirt. Not far behind was captain Ashley Williams, first warning verbally and then physically, and was quickly surrounded by his teammates ready by his side. This was a team ready to stand up for each other.

"You always try and stick up for mates in games but it just felt we'd reached this point where no-one was going to be able to make a challenge or have a go at one of us without having to answer to all of us," says Ledley, who had grown from the boyhood Bluebird at Cardiff into a serial winner at Celtic and was now benefiting from the extra demands of the Premier League with Crystal Palace. "Before, as young lads all finding our own way, perhaps there were times where you felt a bit alone out there and maybe it could affect you. But that night summed up where we were as a team with so much determination and emotion. Even if we were not playing well in a game, we knew we were there for each other, that we don't dig anyone out, that it's about lifting each other. We were there, around the referee, around their players and I think it was a good example of what we felt as a team: this is our home and you're not taking points off us. This is our land."

It symbolised a team who trusted and believed in each other. As a result, they found the trust and belief from the crowd.

Wales had also found a class act in James Chester, partnering Williams at the back alongside Ben Davies, who had moved to Tottenham in a £10m-valued swap deal before the start of the season. It was Hull defender Chester's first home game for his adopted country, taking Coleman up on his offer to represent the land of his Rhyl-born mother ahead of the June friendly in the Netherlands. He had looked a class act in Amsterdam, showing the kind of quality and confidence that made obvious his upbringing at Manchester United, and even with the dangerous Edin Džeko attempting to pull him out of position, the expression worn by the 26-year-old was one of impressive calmness rather than concern.

Yet when the chances did come the visitors' way, they found a man repaying faith rather than simply earning it. Wayne Hennessey had been talked about by Neville Southall for some time as his true goalkeeping heir and had been mentioned in the same excited tones as Bale and Ramsey when first fast-tracked into the senior side by John Toshack. Gaining the first-team shirt at Wolves, and winning promotion to the Premier League, it seemed the somewhat slender 6ft 6in stopper was fulfilling his potential. Then came knee ligament damage, not once but twice, with the Anglesey native admitting he went to 'some dark places' laying in the hospital bed watching Wales from afar. It said everything about his journey that he spoke of his delight at playing at Huish Park, the modest home of Yeovil Town where he had moved on loan, having played at some of the biggest and best stadiums in Europe with his country. He had made his return at the end of the previous campaign, proving he was fit against Macedonia and then proving he was back with a fine performance out in Belgium.

Hennessey had since moved back to the top-flight with Crystal Palace but was without a single league minute to his name when he stepped between the sticks against Bosnia, and yet looked every inch the top quality keeper Southall had believed in when first watching him come through the ranks. Three times Hennessey pulled off saves from attempts you would not blame him for misjudging, his agile expertise helping provide an opportunity for Bale to try and snatch it at the death. After Ashley Williams missed the chance to head home unmarked – something he agonised over in the following days and, indeed, the remainder of the campaign, as replays reviewed the opportunity again and again – Asmir Begović needed to be at full stretch to push away a trademark Bale shot powered by left-footed venom across his goal.

The 0-0 did not provide the win the rejuvenated public had hoped for, but they believed again and they believed in this side, the cries of their country's name sounding around the stadium that Friday night as Wales players grouped together in the centre of the pitch, heads bowed, arms linked.

The huddle had been called together by Bale, repeating the message that that level of performance and effort was what they had to do as a team as they listened to the roar around them and were reminded that this was what it was about. As they looked down at their shirt and then up to the stands, there was no conflicting emotion.

The challenge was to do it all over again in quick succession and retain what they had waited so long to grasp. Historically, Wales had struggled in the second of double-header matches with one-off performances and results undone as injuries and niggles took their toll on a nation traditionally without the strength in depth to challenge. Wales felt they had answered some of the questions of such depth – Leicester's Andy King and Palace's Jonny Williams stepping in for the absent Ramsey and Allen with Hal Robson-Kanu giving something off the bench in place of Simon Church – but this was a chance to show they had also addressed those problems of player withdrawal.

Yet, again, Wales had built upon the off-the-field foundations laid by Speed. Slowly the side had developed a medical and backroom team with huge expertise and experience. The medical databases remained of the highest calibre with painstaking detail of everything from players' training load, their heart rates, to quality of sleep and even whether they had taken paracetamol.

They kept with the traffic light system, used not to get players fit but to get them ready and to avoid the danger of injuries. As players woke the next morning after Bosnia, like every morning in camp, they filled in forms detailing their energy levels, how they had slept, their lower body soreness, how ready they were to train and – interestingly as part of the continuous self-evaluation and desire to improve – how they rated the previous day's training session.

Head of performance Ryland Morgans, who had come to prominence first at Swansea City before moving with Brendan Rodgers to Liverpool, had the complete trust of Coleman who would heed the words of advice about which players were able to do what in training to keep them at peak condition going into the demands of a qualifying game. He was not alone, Coleman showing an increased confidence in his leadership by delegating power to many others in his support

189

staff. Meetings would often see Coleman take a back seat, encouraging others to come forward with their thinking and saying little before a final call on the direction to be taken. The mantra was to develop, to improve and evolve, prepared to embrace new ideas.

The varying backgrounds of those involved helped. Masseur Dave Rowe, who had been attached to the national team since 1997 as well as working with West Ham, doubles up with work with elite athletes at Sport Wales and so was able to bring an angle from different sports while chief medical officer, Doctor Jon Houghton, has a background with the armed services. Rowe's fellow masseur, Paul Harris of Cardiff City, was a former international gymnast. Ronan Kavanagh came on board as sports science analyst having previously been with Statsports, an Irish company that developed GPS monitoring of players' performances in training.

The ethics of wanting to be the best and the idea of being part of something overcame the financial restrictions, the posts becoming attractive to the likes of Chris Senior, a masseur with Arsenal, and David Weeks, who had previously worked with the English FA. There are those, like fitness coach and former Celtic and Rangers conditioner Adam Owen, who are Welsh and have that duty of their country's call, and then there are those who have become to feel Welsh like Sean Connelly, the former Cardiff City physio who had come on board under Speed, as had his old Bluebirds colleague and ex-Wales international Martyn Margetson who served as goalkeeping coach.

All highly capable, an atmosphere of honesty was created and expected with the team adopting the New Zealand rugby approach of wanting people to stab you in the stomach rather than the back. In other words, issues were addressed head on to make sure the team benefited above individuals.

"We come from a lot of different backgrounds but we're all here because we want Wales to do well," says Rowe. "There's a real pool of experience. There's a strong football basis but there's also different backgrounds and multi-sport experience too and it all adds into a greater understanding and complements each other.

"And everyone is willing to go that extra mile because we feel very much a part of what is happening, we see how hard everyone works from players to colleagues. There are great relationships right the way through, those bonds you build up in camp where you are with each other every day and then start back up again after time apart mean that there is a real drive from all of us."

Staff meetings would stretch through the day creating a genuine intensity to the international camps, all aimed to create this club environment where Premier League players not only received Premier League treatment but above and beyond. All designed to give this Wales team the best possible chance.

The trust of the clubs continued, with the days before the Cyprus game seeing both the work and the rewards played out. Bale had struggled with a minor back strain and received treatment following the Bosnia game; past years would have seen the car waiting and the flight booked for the next morning, and yet instead he was among the others going through their recovery and rehabilitation at St David's as high winds and harsh rain battered Cardiff Bay. Williams and Bale, those who had led the committed charge against Bosnia, both sat on a sofa with legs wrapped in inflatable compression boots designed to enhance blood flow and speed up recovery to reduce the 'heavy leg' factor.

Not that any of those who had sampled the sounds and stirring emotions of the Bosnia game would have easily given up on the chance to figure against a Cyprus side who, after their success in Zenica, had lost at home to Israel.

"The camp had been buzzing for a while," says David Cotterill. "Training still had that level of professionalism we had felt since Speedo came in and Chris was carrying on that feeling of respect. Perhaps it wasn't in the same way, but he did have that aura about him and he was a likeable guy too so we wanted to do well for him. We were going into games believing in what we were doing and when you have that, you have a great atmosphere in the group because we knew we were doing the right things.

"You'd look around the squad and everyone was moving up in their careers or gaining more experience at the top level and even when we had players pull out we'd have Premier League players come in. There was never a sense that when we lost Aaron and Joe we would struggle, we'd changed that mentality, and the more momentum we gained the more we felt we could just handle anything.

"And the more the fans bought into it, the more that came. We had been playing at the Millennium in front of 10,000 when this was supposed to be the best you can get in football, and then you'd turn on the telly the next week and see the rugby and think 'Is there any chance we could have the same crowds?'

"But there was this feeling that was starting to change and we had the chance to make sure of it. It wasn't a pressure, there was almost a relaxed feel to things because of our confidence, but when you were at training you'd even see a load of cameras that just wouldn't have been there a few months earlier. You knew then it was turning into something special."

Although perhaps not of the same level, big things had been expected of Cotterill having taken his first steps with Wales in the same season as Bale on the back of a £1m move to the Premier League.

The promise was never quite fulfilled, yet his 13th-minute goal against Cyprus was an example of how even those who had struggled to show their worth with Wales were prepared to haul themselves to a higher level to meet the growing hope and expectations.

"I had actually been warming up right in front of Churchy when he went down heavily and it turned out he had dislocated his shoulder," Cotterill explains. "My first thought was 'Bloody hell, I'd better get ready' but then there was just excitement because we had started so well and were already putting them under pressure. The crowd were up for it, we were up for it, and I wanted to get involved, although I couldn't have imagined making the impact I did.

"I'd taken a corner and they hadn't cleared it properly so when Kingy headed it back across to me I could just swing one in. Hal ran across the keeper and it just squeezed into the far post. I would have taken just being part of it on the pitch that night but scoring was so special for me, not just for what it meant for the side but what it meant personally.

"It had been a hard few years for me. I felt I'd been treated quite badly by Brendan Rodgers at Swansea, being made to train with the kids on a Saturday morning, and it had got to a point where I wasn't enjoying my football and even had thoughts whether I should continue playing. Not many had realised what I had gone through but I got the moves I needed and it was with Wales in mind that helped me through it. That goal was an incredible moment for me after all that."

The belief that had grown from Bosnia soared higher still, screaming from every corner of the stadium when King played into a tightly-marked Bale on the half-way line who, having been targeted understandably but with unseemly challenges, took out three Cypriots with a flick of the ball to see Robson-Kanu race through and slot home.

Showing their new-found adaptability in a switch to a flat-back four, Wales were coasting with only 23 minutes gone, although those who thought taking top spot in the group going into the fourth fixture would come without worry needed to remind themselves that this was Wales and it is rarely that straightforward. Hennessey, the hero a few days earlier, misjudged the flight of a free-kick to allow Vincent Laban to pull one back before half-time. After the break, King's attempt to win back possession near the half-way line only succeeded in catching the ankle of Constantinos Makridis and resulting in Coleman's men needing to play the best part of an entire half with ten men.

Wales had been guilty of allowing adrenaline to overrule cool heads, perhaps in retaliation to what they saw as overly-robust resistance from Cyprus, but they were now required to show discipline as they somewhat naïvely sat off and invited pressure.

They found it, but enjoyed the luck teams always require at times, when an unmarked but unbalanced George Efrem headed over in the only real chance the fifth seeds could muster. It had been more of a battle than Wales would have wanted but, again, this was about delivering and, with seven points from three games, the belief was that this would not be the end of the optimism.

The irony was that Wales had played – at least in terms of passing and possession – far better under Coleman but would have to be better on the ball as they prepared for Belgium the following month.

Yet they had come through a major test where so much of the work inside the camp had paid off, the desire to have the nation's trust rewarded and repaid. Make no mistake, even if the scalp of Cyprus may not be considered much to shout about, it was significant, signalled in Bale's guttural roar to the Cardiff skies. Eyes closed, fists clenched, the relief, delight, passion all aimed into the October air. If there had been doubts about whether the £85m *Galactico* wanted this, they had been blown away by all who not only saw such raw emotion in his celebration, but who had witnessed how he had performed.

The game had been only six minutes old when he had been brutally scythed down by Marios Nikolaiu in an example of the devious desperation Cyprus were prepared to employ to stop him, yet he would not hide and seemed only fuelled to fight back. When King's dismissal asked questions and threatened to swing the game away, he helped a team answer them by leading by equal example, his work-rate leaving no doubt that there had been nothing left on the pitch.

"If you see your main man, this superstar of a player, coming off exhausted or suffering with cramp then you know what is expected of every one of you," says Gunter. "He showed in those games how he had become a leader but also, at the same time, staying very much part of the team.

"He was part of those huddles and he said a few things but to be honest he didn't have to say a word. He's just him and we are us. There are those in a dressing room who will charge around and will try and get you going, but in our dressing room it's quite quiet. I think that's because you look around and you have a respect for everyone in there, that you know they are good players. We know we are prepared and that if we all do our jobs we will do well.

"We believed that if we all performed as we can and gave everything we had, then we would get where we wanted to be. After those games we believed it even more."

Now others believed them too.

10

Together

"There are fantastic players in this side, but it's that spirit that reminds me of us and what we did" – Cliff Jones

Ashley Williams had just finished his final answer as he sat facing the questions from those in the Welsh media who had travelled to Brussels.

There was the odd journalist from Belgium, though they seemed more concerned with team news and impending deadlines than what Wales' captain had to say late on this Saturday evening.

The Swansea City defender had become a seasoned hand dealing with the standard fare before games, UEFA rules stating the manager and the captain must give time to reporters the day before a qualifier. He still offered up enough to satisfy the space left on back pages ahead of a game that had captured the imagination; a Sunday showdown with the star-studded group favourites in their own back yard. As Williams had put it, it was indeed a test of how good this Wales team were. There would be no fear, he added.

The centre-back seemed distracted though, not quite as smiling as he can be, not quite as relaxed. As he walked out of the business room set up for the press conference in the Wales team hotel in the leafy outskirts of Brussels, there was a quick check to see all was okay, that there wasn't some issue that had cropped up for the first time in this campaign that was suddenly going to undermine the surge of optimism. There wasn't, Williams replied as he stood in the corridor with the dictaphones put away. "I just want to be out there. I just want to get into them," he said. No matter that this was a Belgium team – ranked fourth in the world at the time – with players of the calibre of Eden Hazard, of Marouane Fellaini, of Kevin de Bruyne and several others whose recent transfer fees had made them quite possibly the most expensive team in international football. Williams simply couldn't wait.

He was not alone. The side had travelled to Brussels late, shunning the chance to train at the King Baudouin Stadium the night before the match and preferring to go through their final session at home. Ensconced in their plush hotel a 30-minute drive outside the capital, they would not have witnessed the Welsh invasion of the cobbled streets around the city's *Grand Place*. The songs had lasted long into the night, though had not stopped swathes of supporters rising early to book a prominent place at the cafés or bars on the side of the streets the next morning with their cardboard pleas in front of them: 'Ticket Wanted'.

The Belgians had been warned when they had asked the FAW how many tickets they would require for the game. When they were told 4,000, they almost refused to believe the request and provided enough for half the amount. Whether they liked it or not, 4,000 were coming. Like Williams, they could not wait, the chance of taking on a major nation with momentum behind them rather than flat-lining disappointment was just too good to miss.

There had been some fears that the significantly-larger contingent would bring with them tensions of inter-club rivalry – in particular Cardiff and Swansea – yet, as it had been on the field, there was a sense of something different that wafted around the Brussels air along with the smell of freshly-fried waffles available on what seemed like every street corner. There was a togetherness not always seen in such numbers – and it was matched inside the team they followed.

"It can sound a bit of a cliché when you talk about things like that but it's there with this side and I think that's obvious to anyone who has seen us, either on the pitch or off it," says Neil Taylor. "You have to go back to the age a lot of us were when we first came in; if you're a youngster you will naturally get closer to those who are the same age as you. Over the years, a lot of the older members of the squad were phased out and we became more and more tightly-knit because it was almost a case of us becoming senior players before our time. You'd look around the dressing room and you'd know the lads sitting next to you, opposite you, right the way through the squad. You trusted them because you'd been through a lot together even at a young age. No-one has had to force a bond on us – it was just there."

It had also been highlighted by an FAW marketing campaign that hit the *zeitgeist* with an accuracy that resonated right the way through the squad, staff and supporter base.

Under Jonathan Ford, there had been genuine attempts to drag the association into the glossy 21st century and to reinvent the brand that had been damaged by past failures, apathy and the odd embarrassing moment.

"We'd gone from filling the Millennium Stadium to almost falling off an edge of a cliff," admits Ian Davis, appointed the FAW's head of commercial and marketing by Ford after a spell at Sussex Cricket. "Of course, we knew success would be the key driver to bigger attendances and a greater excitement around the team, but we knew we needed something else, a better brand that people could buy into it. We had to change perceptions and make sure the image of the association was a positive one so that when we were in a position of success we would be better placed to make the most of it."

One of the ideas – not without controversy in the minds of some more traditionalist fans – was to revamp the historic badge, to freshen things up and symbolise that the FAW were prepared to change for the better.

Yet it was the old crest – that of the rampant red dragon on a green shield – that provided the inspiration for a advertising slogan that quickly turned into a team motto and a byword for the team's greatest characteristic.

They had attempted slogans in the past; 'Your Game, Your Country' had been a previous effort while the 'Time to Believe' of the previous campaign had captured a sense of feeling before a ball had been kicked, only to look dated by the time the team had flown back from their 6-1 beating in Serbia.

"'Time to Believe' worked well at the time but when we knew we weren't going to qualify the message wasn't as strong," says Peter Barnes, one of the members of the media and marketing team at the FAW. "When we looked at this campaign we wanted something that wasn't so much about success but a mentality."

They found it on the aforementioned badge. In the strategic plan launched around the time of Coleman's appointment, the FAW had utilised the traditional Welsh language motto of 'Gorau Chwarae, Cyd Chwarae' to underline the need to work together at all levels for the success of the game in the country. Translating as 'Best Play is Team Play' the Welsh wording had stood proudly on the chest of many of a Wales star since the crest was commissioned as part of the FAW's 75th anniversary celebration in 1951.

A brainstorming session at Dragon Park saw the notion of 'Together. Stronger' rise from the flip-chart onto billboards. The team, resplendent in new adidas kit, were photographed in determined poses against dark atmospheric backgrounds. To reinforce the message, players from the Under-21 sides, the women's team and the deaf team, as well as supporters, were all included as the posters sprang up around the country. Though it caught the eye, it was a social media push from players that created the sense of the slogan actually standing for something.

"The reason it took off was because the team bought into it in a way we could never have dreamed of, let alone asked them to," adds Davis.

An initial promotion for fans' social media profile pictures to be used as part of a mosaic of Ashley Williams, Aaron Ramsey and Gareth Bale brought the first awareness and a huge response – reaching 10.9m 'users' and with 208,000 fans responding, enough to fill the mosaic five times over – with the trio of stars using the hashtag #TogetherStronger on Twitter and Facebook accounts.

But what happened next was natural, players right through the squad using the phrase under no instruction, with fans following suit.

"I think it struck a chord with the players and with the fans," says Davis. "In sports marketing you try and sell emotion, sell a dream and you sell it through a message. The stars aligned for us a little bit because the way the players got it and the way the campaign played out it developed that connection – and you can't buy that. I think it tapped into the Welsh DNA because we're a nation of believers but we're a small nation and we all have to be pulling in the same direction to have success. I think the players sensed that it summed up what they were about and the fans saw it in them. It didn't cause the success but it did seem to stand for what the success was based on – and the more it happened the stronger the message became."

There were no arms twisted as players tweeted out pictures of themselves in training or in camp with the hashtag, the natural feel of the slogan's evolution creating even greater connection between the supporters. It was used regularly in press conferences, the dressing room feeling it fitted what they were about. Then, with the team staff still eager to find the little inches to help the side take that next step towards success, it was seized upon.

"We had used branding around the hotels and camps under Gary, pop-up banners with quotes like 'It's amazing what you can accomplish when you don't care who gets the credit' (from Harry Truman the former US President)," says Osian Roberts. "But like every element, it evolved and expanded and went to a new level. The 'Together. Stronger' thing felt like our principles and we made the most of them."

Mark Evans, the association's long-serving and popular head of international affairs – effectively the go-to guy when it comes to the organisation of the senior side – is credited with pushing the idea to use the marketing campaign as a means of reinforcing the team's values with visual cues around the hotels stayed in by the side both home and away. In Brussels, just as it would be in St David's, large images of individuals and the collective were placed all around, from inside elevators to a huge draping banner that greets you the minute you walk through the revolving doors with the words: 'Together we are Stronger'.

It was everywhere, that constant reminder of what the team was about, from standing backdrops in the recreation rooms where players would relax between meetings and sessions, to the headrests on the chartered flights for away games. Not only was it a polished symbol that this was a new Wales set-up, but it was a continuous visual cue of what they were playing for.

Staff didn't rest there. There had also been conscious decisions to drive home what it meant to wear the shirt and play for this side. While it was clear players had forged a spirit around each other, efforts were made to remind them that they were also playing to represent a nation.

"It's something we were made aware of with different stories on different camps, even from when I was with the Under-16s and the likes of Ian Rush were involved with Osian coaching the side," says Jonny Williams, one of the 'Anglos' in the squad but whose father, from Anglesey, made trips to follow the side in the campaign despite the absence of his son through injury. "Little things just gave us a context and we'd hear about the big games in the past. It just all added to that strength of feeling when you played."

The singing of the anthem continued, new boys like James Chester conscious of the need to get to grip with it as his teammates had managed. As a talking point to break up some of the boredom that can creep into camps and hotel life, rooms were renamed so rather than Wayne Hennessey staying in Room 205, he'd be placed in the 'Shirley Bassey Suite', the 'Tommy Cooper Room' or rooms temporarily named after other Welsh icons.

Information on different aspects of the country's history was made available to players, stars standing shoulder to shoulder in remembrance events such as the Senghenydd mining disaster while the morning after the game in Brussels, players shunned an early flight home to make a four-hour return journey through Flanders to the Artillery Wood Cemetery outside Ypres where 1,307 soldiers are buried or commemorated, many of whom were Welsh, and the nearby Wales War Memorial at Langemark. The FAW's Head of Public Affairs, Ian Gwyn Hughes, was on hand to address the squad to explain the relevance to some who didn't know what to expect.

It might provoke an image of school visit, yet the maturity and humility of the squad was illustrated that morning where there was just quiet reflection and discussion of the sombre sights rather than the moans and misbehaviour sometimes associated with footballers in terms of public perception. Those who saw Wales players sat at the trestle tables in the service station style café across the road from the memorial would know that not all can be tarred with the same brush. Indeed, Hughes has told of how Bale had specifically asked him to show him the grave of Hedd Wyn, the Welsh poet who had been killed at the Battle of Passchendaele just weeks before being posthumously awarded the Bardic Chair at the 1917 National Eisteddfod, Bale having been intrigued by the story told to him by his mother. The staff weren't sure of how the players were to react to the attempt to underline the importance of the history of the country and the people they represented in the red shirt, yet saw a team who were eager to understand together.

Other elements of Welsh history were outlined to try to encourage a greater meaning. Asked to sing a song by the rest of the squad, Hughes chose *Yma o Hyd* – the patriotic folk song by Dafydd Iwan that translates as 'We're Still Here', referencing Wales' unity and defiance as a nation from even Roman times – and then explained the words and historical relevance of it to the players.

They were ready to harness that spirit of defiance in Belgium. Williams' determination had been shared by the rest of the squad, a mixture of the increased support and the size of the challenge bringing an obvious edge to the team. Even as they disappeared down the tunnel after the warm-up, a quick glance into the steeled eyes of stars said everything about their mindset.

"There was something different about that camp," says David Cotterill, picked to start as Wales went with another switch in formation, looking to contain and counter against their high-quality hosts. "I think everyone sensed we just weren't going to get beat that night. You always go into a game with a feeling you can win it, but there was a real mood among the boys that we had gone in the right direction, we had built up well and we were ready for this. No-one really spoke about it; it was just there all week, this determination. Normally Ash is the loudest around but I remember him sitting down for dinner the night before the game and me saying to him 'You're quiet, I've not heard you for two days.' He just wanted to be out there in the battle to get the job done."

That they did. To a man Wales were excellent as they took home a point that felt as good as a victory, a statement that they could go toe-to-toe with the best in the group – among the best in the world even – and not be overawed or undone. There were moments of nerves, such as when Nicolas Lombaerts fired a shot against the post in the opening half, yet not enough to undo the discipline and organisation, attributes that had previously been lacking but were now shining through from every player. Joe Allen was again immense, taking pressure away from the defence by accepting the ball regardless of the red shirts of the Red Devils surrounding him, and quickly moving the it on. Not even the swinging forearm of Fellaini could stop the desire packed in his diminutive stature, a bloodied lip and nose a suitable scar of the fight he was prepared to put up.

Effort and energy everywhere, Chester again oozing class with neither he nor Williams alongside him willing to entertain the thought of concern when Christian Benteke was brought on, Belgium manager Marc Wilmots altering his system and personnel to try and force a way past the Welsh. They found none; Wayne Hennessey not having to make the same kind of saves Thibaut Courtois did at the other end as he batted away a Bale free-kick and watched a Hal Robson-Kanu shot whizz by.

The previous summer's World Cup quarter-finalists had been reduced to hopeful balls, subdued despite all their stars and greater possession of the ball. There was one last throw of things from Belgium, a Benteke header saved by Hennessey but causing one of those late-in-the-game scrambles which Alex Witsel, the Belgium midfielder, looked ready to pounce upon. On the line was Bale, all too willing to share the burden of the nuts and bolts at the back.

When the whistle went, for all the individual performances of excellence that had produced a result as good as anything since the win over Italy in 2002, it had been the collective will and work that had mattered. They celebrated together.

Bale had been close to grabbing a late winner, though Coleman accepted afterwards that if a point was deserved then a win would have amounted to theft. Still, no-one was going to take this moment away from the delirious, dancing fans in the away end.

Before the game, during half-time and then at the final whistle, the music that bounced around this brickworked bowl of a ground was straight out of 1990s trance and dance collections. Whether fans of the music or not, whether old enough to reminisce and recall the throbbing tunes or not, the away end jumped and raved as one, singing along where possible to the simple melodies in this surreal scene of joy. It was only a point, a 0-0 draw, and yet it felt as though a huge step had been taken, a mental challenge overcome and that it was still all possible. Coleman knew it, just as he would have known that the team would have buckled under the pressure of both the opposition and the occasion a year to 18 months beforehand.

In public he played it down, even if his smile, sat in the bowels of the King Baudouin Stadium, threatened to give it away.

"If you're a Welshman, you never get too confident," he said to the assembled media. "We've always been a little country that's never done much and when we've promised to do something we've never done it. But by the same token I don't want anybody to underestimate us; teams need to take us seriously because we're serious about qualifying."

The fans were convinced of it and the players embraced it. As one they walked over to the corner where the travelling support celebrated and joined with them. One by one the yellow change shirts, no doubt soaked in the sweat of the effort just given, were thrown beyond the fence towards the fans as they applauded each other. Standing alongside the dozens of Welsh flags placed on the running track floor in front of the fans, rarely has there been a moment that spelled such a connection between a team and its followers. The marketing slogan was being lived out between players and public.

They had again seen a team so together in their belief and trust in each other that it had dragged them to a result. It went beyond the 11 players on the pitch too, the sight of James Collins racing onto the field at full-time to celebrate with Williams a notable one.

It could have been easy to assume that Collins, this Premier League player and part of the Wales squad for a decade, would not have been in the mood to celebrate. He had lost his place in the side and it had been little more than a year from his fall-out with Coleman. Here, even without kicking a ball, he was showing things had moved beyond individual concerns.

"Me and Ginge had our fall-out but when we met he told me what he thought, I told him what I thought but we were both big enough to move on and he's been fantastic for me and for the squad ever since," says Coleman of the experienced defender. "He wasn't playing in Belgium so I had pulled him to one side beforehand. I knew this was a big one for us, that we couldn't have any shrinking violets, and I knew he could have a big role in that. Even though he wasn't playing, I needed him being part of the squad, part of that dressing room because everyone was in it together. I told him I needed to hear him being loud and brash, laughing and joking because it's big and I wanted them to have that right level going out there. They were determined, they were clear what they had to do, but I didn't want them going crazy and quiet in those last few minutes so I looked to Ginge and the experience and personality he has.

"My room was across the way from the dressing room and, as I usually do, I said my little bit and disappeared. I don't like being around them all the time, I like them to have their own space. From

203

across the corridor I could hear Ginge, I could hear laughter and the room being noisy – and that was a good sign. He was a revelation for us."

He wasn't alone. Danny Gabbidon had done the same when in the earlier squads. Sam Ricketts was credited for a similar attitude of experience. Even if it meant that they weren't going to get their boots dirty, they were playing their part. Perhaps there was an element of players seeing the chance of success after all the years of struggle and not wanting to miss out, or perhaps the mood of togetherness was as infectious inside the camp as it was becoming outside it.

There had been previous signs of players young and old being so committed and caught up in the togetherness and targets set that no-one wanted to be away from the squad. The likes of Jonny Williams had arrived in camp despite injury while Chris Gunter had taken it to another level when he had been left out of the friendly against the Netherlands in the summer. Coleman had been led to believe Gunter was in need of a rest after a long Championship season with Reading and surprisingly omitted him from the squad. Gunter wasted little time in ringing the manager to tell him that he wanted to be involved regardless, was duly reinstated and ended up starting at the Amsterdam Arena.

"Of course these guys want to play but they are mature and see the bigger picture," adds Osian Roberts. "They aren't there sulking, they are excellent in team meetings, contributing right the way through the week and showing to everyone that that's the attitude to have even when you might not be playing, though a few have come in and been ready and important for us when we have needed them on the pitch. It drips down then on everybody and there is this feeling of togetherness that stretches far beyond who happens to be on the pitch. It's not about individuals, it's about us."

It was also about making sure the intensity didn't drain the team.

After the blow to Allen's face, reporters sensed an easy story with Fellaini not a stranger to incidents where the awkward arms and elbows have, intentionally or not, made a mark on an opponent. However, a string of journalists regrouped after various interviews in the mixed zone area next to the team bus having found no Wales player either claiming to have seen the clash or willing to talk about it aside from describing it as "one of those things".

Perhaps it was purely coincidence, but it transpired later Fellaini had invited the Wales players to a Brussels bar for a post-match wind-down. There can be smiles and stories between rivals at times.

The willingness to match the focus with the fun to find rewards in performances was another theme of the campaign. The emphasis on enjoyment had carried on from the Speed era, the camp remaining in the Bay with teammates not only free to go out together for a stroll and a chat over coffee but encouraged. Mark Evans holds meetings with senior players about their requirements for hotels yet describes them as extremely low-maintenance, good Wi-Fi in the hotel the only demand while X-Box competitions are played out for those not involved in the darts and the table tennis. They simply enjoy each other's company, an attribute most squads would love to have but might struggle to manufacture.

There are no curfews because there is a commitment, management knowing full well that the Premier League era and the scrutiny on performances means players will not step over the line because of the effect it will have on them, not to mention the effect it will have on their team and chances of victory. There is no laying down of the laws because the players know it will be them who ultimately suffer should they take advantage of the trust shown by national staff and their clubs. It is why, although menus around matchday are geared to generating top performance su ch as slow burning carbohydrates that digest slowly to keep hunger away and help with blood sugar control, the popular chef Michael Knight will serve up treats earlier in the week. There is little problem with players tucking into a curry, for example, with the trust that they won't overstep the mark by keeping portions to a sensible level.

It is at mealtimes where a team tradition has developed with newcomers made to sing for their supper, be they players on their first call-ups, a new member of the medical team or a different bus driver. Neil Taylor and Gareth Bale are among the first tapping the glass to indicate someone is in line to stand on their chair and belt out a hit, Coleman not far behind.

"The atmosphere is so relaxed," says Taylor. "I've asked players at Swansea what it's like with their national side and Bafetimbi Gomis has spoken about being with France, staying in this remote team hotel on their own campus where all they do is train, eat and sleep for two weeks. To be honest, it must be so boring for them and we're grateful that we're able to ease some of the intensity that comes with international camps. Of course, you can't have Karim Benzema from Real Madrid strolling around Paris, but we're able to pop out to the Bay for a coffee, to socialise together and it only increases the good feeling we have between each other.

"The staff have given us a real leeway where you can get away from it for a bit, but that's respected because we are respected by them and no-one is going to take liberties. Perhaps that wasn't always the same and some of the older lads in the squad will have seen the changes in the culture of professional football but that side has pretty much gone. Everyone knows if you're not at peak you're going to be left behind in your career and no-one is going to take a chance on things like that. We have a responsibility to ourselves and our teammates and we all respect each other too much to abuse it."

The club environment Coleman sought meant that players – and fans – left Belgium with the only disappointment being the next game was some four months away, the first four fixtures having come in the space of two months. Israel's impressive 3-0 home win over Bosnia that same night meant Wales would head to Haifa in March with eight points, one point behind their hosts who had won all three of their opening games. If the result meant the threat from the Bosnians was subsiding at a rapid rate even after their home draw with Belgium the previous month, it also underlined that the stakes were even higher for Wales' trip to the Middle East.

What added to a sense of significance was the feeling of history repeating. It had been in Israel where Wales had taken a huge leap towards qualification in 1958 as part of the World Cup play-off, winning 2-0 in Tel-Aviv before finishing the job with a 2-0 victory in Cardiff.

The similarities for one of the heroes of those games did not stop there. Cliff Jones, a legend of White Hart Lane having won the double with Tottenham following a move from hometown Swansea, had seen much of Bale's development with a keen eye given his shared nationality and love of the left flank.

"There's something about this team that reminds me of what we had," Jones said in a *Western Mail* interview before the squad met to make the six-hour flight to Tel Aviv. "We felt we were all good players in that side: there was myself and Terry Medwin and then you had the 'Golden Boy', Ivor Allchurch, a very special player. He was the main person with Swansea, but we also had the main personality, Mel Charles, who was a fantastic player. Just as much as all that, we had a real togetherness and a confidence.

"And then we had John Charles. He was a superstar, there's no doubt about that, but he was very much one of us. He was playing in Italy, but he was still a Swansea Jack through and through and loved playing for Wales – and I see those same qualities with Gareth now.

"He's one of the finest I've seen, but it's that fire he's got in him too. I watched the game out in Belgium where he was close to scoring one minute, but then defending on his line the next. There's a big comparison between him and John in terms of how good they were, but also in their desire and how they gave everything as part of a group.

"We had a wonderful manager in Jimmy Murphy, a proud Welshman who demanded we never gave less than our all in that red shirt. I see those same demands from Chris Coleman and I see the same response from the players and that gives me great hope, like when I see Ashley Williams being a terrific leader and fostering that togetherness.

"There's no doubt, just as we had John, this side has Gareth, as well as wonderful players who could lift a whole team, but what made the difference for us in games like against Israel was the spirit we had. There are fantastic players in this side like Aaron Ramsey and Joe Allen, but it's that spirit that reminds me of us and what we did. It's been too long but, especially with it being Israel again, maybe it's meant to be."

Jones' words, said with sentiment and a real sharpness of mind, fuelled optimism further but there were worries that heightened excitement and expectation would weigh heavily on the side. Before the campaign had kicked off, the games with Israel had been specifically targeted because of their status as the group's third seed; if Wales were to make it at least into the play-offs this was the team they would need to overhaul, come what may. It was a game they were easily capable of winning but now had to deliver.

As much as sides like their homes to be their fortress, success is often defined on what is done on the road. The side that came close to Euro 2004 had their opening win in Finland but crucially lost games in Italy and Serbia. The Terry Yorath side of a decade earlier did not simply fail to get to the World Cup because they lost at home to Romania, but because they collected just one point from three games away to main rivals Romania, Belgium and the RCS. Coleman's crop had taken a step in the right direction in Brussels but had their opportunity to take a huge stride in Haifa. Victory would place Welsh destiny in the side's hands going in to the second-half of the campaign with three of their remaining fixtures at home, including minnows Andorra. Coleman's men had quickly approached the point where the question was now could they turn promise into something more tangible.

"Normally we haven't been able to answer those questions," says Coleman, accepting he could sense the tension around the game though stressed there was little of it from inside the camp. "There's no point denying it because I've been involved in squads in the past where we've promised and promised and then came to a game like that one and blown it. Whether it was the last game or a significant one before that, we've bottled it. But not this group, there is something different about them. There was not once during the campaign, as the games came, where I looked at them and wondered about them or sensed a wariness with them. That week they were the same, the focus fantastic and, as long as we gave them the reasons behind the thinking of what we wanted to do, they were like sponges, taking it all in and carrying it through. There were no nerves that night, only belief."

Belief that poured into a performance that simply blew away the Israelis, their hope ruthlessly taken away by a visiting team convinced that this was their moment. Though Wales had to bide their time in the first 20 minutes, the noise of the home fans quickly died as they sensed that the visitors were sharper, quicker to the ball, stronger and, ultimately, better.

Wales still had to wait until first-half injury time to make it count. James Collins, otherwise excellent on his return to the side, had stood on the ball when it squirmed to the back post from a set-piece and begged to be placed into the open net. So it was left to Aaron Ramsey to open with a goal with more directness that had become associated with Wales. A Hennessey punt that bounced into the box

208

was challenged for by Bale and read by the on-rushing Ramsey, whose run into the area was timed to meet the ball perfectly, looping his header exquisitely over goalkeeper Ofir Marciano.

Within five minutes of the restart, the promised raucous and hostile reception was reduced to little but the odd applause of appreciation and acknowledgement amid stunned silence. Eitan Tibi had been left needing to trip Bale as the only way of stopping the Madrid man as he surged towards the Israeli goal, yet there was simply no stopping him nor his side that night.

"When he was brought down, I actually thought it was a penalty," recalls Coleman. "When I spoke to him afterwards he said it wasn't but that it didn't matter because he knew he was going to score. He said: 'Gaffer, as soon as I got up and saw where it was on the right of the area and where the goalkeeper was standing I knew it was a goal all day long'. Imagine feeling that, imagine having that confidence in yourself to know you can get it up and over the wall and that the goalkeeper isn't going to be able to stop it. I'm not sure there's many on the planet who have that. He's on another level to most."

Those in the sold-out 30,200 Sammy Ofer Stadium knew it too. As Bale stood over the ball preparing to go through his usual routine (four strides back, a nudge to the right) flashes of light appeared dotted all around, the sight of mobile phone cameras being readied to capture a moment of brilliance. Bale's instinct looked accurate the moment his left foot punched the ball; the attempts of the Israel defender to retreat from the wall and help out goalkeeper Marciano futile and likely to have been of no worth even if he had donned gloves.

It did not go without notice that Bale had made the most of the opportunity from a dead ball given his situation at Real Madrid at the time. The side's struggles under Carlo Ancelotti to repeat initial success had seen Bale bear the brunt of much frustration. His car had been kicked as he left the Madrid training ground following an *El Clasico* defeat to Barcelona. His relationship with Ronaldo was being questioned and polls in one Spanish media outlet had called for the £85m star to be dropped as he appeared to be taking the rap for the side's failings. Israel coach Eli Guttman had not helped when he claimed in the build-up to the match that Bale had been not showing the same level of commitment to his club and that he was instead saving himself for Wales. Bale had seen Ronaldo fail to score from more than 50 free-kick attempts and yet here he was proving points all over the place. By the time he added a brilliant finishing touch 13 minutes from time by sweeping home a third having already got Tibi sent-off for a second foul a few minutes after the second goal, the front pages in Spain were prepared. This time they were not questioning Bale but questioning how Real could find a solution to allow him to replicate such international form back at the Bernabéu. It was fitting after Cliff Jones' words that Bale had overtaken John Charles' tally of 15 goals for his country.

Still, as unplayable as Bale had been, this was not a one-man show. Allen was a class act again at the base of the midfield, alongside Joe Ledley as Wales returned to the three central-defender system, while Ramsey produced his best in some time in Wales' best performance under Coleman.

Ramsey, like his high-profile partner in the Wales side, had suffered his own share of critics at club level yet no-one could deny that, given the time and space and the right opportunities, he could be a delight to watch and a devil to stop.

"Sometimes people can forget how good he is, but those of us who see him every day don't need reminding," says Ledley, already established in Cardiff City's first-team when Ramsey made the same step from academy to senior side in 2007. "At the time the club were producing a lot of talent and he was still in school when he first came into the training under Dave Jones. I can remember it because every Friday it would always be young against old in a practice match and this guy slotted straight in with some of the things he was pulling off just incredible. He always wanted the ball even then and was never scared to try things, which is how he is now. He was up against some very experienced players in those training sessions, guys like Steve McPhail and Riccy Scimeca who had played in the Premier League, but as soon as we finished we all knew this lad could be unbelievable.

"He's had to overcome a lot and been through more than most but that skill and that confidence is still there with him which makes him the player he is."

While Wales' defensive players can set a platform and Bale can win games from it, it is when Ramsey is at his best with his vision and verve that ensures Wales control games as they did in Haifa.

Yet he, more than most, spoke of the campaign of the collective over the individual, still speaking with the responsibility of a captain but perhaps playing with the freedom of not having to wear the armband.

Asked soon after if he had raised his game as a result of Bale's brilliance, Ramsey said: "I think everybody in the whole team has had to raise their game and bring that togetherness to make us more of a stronger unit. That's what this team has been built on. You can see everyone is out there fighting for each other and working their socks off and we have a lot of quality as well when we go forward so we're dangerous."

Still, as part of the togetherness, Ramsey seemed stronger. It was his skill on the left flank against tired Israeli bodies and minds that provided Bale with the game-finishing third, but it was his own score that meant more. He looked and pointed to the skies as he celebrated and slid on his knees in front of the away fans, dedicating the effort to his grandmother who had passed away shortly before the trip.

It sparked an impressive end of the season for the Caerphilly playmaker, taking in links with Barcelona and a second successive FA Cup winners' medal. The teenager that Ledley and other Bluebirds had looked at with wonderment was now, at the age of 24, putting others under his spell.

"I am a big fan and I think he has grown as a player and become a man," said Arsenal great and former France World Cup and European Championship winner Thierry Henry, speaking at a Welsh Football Trust event as he prepared for his coaching badges under the watchful eye of Osian Roberts. "He wants the ball more, he wants to command the field, have an impact on the game and for the midfield to be his. I've seen him grow as a man, become more mature, not scared to take control of the game and I see it with him playing for Wales too.

"He now knows what he has to do for his team to be good. What I mean is, when he plays for Wales, he can play behind Bale and he does it because that is what the team needs for the performance. He doesn't play the 'me-card', he plays the 'we-card'.

"And you can see that he is happy with the responsibility with the way he played against Israel, that he knows he needs to be as good as Bale. He knows that Wales will not reach the promised land and have their Holy Grail with only Bale, but they need Ramsey like they need Joe Ledley, Joe Allen, Ashley Williams, the whole squad. I think he has taken that on board and realised he needs to step up and he has grown as a man to accept it and I think he can help take the side to France."

Henry was not alone in talking about Wales in France. It seemed like the entire country was now free from the fear of mentioning qualification, a buzz that had started with fans in Haifa joyously chanting 'We are top of the league'. The other notable song from the away end was one dedicated to Coleman, the man who some had wanted out just five games previously. The manager had seen the banner that night which proclaimed this was now 'Coleman's Red Army' and he had felt the faith. He had appeared agitated beforehand as he felt the need to repay it.

"We had known how big the game was and we talked it up because I didn't want them to fall away like we have done before," he says. "I wanted them to keep it in their mind how important it was and make sure we came away with something, not disappear at the first sign of any pressure."

They didn't, Coleman having warned them about what he called the 'shenanigans' of some away trips he had experienced as a player where little things go wrong in terms of the hotel or the training ground. They had experienced it themselves in that nightmare trip to Novi Sad, when Serbia arrived at the stadium before Wales had finished training. It prompted the FAW to enforce stricter security on those occasions, opting in most cases to do their training at home and fly later in the day without bothering to visit the ground they would play at ahead of an away qualifier.

The FAW had worked hard to ensure the smoothest travel to Haifa which can be an understandably awkward trip, chartering a flight with players whisked away from the tarmac to ease the speed of the security processes. Yet, according to Coleman, the 45-minute journey from the airport took closer to two hours because the escort missed a turn-off. Staff left behind at the airport waited more than an hour extra for luggage meaning players did not have their bags before late in the night.

Coleman said he had been part of teams that were left wound-up by such things, irrelevant of whether they were intentional or simple mishaps, but here he was preaching calmness. Worries over the pitch surface that had emerged on a reconnaissance visit to the Sammy Ofer Stadium were laid to rest as Wayne Nash, in charge of security and operations on such trips, took photos of the now green pitch which were quickly circulated to players.

"It wasn't about getting them up for the match, it was keeping them calm because we knew what the atmosphere could be like," Coleman says. "We needed them to have composure, to be brave on the ball and to make sure we stayed in the game if we came under any pressure. We did all of that. We could have won by more, being honest."

With the manager and his team getting the tactics right as they had done in Brussels, the 3-0 and the three points were more than enough to satisfy, the players included, who had worn black armbands and dedicated the performance to the long-serving kit man Dai Williams who had died of a short illness earlier that month. It was to him that many raised a glass that evening in a celebration that said everything about the closeness of the squad, just as seeing some of the players and staff stood together in mourning at Williams' funeral earlier that month. They were together in good and bad. This was the good.

Sat in the hotel bar in Haifa, stars and staff surrounded Owain Fôn Williams as he strummed his guitar, leading players in song long into the night. Sat close to Williams, then goalkeeper at Tranmere at the foot of League Two, was Bale, the world's most expensive player. In that moment though, with Wales, and in the midst of Elton John's *Your Song*, they were equals, together. When they returned, one of the first requests to Mark Evans ahead of the Belgium game was to make sure the FAW purchased a team guitar for future post-game gigs.

The next opportunity came in June – some five weeks after the final Football League games and a fortnight after the end of the Premier League season – with Belgium the visitors to Cardiff City Stadium, long sold out with this unusual mix of expectation and excitement that had rarely made it to this stage of a Wales qualifying campaign.

The Belgians would arrive in south Wales top of Group B by the virtue of their win over Israel in Jerusalem a few days after Wales' own success in Israel. Unlike Wales' win, Belgium – who had crushed Cyprus 5-0 in Brussels beforehand – looked far from comfortable in their 1-0 victory, captain Vincent Kompany's dismissal meaning he would miss the meeting between the teams tied on 11 points after five games.

Not having to share the spotlight with any other sporting event meant the game was the only show in town, the only thing worth talking about. No Olympics, no summer rugby tour, no major football finals, just Wales returning to the height of public awareness after all those years of apathy.

In truth it had begun before the team had returned from Israel, plenty quick to suggest that the game should be played at the Millennium Stadium. Regardless of the fact that the deadline to switch venues with UEFA had passed – and that Rugby World Cup events clashed with the remaining autumn home fixtures with Israel and Andorra – Wales were in no mood to jump onto the bandwagon. Plenty were quick to have their say about staying at a stadium less than half the capacity of the Millennium was denying many the chance to support the national team and perhaps capture new fans.

Yet while the idea of switching was ignoring the facts on offer, the FAW seemed keen not to start straying from the path they had taken to success thus far anyway. While the Belgium game sold out quickly, the 'season tickets' and then 'half-season tickets' – the latter covering the Belgium and the final two for just £50 for adults and £12 for seniors and juniors – had been on sale for some time in advance. Many had taken advantage of the generous pricing and there was a feeling to want to reward them. Perhaps above all, though, was that the players had long made it known how happy they were at Cardiff City Stadium. Previous experiences at the Millennium had not been great ones for them and while problems over the playing surface at the 74,000-capacity venue should have been eased by a new modern 'Desso' surface combining natural grass with artificial turf, there was no want to return. There was a sense that Cardiff City Stadium had become home, that the players felt comfortable in its surroundings and that moving would be more of an advantage to opponents. As some continued to clamour for a move to the Millennium, it did beg the old question of why change a winning formula?

Ramsey was quick to back the refusal to consider switching, voicing the players' opinion and, to the FAW's credit, they helped make sure no-one would question the call once the final whistle sounded on a memorable June 12 night.

Sensing the moment was there to be seized, association officials backed extra spending to brand the entire stadium. Outside the prominently grey and blue ground hung giant images of the likes of Williams, Ramsey and Bale with 'Wales' and 'Cymru' reading loud and proud in dramatic red. Inside, the 'Together. Stronger' motto circled on the digital sponsorship hoardings. Alongside and above, headshots of each member of the squad saw the faces of Gunter, Allen *et al* staring out menacingly. As Ledley mentions, it was a case of this being their house, their land.

As it had been previously, the dressing room was full of the branding, the messages rammed home in Welsh colours and the words the final visual cues for players before they stepped onto the field: 'Together, we stand on the brink of history'. Some may argue that such things make little difference, that it is simply about what players do on the pitch that counts. But the little differences, those inches, add up to the strides that Wales were seeking to take. Just ask Gabriel Riera.

Sometimes such ploys by sporting outfits can seem fake or give off a stench of trying to artificially create an atmosphere, but there was a buzz of authenticity around the whole stadium and squad, flowing through supporters and back again.

There was a confidence too that went beyond going into the game on the back of positive results. Coleman had got his men into camp early but opted against a friendly game; there had been talks to play Northern Ireland but the closer the Belgian challenge came, the more unattractive a potential blood and thunder British derby became. Concerts in the Welsh capital featuring One Direction and the Manic Street Preachers gave complications to the dates available, but the greater feeling was that Coleman could prepare his side better without the need for a full-on friendly.

Furthermore, calculations from FIFA rankings boffins had made it clear that a home win over a Belgium side now placed second in the world would see Wales rocket into the top ten at a pivotal point; the seeds for the summer's World Cup qualifying draw were to be based purely on the rankings and victory would ensure Wales being among the top group of seeds having been in the lowest pot just four years previously, increasing significantly the chances of a favourable draw in the bid to reach Russia 2018. Because of the way points are worked out over an average of 12 months and the lack of value given to friendly fixtures, playing Northern Ireland would have stopped that scenario whether they had won or lost.

Questions were asked whether it was a danger going into such a game with players having not been involved in competitive action for so long, Belgium going to the other extreme of playing neighbours and rivals France five days before the Cardiff clash. Coleman opted to play an inter-squad game behind closed doors at Cardiff City Stadium with staff making attempts to turn the red versus yellows into a true match, assistant Kit Symons (in his last camp before concentrating on duties with Fulham and being replaced by Paul Trollope) in charge of the 'away' team who used a separate dressing room, performed separate warm-ups and so on. It seemed even knowing first-hand Bale's strengths and weaknesses meant little as he scored a hat-trick for the 'home' XI.

Belgium had their own friendly victory to spur them into the first against second showdown, impressing in a 4-3 win with the *Stade de France* hosts scoring two of their consolation goals in the final minutes. It underlined the size of the test and the strength of the opposition, yet it did not go unnoticed how Belgium players on social and mainstream media seemed clearly pre-occupied with their derby, while Welsh focus was firmly on the fixture that mattered. It was picked up upon in the Wales camp too, together with the suspicion that, while Wales had been building towards this game, it came for the Red Devils after a long year that begun with the World Cup and saw the majority of them involved in title-chases, European demands and even end-of-season tours with their clubs to Asia and Australia.

"For us it was a cup final," says Coleman. "We had been chasing and climbing to get to this point, but you could ask questions about whether Belgium had that same feeling about the game. We talked about exactly that in the build-up and the two weeks we had together beforehand. We mentioned to the players that we all knew Belgium would qualify because they are a top team, that they would get the points they needed somewhere along the way and, whatever happened in our match, that they'd be there when they needed to, they could just put their foot on the gas to get there.

"Bosnia were different; they had reached a high in getting to their first World Cup and we felt they were coming down from their graph a little, while we were on our way up. Belgium seemed to be just nudging along, doing what they had to without really having the urgency perhaps they'd had in the previous campaign where they hadn't qualified for a long time. Now it was us in that position and we were ready for it."

The feeling was shared by those outside of the camp. Usually, the arrival of a top-class side with high-profile players sees the discourse become all about how Wales would stop player 'x' or 'y'. Yet no-one was really talking about Eden Hazard while the only mentions of Kevin de Bruyne were over a potential move to Manchester City from Wolfsburg, a subject that brought a tetchiness out of Belgian officials and manager Marc Wilmots in the final pre-game press conference. Wilmots was also the subject of speculation over his future at the time with the real possibility of him leaving the national set-up for Bundesliga club Schalke high on the agenda.

Wales had no such distractions, Coleman knowing his side were focused and firmly prepared to make the most of a game that already felt like a once-in-a-generation type affair.

"We had reached where we had wanted to be as a group," he says. "We had asked how we could make it feel more like a club, to have that atmosphere and spirit. All the little details in the backroom, by administration staff, media staff and the players themselves had got us there. Most importantly, everyone had bought into it. I remember walking into the team room at the hotel where the boys play darts or sit around and it was all decked out in our colours and our messages, and in it you could just feel this spirit and vibe about. It was magnificent. They were up for this, they were ready. You could smell it on them.

"It had taken us a long time and a lot of improvements along the way to get there but everything was there for them. It was not so much about spoiling them but giving them that environment where they felt they could be successful and keep coming back to us to be successful.

"When that happens and you have a challenge like we did that night, there is no fear, they just know what the demands are, what is expected of them."

Toshack's teenagers were all grown up. The golden generation were ready to shine.

"We had obviously seen it building for a while, you saw it in the dressing rooms where they are all accountable, they all take ownership," adds Coleman. "It's their team almost. When we were

217

having unit meetings, and it's not just the guys starting the game but all the squad involved, you could see them speaking among themselves, disagreeing perhaps on different things but that is so healthy. We'd got to a stage where there was no embarrassment about things that were said – which is significant because you'd be surprised how insecure footballers are. Here everything could be out in the open. Even when mistakes are made we accept them. I accept I make mistakes, things we shouldn't have done, but as long as you know you've made one you can move on. There is no inhibition. They feel safe, no-one is trying to trip them up; we all want them to succeed. I think they feel that closeness.

"You felt it that week, that sense was huge, and I went into the game not once thinking we would lose. I wasn't sure if we would win but once we scored first I thought it would take something spectacular."

What followed was certainly spectacular, a night that will live long in the memory to all those who witnessed it.

The atmosphere had been incredible before a ball was kicked. As images and videos of the raving in Brussels had swept social media, a new anthem had evolved with Zombie Nation's *Kernkraft 400* capturing the ecstasy of that night. The trance track had been the one blaring over the King Baudouin PA as the team celebrated with fans, and supporters had then commandeered it as a chant of their own.

The players had quickly cottoned on, gleeful when they were told in Brussels the fans wouldn't leave the stadium despite police asking them as they danced and chanted away to their new party-piece. The FAW did not miss a trick as they ramped up the volume before kick-off, the same tune blaring away. Clapper banners had been placed in every seat to add to the noise – not that it needed it – while the words 'Cymru' in the shape of the Welsh flag was formed in a mosaic by those in the vocal Canton End as the anthem was belted out with more vigour and volume than could be remembered by many. Pre-match music blared, the FAW having brought in extra speakers to ramp things up. Perhaps for the first time it did not feel as if Wales were playing at the home of Cardiff City but were simply at home.

And yet all that was just an appetiser. Wales were comfortable in their role, composed against the cacophonous background of the crowd who refused to let a moment pass without chant or song aimed in support of their side. It did not take long for the surprise in

Coleman's selection to look justified, Jazz Richards coming in for his first start in two years in an eyebrow-raising decision to play him right wing-back in the same system that had triumphed against Israel, Chris Gunter moving into the centre-back position as Ben Davies sat out injured. Richards was a midfielder by trade, and brought through at Swansea City thus having a natural ease with the ball at his feet, but the fact he was facing the drifting danger of Hazard concerned many. Within the first ten minutes he had made the kind of tackle on the Chelsea superstar that settled himself and any doubts others had. It was the start of performance that went on to embody how while the leading light of Bale understandably gained the headlines in this side, it was often the roles of the lesser lights that helped write the story.

There were saves for Wayne Hennessey to make in early pressure from black-shirted Belgium, a full-stretch one from Radja Nainggolan perhaps the most significant, but again he was being protected by a team that knew their jobs and the levels to which they had to perform. Ground was covered at an exhausting rate, the tempo of proceedings not stopping the chasing of lost causes and the harassing of visiting players to deny them a rhythm that could have silenced the songs from the stands.

And then there was Bale, at full speed on his 50th cap, charging and driving forward as if it were the first game of the season rather than the final 90 minutes of a long, often difficult, football year. Yet that was the point: it was Wales' final and those suspicions of a lack of Belgian desire crept in before being fully illustrated in the eyes of Jan Vertonghen's expression. As his former Tottenham teammate surged past him at one point, Vertonghen gave away his fear of Bale and seemed to scream out that he did not want to be there.

He was soon joined by Nainggolan. The Roma midfielder had been Belgium's most impressive player up to the 25th minute, just as he had been the Red Devils' stand-out player in the France friendly earlier that week. He had been the subject of teasing questions from Belgian journalists to Coleman the day before the game, asking the Wales manager if he was aware of the mohawk-haired 27-year-old without mentioning his name, perhaps in an effort to try and get the Wales manager to attempt a pronunciation of his awkward-sounding surname. All they got in response was a knowing smile and the reply:

"Don't you worry, we know all about your players." Coleman might as well as rolled his sleeves up as he said it, such was the indication that Wales were ready for this particular fight.

What Coleman might not have expected was Belgium to have bloodied their own nose. Errors were being made, many enforced under the pressing and pressure being applied by a crowd-fuelled Wales. Courtois, normally so steady, hashed a clearance and, soon after, Jason Denayer allowed Hal Robson-Kanu to beat him to a loose ball down Wales' left. With little on, Robson-Kanu held up the ball and then tried a drag-over only to be wrestled to the ground in a minor tussle. Ramsey swung in the free-kick towards the near post where Bale and Williams were lurking, the defensive header only reaching Joe Allen on the edge of the box who headed upwards. Alex Witsel seemed to have got enough on it in his aerial challenge with James Chester to end the danger yet, inexplicably, Nainggolan, facing his own goal, headed back to Courtois. He might have seen Bale seconds before the contact though it would have been too late. Wales' main threat had shuffled off the pitch and was returning as the ball dropped to him with not a Belgian player near. It seemed to happen in slow-motion when in reality it was Bale's ice-cold reactions that made it appear so, chesting-down with his back to goal and swivelling in one fluid motion to slot home with his supposedly weaker right foot. Players' of lesser calibre would have panicked, would have rushed, but not Bale as the prone Courtois knew. For a second before he eased his contact with the ball, there seemed to be silence, perhaps caused by 33,000 inward breaths. Only one person in the stadium had not been stunned.

Bale did not wait for the ball to reach the net, turning and sprinting to the sideline as the roar told the world of the score. On his knees in screaming euphoria, he was joined first by Ramsey, then Robson-Kanu before the rest of the red shirts joined him celebrating a goal that meant so much to so many. The commentary team on Welsh language broadcasters S4C included Nic Parry, who has also served as a High Court judge. His recommendation to make Bale a saint as he described the immediate aftermath of the goal would not find many in Wales seeking to lodge an appeal.

There were chances for Ramsey and Robson-Kanu in particular to double the advantage, but what would lead to Wales' victory was their refusal to give real chances at the other end. The lead had given extra energy to legs and greater concentration to mind, Williams taking personal pride in his individual battle of the physical with Christian Benteke. It felt at times Wales were down to ten men such was the way they were prepared to retreat into organised lines and shut off space, increasing Belgian desperation – and yet there was a twelfth man that night.

With 20 minutes remaining, Bale had moved to the sideline attempting to stretch out the cramp starting to build in his calf and to receive an energy gel as tiredness began to take its toll. As if sensing the need, the crowd struck up an impromptu, *a cappella* rendition of the national anthem. Belgian journalists in the press seats looked around unsure what was happening. So did their team, seemingly awestruck by the emotions flooding down from the seats around them and close to being stopped in their tracks. The ball was stroked side to side as the chorus of '*Gwlad, Gwlad!*' roared harmoniously around the stadium. Sky commentator Bill Leslie simply stated: "These are special scenes.....something is happening in Welsh football" as he let the moment speak for itself, the silence between the lyrics as deafeningly pronounced as every word of *Cymraeg* belted out by the 33,000 present. There was a now a truth to the clichés of hairs standing on the back of necks and seasoned reporters were unable to find the words to do that moment justice.

"It was tribal," admits Coleman. "I'd never witnessed that, none of us had. You could see Belgium didn't know what was happening. It affected them. It was just this incredible moment that probably won't be repeated or bettered because it was just so spontaneous. I've actually got the match recorded at home and every now and again I will put it on and fast forward it to that last 20 minutes and it has the same impact on you. It was just special."

Mae Hen Wlad fy Nhadau was sung again that night as the clock ticked down and red shirts scattered around, closing down and edging themselves towards one of the finest nights in the history of the national team. Indeed, the anthem has been sung mid-game ever since but not quite with the same resonance of that June evening where the fans played their part in this incredible sign of togetherness; one team, one nation, one dream.

One man could not last the full duration, Bale finally limping off as his calf cramp got the better of him. Incredibly, he apologised to Coleman has he came off with two minutes to go.

"I hadn't played for three weeks as I didn't play the last game for Real and we'd had a two-week break, plus I'd been ill the previous week so I really wasn't in good shape to run as much as I could," Bale said of the moment when speaking after the campaign. "The manager had said before the game as long as you give everything on the pitch there are people to come on and do the extra leg work. I did as much as I could. I think I had cramp 15 minutes before I came off, I was just hobbling around. I tried to run and then it got to a point where it was like, 'I can't.'"

It summed up the lengths every member of the side were prepared to go to as they sought the result that would put them five points clear of third-placed Israel with four games remaining. When the whistle went to confirm that scenario, Bale leapt from the dug-out and into the arms of the coaching team as they hugged and celebrated as one with players, the togetherness there for all to see.

Williams was helped up off the floor having been embraced on the ground by a clearly emotional Gunter, no-one left in any doubt that every ounce of effort was given in Wales' cup final. Supporters somehow had enough to bounce and bellow from the stands, daring to sing of a summer to come: "*We like to sing/We like to dance/We've got our passports and we're off to France*". Zombie Nation played again, unintentionally summing up how this football nation had risen again, that this was a resurrection of a team that so many had lost faith in.

"It was incredible," says Neil Taylor. "None of us had experienced that, not with Wales. The noise had just been unbelievable and such a long way from what a lot of us had tasted before. It was what we had worked for, what we had dreamed about and, when it came, we raised ourselves. I think when you hear the anthem like that and the backing we had then it just gives you that extra lift for that extra effort we needed, to make sure no matter how we were feeling we could go the extra mile.

"We got into the dressing rooms and we had the odd beer to celebrate with as it was the end of the season; we thought it was important because we needed to unwind and reflect together and there's not always the chance for that. It was a special moment but, to be honest, it wasn't a huge celebration because so many of us were dead on our feet, just physically drained. Even that was good to see though, because when you looked around and saw what every one of you had given it made it that much better."

To a man they had made the difference.

"Together Stronger means what it means, it's not just words to us," adds Gunter. "But if you could add another word it would be 'respect'. We all respect each other. Whether you're in the Champions League or League Two we were all the same in that dressing room, all part of it."

This was Wales F.C.

The mantra when they emerged from the dressing room to face the media was that it was an important step but not the final one. It was true, there was still work to be done, but deep down there was this growing acceptance that the fantasy was soon to become reality. Coleman called it his biggest night, but spoke of bigger ones to come as he faced reporters with smiles to match his own.

"I said that and it was true, but I knew," he says. "After the game me and my wife Charlotte went down to the Gower in Swansea to stay in my friend's house for a few days to get away from it and try and unwind after such a big build-up. I remember sitting down there on the beach, with the rain absolutely pissing it down and not being able to stop this huge smile come across my face as I looked out over the sea. Right then I knew. We had games to come but one of them was Andorra at home and I knew it would take a nightmare for us not to do it. We were all but there. We all but qualified that night."

11

Stronger

"We know each other like brothers, we fight for each other, and that togetherness is really special. We knew how good we were and we've proven how good we are" – Gareth Bale

A Welsh summer spent thinking about the next.

If the euphoria felt that night against Belgium did eventually subside, it never really died. Days were spent by those with calculators and pieces of scrap paper trying to work out the permutations of points needed to qualify, even Chris Coleman admitting he had spent time scanning the different scenarios regarding the final four games.

Adding to the anticipation was the confirmation from the world's governing body, FIFA, that Wales were indeed one of the top ten nations in the game as their soaring climb up their rankings continued apace. It had been timed with the unerring accuracy of an Aaron Ramsey pass, although in truth the fact that the July rankings in which Wales had found themselves at a record highest tenth-place was being used to determine the World Cup seeds was simply a happy coincidence. Having been down among the also-rans and the rankings a source of embarrassment for Gary Speed before he helped spark the rise, Wales were now above former world champions Spain, Italy and Germany.

Chris Coleman led the FAW delegation to Saint Petersburg and the grand Konstantin Palace for the 2018 World Cup qualifying draw with Wales no longer the minnows to be mocked. Of course, there were those quick to question the accuracy of the rankings and scoff – something that became louder in the months that followed when Wales edged above old rivals England for the first time. But, given the rankings are essentially elongated form guides, Wales' run without competitive defeat stretching over a year showed that they were there on merit. Furthermore, given that plenty had laughed loudly when Wales languished in the three-figured places next to nations few realised played football, fans had every right to make the most of their current standing and enjoy the high, whether it meant much in the grand scheme of things or not.

The draw, as it turned out, could have been better and might not have been the group Wales would have chosen if given the opportunity: the emerging force of Austria as the second seeds, a Serbian side who had lost their way since Novi Sad from the third pot, Home Nations rivals, the Republic of Ireland, from the fourth batch of seeds, and ex-Soviet states Moldova and Georgia; if nothing else, it provided three bites at a cold dish of revenge given the infamous 1994 defeats to the latter two and the more recent shambles in Serbia.

Still, there was no powerhouse, no traditional big gun that could shoot down 2018 optimism before a ball was kicked, the likes of France and Italy – who had been pushed into the second seeds because of Wales' rise – being avoided. So although making it to Russia would not be easy, neither could it be viewed as impossible. Even if it was, such was the buzz around the ongoing campaign that Wales felt ready to take on the world regardless. Coleman and those in blazers with the dragon embroidered on their chest would have sensed their football nation being treated a little differently, UEFA's decision to award the 2017 Champions League final to Cardiff's Millennium Stadium announced just a few weeks beforehand.

Of course, there was a danger of getting carried away on this wave of excitement. The past had taught plenty to be careful of assuming success when defeat and despair could still be snatched from the jaws of victory. Coleman had spoken with caution, regardless of his feelings on that Gower beach, and told of the challenges still to be faced to reach Euro 2016 before thinking of tournaments beyond France. As regards to the rankings, he urged supporters to enjoy the deserved moment in a similar way as he had told them to get excited about qualification prospects following the Belgium win, but he stressed that he and his team would be remaining grounded and guarded.

"There's a feel-good factor which helps us; it means we have to keep producing and pushing the bar and see where we can improve again," he said at the time. "There has been a lot made of the rankings – and it is pleasing on the eye – but it's about success for us. We have got to qualify and we haven't done that yet. I am in the same position as Mark Hughes or Terry Yorath when they were sat here. They were nearly there, but, unfortunately, it never happened. As yet, we've done nothing different from anyone else. But we've now got the chance to go and do that because it's all about getting to France – by hook or by crook – and it's only ever been about that. The rankings are not relevant. If we are eighth in the world but we don't get to France, so what? We've got to get there, no matter how we do it."

It underlined the new steel and focus that had flourished during the campaign, forged in those backs-to-the-wall results and the feeling of going to the wire yet emerging unbeaten. Like so much about the side, it had not happened by accident. Heading into that first match with Andorra, there was always the thought that this was a team made of stronger stuff. Aside from coming through together, the side had undergone very few changes over two campaigns and, thanks to individuals' progress with their clubs, they were far more experienced in terms of high-pressure and meeting expectations. Entering the campaign, Gareth Bale had lifted the Champions League, Aaron Ramsey the FA Cup final matchwinner while Ashley Williams, Neil Taylor, Ben Davies, Joe Allen and Joe Ledley had all recently played European football. There were proven track records of mental toughness; Bale and dealing with the demands of being a *Galactico*, Ramsey and his battle back from serious injury, so too Neil Taylor, Wayne Hennessey, Sam Vokes and David Edwards. Coleman knew he had a group who were comfortable with all the mental challenges that come with the game at the highest level. However, to do something not done before, Coleman felt they needed to be pushed. Perhaps more significantly, he felt he needed to be pushed.

"In football we are quite arrogant that we don't want to hear from different angles, that 'this is the way we've always done it' and that's that – but why are we right?," says Coleman of the appointment of whom he described as 'the final jigsaw' ahead of the campaign, sports psychologist Ian Mitchell.

"We wanted that fresh angle and we thought Mitch could bring it. Most sports have sports psychologists attached but football has an arrogance – and God knows why – yet we were keen to see the benefits."

'Mitch' had been a young hopeful at professional level himself before a serious knee ligament injury ended a career that began as a schoolboy with Chelsea before taking in spells with Hereford and Merthyr. It was his injury that saw him focus his energies on academia, undertaking a PhD and becoming a senior lecturer in sports science at Cardiff Metropolitan University, while remaining in football through coaching and as part of Osian Roberts' pro-licence courses where he would speak passionately about his beliefs that there were ways and means that teams and players could benefit from being challenged.

"The brain can be trained," Mitchell insists. "I remember having a conversation with an elite player on a coaching course who was adamant that mental toughness can't be developed, that you're either born with it or not – but it can.

"Mental aspects of performance have to be trained and if you don't train them how can you improve? Self-belief, attentional control, emotional control, the ability to perform when you're challenged at a high level, they can all be stripped back and worked on."

With his football background meaning Mitchell was found on the training field rather than in a remote and unrelatable office environment, he would soon be credited with helping Garry Monk's side to success at Swansea City, having already worked with Taylor through the serious ankle injury suffered in 2012. Players do not have to knock on his door, but see him as part of the management team where a mixture of informal chats and formal analysis is done in the language of football and as a natural part of the build-up to games.

"I'd been involved with the Trust so had that basic flavour of things and tried to help look at different ways of working, being critical in terms of coach effectiveness and helping create an environment where you would question everything we did, from how we would plan sessions, how we would give feedback and getting players to reflect and challenging them," says Mitchell, who had worked briefly with Gary Speed beforehand. "I'd been invited to deliver a presentation to the international committee of the FAW with the coaching staffs from the senior team to the Under-16s present.

"It was after that Chris pulled me to one side and said he had been taken by what I had said about getting people to step out of comfort zones and working in a vulnerable way because I feel when you do that, you become more aware and work with a heightened level of focus and energy. I think he liked what I call risky work because that's where the rewards are.

"And I think he saw that there didn't need to be that stigma attached to what we wanted to do because the mental aspect of international football is huge. The psychological demands are too big to ignore, from the intensity of training and perhaps two games in a short space of time – you wouldn't put a player on the pitch if they were not physically prepared for that, so why would you put them out there if they were not mentally prepared? When you are mentally fatigued you make poor decisions, you don't communicate effectively and you come away from game plans. I think Chris saw that and wanted to see how we could work."

Coleman, though, was perhaps just as attracted by how Mitchell could make him better. Aware the lack of time spent with players – and that Wales in effect borrow them from clubs for international duties – the notion was to have an indirect impact on the players, via the manager.

"Going into the campaign and being clear on what we needed to do if we wanted to achieve anything, I knew I had to make the most of the time I had with the players, which is not a lot either over a year or between games," says Coleman. "To do that I needed to be better, so I basically told Mitch he needed to improve me. Not in terms of as a tactical manager, but in addressing people, getting the right messages to them and how to deliver those messages effectively. Basically, I needed to squeeze more out of myself and Mitch helps with that."

Before that first match, Mitchell slotted in to the backroom team with little problem, helped by the acceptance and recommendations of Taylor and Williams who had seen his work first-hand.

"We can go and see him on an individual basis if we want, but no-one has to – he's just there if anyone feels they need him," says Taylor. "But we will all do little things with him, simple stuff like problem solving with a tennis ball where it has to pass around so many hands in a certain number of moves. They are only little things, things that help with the team bonding and getting you thinking. But much of his work is subconscious; I'd say 10% of his work is with the players but I think the actual impact has been a lot bigger with the way it's come through the manager."

One key factor Coleman wanted to better was his communication, knowing how vital it was to pass on information to players ahead of big games without seeing stars lose focus. With Mitchell on board, the coaching team opted to ensure that talks with the squad lasted no longer than ten minutes.

"Mitch, Osian and Ryland will be stood at the back of the room behind the players with a stopwatch held up so I know when I need to stop before I lose them," says Coleman. "You can give them information all day if you want but they will start looking around after ten minutes. We have to give it to them in bits.

"It's things like that we needed to be prepared to improve upon and Mitch was very much part of that. I wanted him there for me and the staff, pushing me and not being afraid to question decisions or warn of the potential pitfalls to be prepared for. I like that and we needed it, especially at times when things are going well because that can be dangerous."

It was something Wales were wary of post-Belgium, the September trip to Cyprus representing the first of the final four fixtures where Welsh destiny was very much in Welsh hands. Much of the first part of the campaign had been about dealing with coming through adversity, with the coaching team playing heavily on the 'Together Stronger' ethos, backing up the branding with specific use of vocabulary when speaking to both players and the press.

"Before camps the coaching team talk about everything, every detail and how we can then influence the players mentally," says Mitchell. "It's not a case of me standing up giving lectures, but with the staff it's about making sure what messages we present when we're in front of the players and being consistent with it, so everything is clear from day one. Whether that's physios, doctors, masseurs, kit men, coaches, technical staff, there is a consistency on what we're about and that 'Together Stronger' line underpinned everything.

"Communication is huge so we don't just tell the players 'This is what we're doing', it's why we're doing it too. If we have quite a heavy physical session, the coaches will make sure they explain why so everyone understands and buys into it more.

"What stands out, though, is that identity which Chris has a strong vision of, so that anyone coming into the camp is clear about it. Seeing the branding, speaking about it and just reinforcing those values is huge because when you face adversity, it's those values and beliefs you fall back upon and it can be a very powerful thing.

"We saw it in the first part of the campaign and the games against Bosnia and Cyprus at home were turning points. We knew it would be a challenge with players missing but the message was to embrace it, to push everyone, and every time we spoke to the players it was reinforcing that. Before games, at half-time, at every opportunity there are reminders about the goals, the campaign, what we are about and what we want to achieve."

Players not only took it on board but embraced it and revelled in it, yet it was through Coleman that the greatest message came.

"He is at the front, a fantastic leader who truly represents what the group is about," adds Mitchell. "Ask the players and they will tell you the tremendous respect they have for him and the trust he has earned – and when he stands and talks he is believable. I think the group have grown stronger and have grown more confident because of that."

Coleman, though, was wary of over-confidence heading to Nicosia. Wales had turned themselves into outright favourites to qualify, a status that has rarely sat well with the nation as a whole; one that prefers to fight against the odds. As a result, Coleman did his bit to make the most of his September surroundings. As Wales landed in the late summer heat of Cyprus, there were not only reminders of how sides of the past have thrown away such positions of opportunities to qualify, but also of the national team's last visit to the city. Eight years on from the likes of the Joe Ledley and Gareth Bale being part of the John Toshack team that hit a Cypriot low, Coleman was given the perfect backdrop to guard against complacency.

"Before each camp we discuss what we want the theme to be," says Mitchell. "We knew going into those games, off the back of the wins we'd had, that complacency might well have been a danger for us, so we wanted to address it. Then, when it comes to the pressure of the game, the players have the right mindset. Going into that Cyprus game and with Israel at home a few days later, we played on being an underdog because we knew if we framed it like that it could help us stay away from any complacency.

"The messages, inside and outside the camp, were not about qualifying or what we needed to do in the two games in terms of

230

results, but about how we didn't have a good record in Cyprus, that we would need to fight as underdogs and be better. We front-loaded our meetings that week to show how dangerous Cyprus could be, and our previous records there.

"Chris was excellent on playing on the emotions of the group, reminding us how we had felt the night of the Serbia game, another place where we did not have a good record. He reminded them how far we had come and what it had taken – and how we didn't want to go back. That week we had a huge level of focus on what we were going to do to put on a performance; we didn't speak about winning."

The 3,000 fans who had spread from Wales to the various holiday resorts in Cyprus were not so cautious. The game had been one the Wales management had been wary of at the time of the automated draw – the seasonal heat, its effect on the pitch and the long journey at an early part of the football season – yet fans had not stopped singing in the pool parties of Larnaca and Ayia Napa. Few had opted to stay in Nicosia itself yet, on the afternoon of the match, thousands arrived *en masse* via coaches, swamping the old town in song and sunburn. While Coleman kept his underdogs hungry, supporters were gorging themselves on this taster of watching their side in the summer sun. To them at least, the journey from Paphos to Paris seemed a short one.

Yet just because of the caution against complacency Coleman was injecting into his squad, it is not fair to say Wales had suddenly started to freeze under the pressure, even if the medical team had brought with them an ice-slush machine and portable inflatable ice baths to aid both against the high 30-degree heat and with post-game recovery. The late withdrawal of Joe Ledley, who suffered a hamstring strain in the training session before the flight, had affected plans with Joe Allen already missing through suspension. Still, confidence remained.

As they had done all campaign, the week of build-up had shifted from motivation and focus on international matters away from club concerns, to building belief. The early clarity of opposition analysis gave way to the attention of roles and responsibilities of individuals and units, Osian Roberts coming into his own as triggers and visual cues about jobs in positions in and out of possession were outlined, all feeding into a tactical confidence.

"There's a real calmness to it, a coldness almost," says Chris Gunter. "Things had got bigger and bigger since Andorra, questions being asked from us on every step: a first win, could we back that up? Then the results at home but ones we might have been expected to do well in, so could we go to Belgium and get something? Then it was Israel which was called our biggest game in a decade which went up a level again with Belgium at home. It had got bigger every time and yet it never felt like that in the camps and within the squad. We pretty much prepared the same way every game and we never once talked about anything other than the performance. If you had gone into the team hotel in Nicosia you would not have known that if we were to win both games that week we would qualify. It was all about that game, preparing for Cyprus and playing a certain way. Not once did we think about Israel on the Sunday or even getting a result, it was focussing on the performance and the rest would take care of itself."

There were times where it did not seem as if that would happen. The locals did not see Wales as underdogs with the home support sparse and overshadowed by the packed away end of permanent smiles, but there were visiting chances missed to encourage a Cypriot charge. Ramsey fizzed a shot just off target and Taylor failed to angle his rebound accurately when Bale's free-kick was fortunately saved by Antonis Giorgallides. Much talk before the game had been about the overly-physical nature in which the Cypriots looked to thwart Wales – and Bale in particular – leading to recalled Andy King warning that the side were ready to stand up should the referee not control matters. Polish official Szymon Marciniak did indeed make some questionable decisions, none more so than the one to rule out David Edwards' first-half header for an apparent earlier push from Hal Robson-Kanu as both attempted to meet a Bale cross. With Cyprus given some leeway in their attempts to bully, Wales were in danger of being dragged into self-pity and away from their game-plan.

Defensively, though, Wales remained as solid as they had increasingly become. Though Cyprus' hopes of a goal of their own came mainly from attempts at crosses or high balls, each one was batted away with a team of organisational discipline and determination. If a block was there to be made, there was a body there. No tackle was shirked, no inch given – Wales were too close to their summit to start backing down now.

Still, on the media benches the scores from elsewhere – Belgium coming from behind to beat Bosnia and Israel winning 4-0 at home to Andorra – meant the need to capture the mood in the reports to be sent home on the stroke of full-time saw the frantic figuring out of whether a draw at Nicosia's GSP Stadium would still give the golden generation the chance of their crowning moment in the home game against the Israelis three days later. Eight minutes before that deadline, Bale rewrote the reports.

Wales had continued to play, continued to probe and, while never looking at their best, continued to plug away. Few had looked up when a delicate piece of Ramsey play on the right flank was passed into Jazz Richards who swung in a cross invitingly. As Bale had risen above adversity in Andorra, he rose above the white Cypriot shirts around him to power a header home that John Charles, and the Wales side of 1958 this team were set to emulate, would have all smiled at.

It had not been Wales at their best and Bale had looked more frustrated than he had done throughout the campaign on the hard surface, yet now he was roaring again, racing towards the dug-out where a coaching team and substitutes bench enveloped him in collective euphoria. A blur of red soon joined in, scenes on the sidelines mirroring the bedlam behind Wayne Hennessey's goal. Pure joy, not even in the context of qualification and its significance towards the Sunday game with Israel, but just one of those moments that make the sporting suffering worth it. As if to signal that they didn't want that moment to end, another of the campaign's new anthems was soon roared out. *"Don't take me home/Please don't take me home/I just don't want to go to work/I want to stay here/Drinking all your beer/So please don't, please don't take me home."* As they danced with strangers and friends alike with the Cypriot sun long set, no-one wanted it to end, and yet the end was in sight. One more win, one last victory – be it against Israel or in the two further matches to come – would see *Y Ddraig Goch* flying atop Welsh football's Everest.

If Bale was the flagbearer, captain Ashley Williams was the one driving the momentum from the back. He had been superb in Cyprus, living up to the machine moniker given to him by Garry Monk as his commanding consistency continued with almost unnatural reliability. Still, the human side peaked through. He struggled not to smile as he was asked the questions of what was potentially lying in store just 90 minutes away, trying his best to quickly speak of jobs not being done and focussing on what was still required. Williams knew, though. He, like anyone would, had allowed himself to dream of that moment – of the final whistle sounding – and the door to a major finals swinging open. Indeed, as Coleman's skipper he would be the man leading Wales out in France and firmly into the history books.

Yet Williams, unlike Bale, unlike Ramsey, unlike several in the side, did not grow up dreaming of that moment of wearing Welsh red on the biggest stage. If the centre-back wanted to hide his West Midlands background he would struggle, most hearing his booming Brummie-esque tones before seeing him, and he admits it would be foolish to try and claim that when kicking a ball around his local park he pictured himself playing at the old National Stadium and not at the old Wembley. He had thought of Three Lions, even been a ball boy as a 13-year-old in a game against Moldova. Had it not been for another one of Brian Flynn's chance wonderings and willingness to ask questions then it may never have been a case of England's loss and Wales' gain.

Flynn had travelled to Stockport's Edgeley Park to watch a 19-year-old Wayne Hennessey playing on loan from Wolves and had been taken by the performance of a centre-back named Williams, the surname enough to pique an interest and prompt a question.

"I can remember the text I had," recalls Williams on the message that arguably changed his life. If he had not longed of playing for Wales, he had been long aware of his mother Lyn's Welsh heritage through her Rhondda-born father. "It came from the assistant manager at Stockport, Pete Ward, who had played for Flynny at Wrexham. All it asked was if I had any Welsh in me? That was it, no explanation. I answered and the text came back: 'You could nick a cap here.'

"That was it for a while, then Tosh came to watch me for play at Hereford and reckons he left at half-time because he'd seen enough and knew I was good enough. That's what he tells others anyway; what he's told me is that he thought I was shit! Anyway, he picked me and that was the start of it really."

Williams made his debut in Luxembourg, persuaded during the journey to opt to sign for Swansea City with Cardiff City also showing an interest, racing back from arrivals at Rhoose to the Liberty where forms were waiting and signed on the bonnet of his car to beat the transfer deadline. A defender who could flick between ball-player and battler, the speed of his progress rarely slowed from that moment. The kid released by West Brom and who had to turn to non-league football and part-time work as a waiter, petrol station server and theme park assistant, was now becoming a man many wanted in their sides as he won promotions and proved points at every level he stepped up to.

The background has helped forge Williams' personality on-and-off the pitch, humble and hard-working to underpin an obvious talent.

"Ash has seen real life," says Coleman of his skipper. "In football you can be used to having it all there for you, but Ash has been on the other side and I think you see it in how he approaches things and in his performances. He relishes every challenge and makes the most of every opportunity.

"When I made the decision over the captaincy, we knew what we would get from Ash aside from the fact he was experienced from captaining Swansea. Of course there were some asking questions because he wasn't born in Wales, but my argument was that when he puts the jersey on, when he's putting his body on the line, he's Welsh enough for any of us then. I had no issue with it, none of us did. For where we were at the time he was perfect for us, and still is."

Williams never went down the Vinnie Jones route – there were no dragon tattoos done to play to a Welsh gallery – and has previously said he is careful to call himself Welsh, perhaps not to trivialise the often emotive issue of nationality. Yet that alone speaks volumes for the man and his understanding of the country he is clearly proud not only to represent, but to call home.

"I was born where I was born," he says. "But I know what I feel. I know where I live, where my kids were born, where my roots now are, where I will probably live when I finish playing. I know what it means to play for this country because I feel it. I feel Welsh."

Taylor, the player who shares a defensive responsibility for club and country with the left-sided centre-back, has no doubts.

"Like everything with Ash, as much as he's a loud guy, he's always done his talking on the pitch and never lets anyone down," Taylor says. "He's a good captain as he can approach people in different ways, he senses that side of things, but the biggest thing is how he is when it comes to the game. If you can't perform on the pitch then it doesn't matter how well you talk or anything like that, it is not going to mean anything because no-one will follow you – but you'd follow Ash.

"I've played with him for years and he's just someone who you can rely on in more ways than one. I mean, when does he miss a game? He's someone you can depend on and look to and he reminds me of Speedo like that. He's someone who's not fussed about plaudits but just wanting to achieve things."

That's an attribute that leads Williams to often playing through injuries or opting against the rests and withdrawals. Before the Cyprus game he had missed only three Wales games through injury or suspension in seven years, and on the pitch in Nicosia was seen downing painkillers having taken an elbow to the windpipe. Just as Bale inspired in his way, so did Williams in his.

"There's a responsibility wearing that shirt, something I'm aware of," he says. "And I think far better players than me have not been in this position. Perhaps the fact I wasn't born here means I could never go out giving it half-hearted because I know I'd be letting the Welsh public down. It's not even about proving you're a good player, but proving that commitment, that I'm worthy to wear the Wales shirt.

"I've played through pain and there are times where you strap yourself up to go on international duty when others can rest at their club. Even my family ask me why I put myself through it, worried I won't be able to walk or play with the kids when I'm older.

"The only thing I can think of is that it's the way I was brought up, the way my dad was, the way the guys were I played with at Hednesford in non-league. Back then if you could get on the pitch you did. At the time it meant a lot getting your appearance money because, well, you needed it.

"And that buzz of playing for your country is still the same. There's been tough times and there are moments and matches when you question why you're away from your kids. But when you retire ... there are players who will retire with a lot of things, memories and money and lifestyle – but not many will have international caps. There have been some real lows; it can be quite lonely after defeats in the hotel room away from family and home, but the highs are incredible. It makes the sacrifice all worth it."

The sacrifice led to a Sunday afternoon in Cardiff when many couldn't quite believe was happening. The maths was simple, or at least that was how it seemed. A win would mean a summer in France, that much was clear, but it was only in the final hours before the game that it became apparent that a draw could be good enough, should Belgium fail to win in Cyprus later that night.

"We didn't know. We were only thinking about the game and trying not to think of all that, however much what it would feel like to qualify would try and creep into your mind," says Gunter. "Because you couldn't escape the hype, as much as we had dealt with it well. You had people asking for tickets, you knew what times your mates were meeting in the pub, you knew the whole country was watching. It was strange because it wasn't something any of us had experienced before, but we'd kept it quite methodical, kept the focus on the performance and the game plan. No-one talked about qualifying even if we knew what the situation was."

The hope from all – fans wanting to party, players wanting to finish the job and newspapers wanting to push buttons on qualification supplements – was that Wales would make it simple, and the fact Israel were in need of victory to keep alive their own hopes suggested it would play into home hands.

What followed, though, was an Israel side prepared to sit deep and frustrate, with Wales caught a little by surprise and not quite able to provide the breakthrough as the physical and emotional drain of three days earlier took its toll. Aaron Ramsey did more than most to try and find that moment of magic and there was a huge handball shout ignored – how Paul Bodin must have wished more than most for the spot kick to have been awarded and to have seen Bale slam the ball home and the coffin lid shut on those ghosts of 1993.

No-one was spooked though, and the fans would not be quietened – a ten-minute brass band-backed chant in Hal Robson-Kanu's honour to the tune of Salt-N-Pepa's *Push It* summing up the surreal, almost delirious atmosphere – even if Israel would not be beaten. There was a moment when Simon Church thought he had answered a nation's prayers when he headed home late on, yet the linesman's flag had stopped the fuse short of igniting Cardiff City Stadium into an explosion of noise. It had taken Church a few seconds to realise he had been denied a place in the record books, but Coleman hadn't moved, aware the striker was indeed well offside.

The ensuing 0-0 had extended the record number of successive clean sheets to five and the longest unbeaten run in competitive games in the national side's history to ten, yet it meant Wales weren't quite there. Granted, only one point was needed from the final two games – away to Bosnia and, crucially, home to Andorra – but the country knew you can't be almost qualified in the same way you cannot be almost pregnant; you either are or you are not.

While the supporters still sung, the squad were subdued, telling themselves and the media that four points from the two games was a return to be happy with but unable to disguise that touch of anti-climax and disappointment.

"We were in a bit of limbo, like we had been in the match," says Coleman. "It wasn't a case of the players being caught up in it because not once had we told them we had to win a game. They knew what the consequences were, they could see the carrot there for us, but we never mentioned it. It wasn't a case of the word being banned but they were brilliant and we kept our focus. Israel came to get a point and frustrate us, and in the past we would have got caught up in that and perhaps lost; that showed the difference and how tactically aware they had become.

"I could have changed it, put wingers out, but I was wary they could have countered us and got the goal to beat us and left us flat and with the damage that would have done. The point was good enough for me because we knew we had Andorra and if we couldn't beat them, well, we wouldn't have deserved it."

They almost didn't have to wait. Slowly the news had crept through to the players about the need to turn to Nicosia. The confusion had arisen in the working out of the possible maximum points left to pick up by sides, without realising that rivals – namely Belgium and Israel – still had to play each other and so couldn't both reach a tally to topple Wales.

"We hadn't thought about it, but by the time we'd gone downstairs at the stadium for some food the boys had started to talk about it," says David Cotterill. "We made sure the TV was on when we got on the coach and as we were driving to the hotel we were cheering every time Cyprus defended their own box – anyone watching must have thought what a bunch of idiots. By the time we got back to St David's we were all set up in our main room watching it together."

Coleman had opted not to.

"I was stood in the bar with Charlotte and a few others and then, from the recreational room across the foyer, you could just hear this roar," Coleman says. "It was half-time and Gunts came rushing in, shouting 'Come on, it's 0-0, we're going to do it'. I stayed where I was and thought just let it happen because I didn't expect any favours. Of course, I would have taken it, but I wanted to do it ourselves – though perhaps I was only saying that because we knew we had Andorra to come. Time went on and Ian Gwyn Hughes came in, smiling, and saying: 'Big fella, five minutes to go, it's 0-0 – it's going to happen tonight'. He walked back out and, I'm not kidding, three seconds later he's back and saying 'Hazard has scored, it's bloody happening again'. It was typical in some ways but no-one was down and I was saying: 'For God's sake don't worry, we're there'."

Hazard's goal in the 86th minute had delayed the inevitable, the momentum and the mathematics simply too great in Welsh favour for this now to be added to that long list of glorious failures. As the Chelsea midfielder pounced to end a stubborn Cypriot resistance, it didn't feel like the same sucker punch to the stomach suffered so many times before.

Indeed, there was a sense that it was fitting for history not to happen via a game being played thousands of miles away; a sense that this fairytale deserved its final triumphant scene. Perhaps it would be in keeping with the past trials and tribulations had Wales' long awaited moment come as supporters made their way home cross country, fans finding out fate via crackling radio updates or waiting for unreliable 3G signals to check scores – hardly the way anyone would have dreamed it. The campaign of Together Stronger deserved better and would get it soon enough; the wait of a few more weeks little when you have already waited 57 years.

Thoughts were already turning to France – the potential opponents after it was confirmed that the seedings used would inevitably place Wales in the bottom pot of the finals draw, the potential team bases, while cheap flights to various venue cities were already being eyed up by fans. Of course, there was still that natural pessimism that wondered what twist the football gods had in store to snatch this away; before the Israel game there had been some concerns – however unlikely – that a good-natured pitch invasion would lead to UEFA sanctions and even a possible points deduction after the FAW were fined and warned for those who spilled onto the pitch in Andorra. In reality it would have meant fans probably banned from going to France, not that the game provided the temptation in the end anyway.

The question was where and when it would happen rather than if, with the first opportunity coming in Bosnia. A draw would seal qualification but Wales could walk off the pitch beaten and still be celebrating should Israel, the only side in the group who could catch them, fail to beat Cyprus in Jerusalem.

If it was to happen in Bosnia, it would be witnessed by a hardy few. As they had done through the campaign, the Bosnian FA had again opted to stage the game away from Sarajevo in the more partisan and remote city of Zenica, an hour's drive from the capital, at the claustrophobic Bilino Polje Stadium. The 15,600-capacity venue, almost British in its hard-edged appearance compared to the circular stadiums of most of Europe, meant that only 700 or so Welsh fans would be allowed to squeeze into its tiny away section housed in the corner alongside flag-waving and flare-branding ultras. Wales were braced for hostility, Coleman clearly framing the game with reference again to Serbia. Regardless of the certitude of the qualification circumstances, the manager was keen for his side to show how far they had come from the low both he and his side suffered that night. He knew they had come so far – tactically, mentally – but so had he.

"I think we definitely saw a difference with him over the second campaign," says Taylor. "How much Mitch had an impact on that, I don't know, but he obviously made a decision to change things and we felt it. There was a different temperament to him. There were games where you would think 'we're going to get a rollicking at half-time' but we've gone in and he's stayed calm, given us the right information and been clear with it, which can make sure the game goes our way or we can put things right."

For the emotional character who shared some traits with the mythical beast on his country's crest, Coleman's mission over the campaign was to keep the fire in the heart, but ice in the mind. There had been previous times, even during press conferences, where you could see Coleman itching to release the old centre-back and misplace his passion. Now he would arrive at press conferences in the final 24 hours before a match with Mitchell stood in the back of the room, a visual cue of the messages needed to be given out. Rather than

240

bemoaning injuries, the strength of the team was talked up. When questions came about individuals, the importance of the collective was spoken about. When controversies came, they weren't ducked such is Coleman's honesty – for which all involved in headline making were always grateful – but they were done without losing sight of the mantra that the hottest part of the flame is blue.

"I knew I had to be better and that was part of it," he says. "I can wear my heart on my sleeve, that's me, but I have to rein it in sometimes. I had to portray the right messages – not being false, but not losing it in that emotion. It was hard for me because when I need to say something the Swansea boy in me comes out. If someone wants to front me up, I'll front them up. I will defend my corner but there had been times where it didn't do me or the team any good. Like Macedonia and the passport when I should have taken it on the chin because I knew what I'd done. Sometimes it works in your favour, sometimes it doesn't, but I made an effort to try and make it more of the former than the latter."

Players felt the benefits of both sides. In him they saw a manager with the same toughness as they were expected and wanted to show, with the same desire to achieve and the same passion about what they were doing. His leadership went from the towering figure stood in the dressing room, to the man able to trust his players in the moments before it mattered, walking away to calm himself and collect thoughts in the heat of battle with a game of 'wordsearch' on his mobile phone. He had led from within and it inspired confidence from all quarters, his faith in the coaching team and the delegation bringing the best out of everyone, as he had sought more from himself. One last extra effort was needed.

It was needed in a country that knew all about hope. The fans who had travelled stayed in Sarajevo amongst its haunting echoes of the past and its crushing, cruel war. Buildings remained with their bullet holes while buses out of the capital north towards Zenica all fell silent the moment the white crosses of the graveyard on the far hills came into view. They were sights to put things into perspective, but this was also a city and a nation who knew much about the pride to be gained from sporting identity. The football heartbreak of Wales does not stand in any comparison to the suffering felt in Bosnia, but it had been in Zenica where it had had its own outpouring of football emotion when the national team qualified for its first major finals two years previously. Wales now had its own chance to turn hope into something more, through a side not weighed down by history, but spurred on by it.

The hosts sensed it, the hostility never really appearing and instead an empathy emerging from the home fans about the desire of a small nation to see its flag fly high on a major stage, atop that mountain. There were nerves, certainly from those outside the camp, though they were strange sensations. The reality was that, with Andorra to follow later that week, there was little to be concerned about and yet the sense of anticipation was gut-wrenching. Much was the feeling of the unknown – not a fear of it but of not being sure how the emotions would take hold.

Fans had been in nostalgic mood in the bars of Sarajevo the night before, talking of their favourite trips, outdoing each other with tales of the worst of times that could double up as the best of times. The more obscure journeys, the biggest embarrassments – the football fan's equivalent of the scar scene in *Jaws* – all being smiled upon with strangers turned soul mates because of their common dream. There was this sense of disbelief about what was to happen, not in the smiling, shaking of heads, but in a strange unsettling way. Suddenly the line from '*Can't Take My Eyes Off You*' made sense; it did feel too good to be true.

Hardened, experienced journalists, felt it too, aware that this potential culmination of a life's work in hoping to cover such a moment was nigh.

The players would have been aware of such emotions – it would have been impossible not to – but the work had long been done to harness it correctly. On the walls of their hotel a short distance from the rain-sodden ground were 48 words that they would carry with them. They were spelt out on a simple poster, standing above an image of the team huddled together, stronger.

We've come a long way together.
By standing together and singing together.
We started believing.
We've been to the wire and prevailed.
We've fought to stay unbeaten.

242

We've dug deep to keep our dream alive.
Now we stand on the brink of history.
Because together we are stronger.
Gorau chwarae cyd chwarae.

In a perfect world, it would have inspired to a straight-forward victory
that would have given journalists time to celebrate and fashion reports
fitting to the occasion. Typically for Welsh football, it didn't happen
that way. Bosnia – needing victory to try and seize a play-off place –
imposed themselves in terms of possession. Pjanić looked every inch
the classy playmaker he had done in Cardiff but, again, was being
kept at arms' length as he had been that night. Ramsey and Taylor
may have done more when they seemed to have combined to create
an opening before the break, but whereas Wales struggled to free
Bale and find a way to test Asmir Begović, the onslaught from the
hosts never came.

"It was difficult because we knew we were there but we had gone
into it determined to put on a performance and show what we were
made of, to do it the right way," says Coleman. "But it was strange;
we had been told it was going to be really hostile, really aggressive,
with the players and fans on top of us, but when we got into it I asked
myself: 'Is this it?' We had been a bit shaky in the first 15 minutes but,
like the rest of the games apart from Andorra at the start, I thought
we looked alright and they seemed to be running out of patience and
ideas, and we were growing more comfortable, stronger. But then out
of nothing really we conceded."

It was nothing, the first non set-piece goal of the campaign
conceded as a high ball was misjudged by Williams allowing Milan
Djurić to head past Hennessey with 71 minutes gone.

Still, news of a goal for Cyprus in Israel slowly filtered through
to the fans. While an Israeli equaliser prompted some final nerves,
by the time Vedad Ibišević stabbed home in the final moments, the
Holy Grail had been found following a further goal in Jerusalem. The
scorer, James Demetriou, Cyprus' Newham-born Walsall right-back,
may never again find himself having to pay the Severn Bridge toll.

Supporters, either unable to trust the scores flashing up on their
phones as the expense of data roaming charges was ignored in the
agony of anticipation or simply unable to get signals, pleaded with

Sky Sports' and long-serving and long-suffering Wales reporter Bryn Law – a fan like them – to confirm the score. He had been earlier positioned by the team bench, leaving the travelling faithful unsure of events elsewhere, but was ready to confirm it to the fans he was now stood in front of. A flash of fingers – a two and a one – prompted Bosnian bedlam and even applause from the home fans.

The scenes on the pitch were equally chaotic, but more in confusion. Williams, so annoyed at conceding twice and losing the unbeaten record, was seemingly not interested in hearing the news. An equally angry Coleman had already started marching, in upset, across the pitch from his dug-out towards the tunnel in the far corner. Some players had spotted the scores flashed up on the screen in the opposite end, some substitutes were aware, yet some seemed unable to take it in or trust what they were hearing. A consensus from the coaching team was to wait until the rumours could be checked out in the dressing room.

Mark Evans, fully bearded like Joe Ledley after urges to the both not to shave until sealing a place in France, strode away from the cover of the tunnel to meet Coleman near the penalty area. There stood the manager, drenched in his suit jacket he has refused to take off during games in superstitious fear since doing so in Serbia, even in the heat of Haifa and Nicosia. Evans, a bedrock of a figure for the national team in bad times, found himself fittingly delivering news 57 years in the waiting to the manager who had helped make it happen. Time seemed to stand still, as it had done when that ball dropped to Bale against Belgium. Coleman had been unable to read Evans' face. He asked if he was sure. The seconds passed, the realisation dropped.

"I had no idea," says Coleman. "I had told them I didn't want to know. Others around me might have done but I was too focussed on what we had to do and what was happening. I had wanted that win and there was disappointment as I was walking off because I was so caught up in that moment, I hadn't thought about anything else. It needed to be Mark who told me and when it did sink in, when I knew, I was gone, I was off."

Coleman's race towards the away end was the signal to the rest, the plans to wait to see the score themselves in the dressing room ripped up as they looked up and saw the manager spark the celebrations, a manager as one with the fans and soon to be joined by his team, Bale leading the way as he sprinted and slid towards them.

"That moment....to see the look on their faces, it is hard to explain," he says having reached out and embraced tearful supporters through the gaps in the terrace fence. "You can't buy it, that feeling, not just for myself but for them, for us all. I knew those who had been able to get there had seen it all, some incredible downs. We had teased them with what we had all wanted and let them down, but in that moment it was all gone. To see some of them crying with joy is something I will just never forget. To celebrate with them was incredible and even more so to see them celebrating with this team that had given them what they had dreamed of. Not just in qualifying, but I think they saw a group of players who they felt it meant as much to, as it meant to themselves. They believed in each other and that was their moment together. It was perfect."

The tears in the away end were real. The small allocation meant those there were the ones who have spent, in reality, far too much time and far too much money following Wales, when success could only ever be seen as an unexpected bonus rather than part of the attraction. In some ways they could be compared to a poor gambler, one that is always lured by the thought of winning big and spending game after game chasing their losses. It was never about the jackpot but the joy of the togetherness, something that made the eventual triumph all the greater to experience. They would have looked around, into a familiar face or otherwise, and known they had been through the same. Together they had seen this side not only bury the ghosts of 1958 and all those years they lingered over, but the ghosts of all those failures, glorious or otherwise. Whatever came after Zenica for Wales, the spectres of Gheorghe Hagi, Joe Jordan and so many others will never again hurt as they once did having been laid to rest in the sodden ground of the Bilino Polje Stadium.

They *cwtched* and chanted into the night, the fears for away supporters' safety unfounded and the Football Supporters Federation Cymru later revealing that the Bosnian Police had praised their behaviour with the only incident being one fan having to pay a fine for rugby tackling a statue and knocking its head off in the process; a surreal image to go with a surreal night.

The players shared it with them. Within moments of the collective realisation they were in euphoric unison as the home fans and players disappeared. Flags were handed over and draped over tired shoulders no longer carrying the burden of history but the pride of history makers. James Collins and Neil Taylor collected signature bucket hats in red, yellow, white and green – a Wales fan staple – and continued to wear them long after media duties had taken place and they had boarded the bus home. Indeed, as the team crowded together for a squad picture, it was Taylor who ordered the photographers to change their positioning so they could capture the tearful throng in the background; they were all part of that moment.

Coleman, who like Bale had spoke of the best loss of his life when cameras were thrust into their faces, was hoisted high by players and thrown into the air over and over again. The manager who had once admitted his struggles to call this his team was now being chaired and cherished in the greatest show of celebratory fondness that he or anyone could have imagined.

The open window of the dressing room in the upper floor of the stadium betrayed the bedlam going on as beer and music flowed to the car park below, journalists understandably having to wait for some of the adrenaline and ecstasy to die down before getting the chance to ask their questions. Few felt able to put it into words but the smiles and the eyes said everything, those same knowing looks exchanged that this had been a long road, a long way from the tentative start under John Toshack and the problems of unfulfilled potential, but ultimately worth it. Wales may have progressed through the campaign with the ruggedness and winning mentality of a perennial qualifier, but there was no mistaking in those expressions that few other nations or groups of players would have known a feeling quite like it.

Coleman felt it, but there was something else. "Relief," he says. "It was incredible, don't get me wrong, but after all that build-up, all that wait, there was real relief.

"After the Andorra game I had it all planned out, to go have a round of golf or two, a few glasses of wine and maybe take the missus away, but I went home and was just floored. I was ill for three days, all that stress in the system releasing and leaving me with nothing. The next week I was supposed to go to some games in Europe with Osian but I couldn't go. My body had kept going but once it all finished I had nothing left. So that showed you the relief."

It would wait a little longer to take over. As supporters made their way back to Sarajevo and on to home, ready for the homecoming party against Andorra, the team took the short coach trip to their Zenica hotel. There was no grand party, no co-ordinated celebration, but just a team – of players and staff – sat together in a room with little more than a guitar. One of the images from that room shows kitman Dai Griffths, a figure there from the very start, strumming away victory songs he and so many others would have wondered would ever have been played.

"We were in this one massive room where we'd eaten together and nobody left, we just wanted to share that moment together," says Coleman. "Players don't tend to sleep after games anyway and we wouldn't normally let them have a beer after the first game of a double-header but having done what we had done we celebrated together, staff and players. It was electric, the best atmosphere I have ever known. I have never witnessed something like that night."

He was not alone. The smiles stayed with all as they journeyed back to Cardiff. Coleman expressed the feelings of a nation when he remarked before the Andorra party how nice it was to see the Group B table and see Wales spelt with a 'Q'.

Andorra did their best to try and diffuse the party atmosphere come the final fixture, though Wales were never going to be denied, goals from Ramsey and Bale eventually making sure they were not. The Zombie Nation had risen and was going to take some stopping now, the excited chatter of going and achieving more in Euro 2016 already falling from the mouths of players and punters together. It said much about the team that they were prepared to talk about greater goals and future aims in the immediacy that followed a triumph more than half a century in the making.

"That's what the aim has to be," says Jonathan Ford. "Of course we will have targets in the campaign but the aim when we started was to put the pride back into Welsh football and hopefully we have done that and we can continue to do that. We've been blessed with a lot of other things we've been working on coming through together at the same time to give what I hope to be a purple patch for Welsh football with Euro 2016, the Champions League coming to Cardiff, and then the World Cup in 2018 and the Euros in 2020. The hope has to be that it's a historic time for us. We've had good spells before but they only seemed to come around every now and again. We know the pride is back and we would like to keep it there."

Certainly there was a pride in the air that washed over from the sea towards Sully the next morning. On an unseasonably hot day for October, the local junior club of the village on the outskirts of Penarth was abuzz all because of this great game of football and the feelings it can create. Standing with them was one of the boys who would be kings, one of the golden generation who had done so much to end the sniggers and the suffering around Wales' national team. Bale had a smile as big as the children to whom he had delivered a training session as part of a sponsorship drive through the FAW's community partners.

He looked back on the past year or so, the bid that began with the threat of embarrassment in Andorra, and spoke of a side that had grown in age, grown in belief and of being swept into a "perfect campaign" by a momentum not felt by many Wales sides of the past. He told of the incredible passion he feels for his country and feels from the country to the team, of the anthem and of a team that "know each other like brothers, ready to fight for each other and with a togetherness that is special".

And he spoke of the future.

"We need to enjoy this," he said to the *Western Mail*. "This is a great moment for Welsh football and everybody needs to enjoy it, but I've said all along it's not just about qualification, it's also about growing football and getting youngsters to play in Wales and trying to get it massive again, get the hype and excitement about it. That's why I like to come to things like this, to get kids excited because one day they could be pulling on a Wales jersey and qualifying. We want to grow ourselves as a country and have more chance of qualifying again."

He could be right. One of those young, starry-eyed hopefuls may well go on to become the next Bale, or Ramsey, or Allen or Williams or Hennessey. That small gesture, that small piece of advice of how to take a free-kick may well make the smallest difference to their chances of making it. Because for all the huge occasions and the momentous nights and the long road, it was always a journey made up by the smallest steps. From John Toshack's insistence with youth to Brian Flynn's chance conversations. From the tragedy to the togetherness. From Gabriel Riera to Jason Demetriou. From Belgium hitting the post to the perfect free-kick in the perfect place in Haifa. Every one of these just a matter of inches, of luck being taken and luck being made. The smallest detail in the backroom, the one per cents that all added up. That one fan's decision to start an anthem midway through a game, which gave a red shirt that one extra surge of adrenaline to make that one tackle or that one extra run. All making the difference to a group of players born at the same time, but bonded with the same aim. Together, stronger.

"We knew, all of us, that this meant so much to so many," says Coleman. "We wanted it for so long, we chased it and we did everything we could to get there, every fine detail we could, every effort we could give. Then to see the reaction from everybody at the end was unbelievable. We had done it. We got there."

Appendix

(a) Results: 2005–2014
(Pre-Euro 2016 Qualification Campaign)

F – Friendly
WCQ – World Cup Qualifier
EQ – European Championship Qualifier

2005

Feb 9	Wales 2 Hungary 0	(F)	Millennium Stadium, Cardiff
Mar 26	Wales 0 Austria 2	(WCQ)	Millennium Stadium, Cardiff
Mar 30	Austria 1 Wales 0	(WCQ)	Vienna
Aug 17	Wales 0 Slovenia 0	(F)	Liberty Stadium, Swansea
Sep 3	Wales 0 England 1	(WCQ)	Millennium Stadium, Cardiff
Sep 7	Poland 1 Wales 0	(WCQ)	Warsaw
Oct 8	N Ireland 2 Wales 3	(WCQ)	Belfast
Oct 12	Wales 2 Azerbaijan 0	(WCQ)	Millennium Stadium, Cardiff
Nov 16	Cyprus 1 Wales 0	(F)	Limassol

2006

Mar 1	Wales 0 Paraguay 0	(F)	Millennium Stadium, Cardiff
May 21	Basque XI 0 Wales 1	(F)	Bilbao (*Non-cap international*)
May 27	T & Tobago 1 Wales 2	(F)	Graz
Aug 15	Wales 0 Bulgaria 0	(F)	Liberty Stadium
Sep 2	Czech Rep 2 Wales 1	(EQ)	Teplice
Sep 5	Brazil 2 Wales 0	(F)	White Hart Lane, London
Oct 7	Wales 1 Slovakia 5	(EQ)	Millennium Stadium, Cardiff
Oct 11	Wales 3 Cyprus 1	(EQ)	Millennium Stadium, Cardiff
Nov 14	Wales 4 Liechtenstein 0	(F)	Racecourse Gd, Wrexham

APPENDIX

2007

Feb 6	N Ireland 0 Wales 0	(F)	Belfast
Mar 24	Rep Ireland 1 Wales 0	(EQ)	Dublin
Mar 28	Wales 3 San Marino 0	(EQ)	Millennium Stadium, Cardiff
May 26	Wales 2 New Zealand 2	(F)	Racecourse Gd, Wrexham
June 2	Wales 0 Czech Rep 0	(EQ)	Millennium Stadium, Cardiff
Aug 22	Bulgaria 0 Wales 1	(F)	Bourgas
Sep 8	Wales 0 Germany 2	(EQ)	Millennium Stadium, Cardiff
Sep 12	Slovakia 2 Wales 5	(EQ)	Trnava
Oct 13	Cyprus 3 Wales 1	(EQ)	Nicosia
Oct 17	San Marino 1 Wales 2	(EQ)	Serravalle
Nov 17	Wales 2 Rep Ireland 2	(EQ)	Millennium Stadium, Cardiff
Nov 21	Germany 0 Wales 0	(EQ)	Frankfurt

2008

Feb 6	Wales 3 Norway 0	(F)	Racecourse Gd, Wrexham
Mar 26	Luxembourg 0 Wales 2	(F)	Luxembourg City
May 28	Iceland 0 Wales 1	(F)	Reykjavik
June 1	Netherlands 2 Wales 0	(F)	Rotterdam
Aug 20	Wales 1 Georgia 2	(F)	Liberty Stadium, Swansea
Sep 6	Wales 1 Azerbaijan 0	(WCQ)	Millennium Stadium, Cardiff
Sep 10	Russia 2 Wales 1	(WCQ)	Moscow
Oct 11	Wales 2 Liechtenstein 0	(WCQ)	Millennium Stadium, Cardiff
Oct 15	Germany 1 Wales 0	(WCQ)	Mönchengladbach
Nov 19	Denmark 0 Wales 1	(F)	Brondby

2009

Feb 11	Wales 0 Poland 1	(F)	Vila Real, Portugal
Mar 28	Wales 0 Finland 2	(WCQ)	Millennium Stadium, Cardiff
Apr 1	Wales 0 Germany 2	(WCQ)	Millennium Stadium, Cardiff
May 29	Wales 1 Estonia 0	(F)	Parc y Scarlets, Llanelli
June 6	Azerbaijan 0 Wales 1	(WCQ)	Baku
Aug 12	Montenegro 2 Wales 1	(F)	Podgorica
Sep 9	Wales 1 Russia 3	(WCQ)	Millennium Stadium
Oct 10	Finland 2 Wales 1	(WCQ)	Helsinki
Oct 14	Liechtenstein 0 Wales 2	(WCQ)	Vaduz
Nov 14	Wales 3 Scotland 0	(F)	Cardiff City Stadium, Cardiff

2010

Mar 3	Wales 0 Sweden 1	(F)	Liberty Stadium, Swansea
May 23	Croatia 2 Wales 0	(F)	Osijek
Aug 11	Wales 5 Luxembourg 1	(F)	Parc y Scarlets, Llanelli
Sep 3	Montenegro 1 Wales 0	(EQ)	Podgorica
Oct 8	Wales 0 Bulgaria 1	(EQ)	Cardiff City Stadium, Cardiff
Oct 12	Switzerland 4 Wales 1	(EQ)	Basel

2011

Feb 8	Rep Ireland 3 Wales 0	(F)	Dublin
Mar 26	Wales 0 England 2	(EQ)	Millennium Stadium, Cardiff
May 25	Wales 1 Scotland 3	(F)	Dublin
May 27	N Ireland 0 Wales 2	(F)	Dublin
Aug 10	Wales 1 Australia 2	(F)	Cardiff City Stadium, Cardiff
Sep 2	Wales 2 Montenegro 1	(EQ)	Cardiff City Stadium, Cardiff
Sep 6	England 1 Wales 0	(EQ)	Wembley
Oct 7	Wales 2 Switzerland 0	(EQ)	Liberty Stadium, Swansea
Oct 11	Bulgaria 0 Wales 1	(EQ)	Sofia
Nov 12	Wales 4 Norway 1	(F)	Cardiff City Stadium, Cardiff

2012

Feb 29	Wales 0 Costa Rica 1	(F)	Cardiff City Stadium, Cardiff
May 27	Mexico 2 Wales 0	(F)	New York City, USA
Aug 15	Wales 0 Bosnia 2	(F)	Parc y Scarlets, Llanelli
Sep 7	Wales 0 Belgium 2	(WCQ)	Cardiff City Stadium, Cardiff
Sep 11	Serbia 6 Wales 1	(WCQ)	Novi Sad
Oct 12	Wales 2 Scotland 1	(WCQ)	Cardiff City Stadium, Cardiff
Oct 16	Croatia 2 Wales 0	(WCQ)	Osijek

2013

Feb 6	Wales 2 Austria 1	(F)	Liberty Stadium, Swansea
Mar 22	Scotland 1 Wales 2	(WCQ)	Glasgow
Mar 26	Wales 1 Croatia 2	(WCQ)	Liberty Stadium, Swansea
Aug 14	Wales 0 Rep Ireland 0	(F)	Cardiff City Stadium, Cardiff
Sep 6	Macedonia 2 Wales 1	(WCQ)	Skopje
Sep 10	Wales 0 Serbia 3	(WCQ)	Cardiff City Stadium, Cardiff
Oct 11	Wales 1 Macedonia 0	(WCQ)	Cardiff City Stadium, Cardiff
Oct 15	Belgium 0 Wales 0	(WCQ)	Brussels
Nov 16	Wales 1 Finland 1	(F)	Cardiff City Stadium, Cardiff

2014

Mar 5	Wales 3 Iceland 1	(F)	Cardiff City Stadium, Cardiff
June 4	Netherlands 2 Wales 0	(F)	Amsterdam

(b) Results: 2014–2015
(Euro 2016 Qualification Campaign)

Round 1

September 9, 2014	Estadi Nacional, Andorra la Vella

Andorra 1	**Wales 2**
Lima 6 pen	Bale 22, 81

Andorra:	Pol; Rubio, Garcia, Lima (Capt), Maneiro; Vales, Ayala; Lorenzo, Peppe (Vieria 53), Martinez (Sonejee 83); Riera.
Wales:	Hennessey; Chester, A Williams (Capt), Davies; Gunter, King (G Williams 77), Allen, Taylor; Ramsey (Huws 90+2), Bale; Church (Ledley 52).
Attendance:	3,150
Referee:	Slavko Vinčić (Slovenia)
Other Group B Fixtures	Bosnia 1 (Ibišević 6) Cyprus 2 (Christofi 45, 73)

Group B Table		P	Pts
	Cyprus	1	3
	Wales	1	3
	Andorra	1	0
	Bosnia	1	0
	Belgium	0	0
	Israel	0	0

Round 2

October 10, 2014   Cardiff City Stadium, Cardiff

Wales 0   **Bosnia 0**

Wales: Hennessey; Chester, A Williams (Capt), Davies;
             Gunter, King, Ledley, Taylor; J Williams
             (G Williams 83), Bale; Church (Robson-Kanu 66).

Bosnia: Begović; Mujdža, Hadžić, Šunjić. Lulić; Bežić;
             Sušić, Pjanić, Medunjanin; Ibišević (Hajrović 83),
             Džeko(Capt).

Attendance: 30,741

Referee: Vladislav Bezborodov (Russia)

Other   Belgium 6 (de Bruyne 3, 34, Chadli 37, Origi 59,
Group B   Mertens 65, 68)
Fixtures   Andorra 0

             Cyprus 1 (Makrides 67)
             Israel   2 (Damari 38, Ben Haim II 45)

Group B Table		P	Pts
	Wales	2	4
	Belgium	1	3
	Cyprus	2	3
	Israel	1	3
	Bosnia	2	1
	Andorra	2	0

Round 3

October 13, 2014   Cardiff City Stadium, Cardiff

Wales 2   **Cyprus 1**

Cotterill 13,   Laban 36

Robson-Kanu 23

Wales:	Hennessy; Gunter, Chester, A Williams (Capt), Taylor; King, Ledley, G Williams (Edwards 58); Robson-Kanu (J Taylor 83), Bale, Church (Cotterill 6).
Cyprus:	Kissas; Kyriakou, Merkis, Dossa Junior (Angeli 26, Papathanasiou 85), Antoniades; Laban, Nikolaou (Alexandrou 67); Efrem, Makridis (Capt), Sotiriou; Christofi.
Attendance:	21,273
Referee:	Manuel Gräfe (Germany)

Other	Andorra 1 (Lima 15 pen)	
Group B	Israel 4 (Damari 3, 41, 82, Hemed 90+6 pen)	
Fixtures		
	Bosnia 1 (Džeko 28)	
	Belgium 1 (Nainggolan 51)	

Group B		P	Pts
Table	Wales	3	7
	Israel	2	6
	Belgium	2	4
	Cyprus	3	3
	Bosnia	3	2
	Andorra	3	0

Round 4

November 16, 2014   King Baudouin Stadium, Brussels

Belgium 0   **Wales 0**

Wales: Hennessey; Gunter, Chester, A Williams (Capt), Taylor; Allen, Ledley; Ramsey, Bale, Cotterill (G Williams 46); Robson-Kanu (Huws 90+5).

Belgium: Courtois; Vanden Borre, Lombaerts, Alderweireld, Vertonghen (Capt); de Bruyne, Witsel, Fellaini; Chadli (Benteke 62), Origi (Mertens 73, Januzaj 89), Hazard.

Attendance: 41,535

Referee: Pavel Královec (Czech Rep)

Other Group B Fixtures:
Cyprus 5 (Merkis 9, Efrem 31,42,60, Christofi 87 pen)
Andorra 0

Israel 3 (Vermouth 36, Damari 45, Zahavi 70)
Bosnia 0

Group B Table

	P	Pts
Israel	3	9
Wales	4	8
Cyprus	4	6
Belgium	3	5
Bosnia	4	2
Andorra	4	0

Round 5

March 28, 2015   Sammy Ofer Stadium, Haifa

Israel 0

Wales 3
Ramsey 45+1,
Bale 50,77

Wales: Hennessey; Collins, A Williams (Capt), Davies; Gunter, Allen, Ledley, Taylor; Ramsey, Bale; Robson-Kanu.

Israel: Marciano; Dgani, Ben Haim I (Capt), Tibi, Ben Harush; Natkho, Yeini, Ben Haim II (Biton 60), Refaelov, Zahavi (Sahar 70); Damari (Hemed 43).
Red Card: Tibi 51

Attendance: 30,200

Referee: Milorad Mažić (Serbia)

Other
Group B
Fixtures
    Andorra 0
    Bosnia   3 (Džeko 13, 49, 62)

    Belgium 5 (Fellaini 21, 66, Benteke 35, Hazard 67, Batshuayi 80)
    Cyprus   0

March 31, 2015
Israel   0
Belgium 1 (Fellaini 9)

Group B
Table

	P	Pts
Belgium	5	11
Wales	5	11
Israel	5	9
Cyprus	5	6
Bosnia	5	5
Andorra	5	0

Round 6

June 12, 2015   Cardiff City Stadium, Cardiff

Wales 1   **Belgium 0**
Bale 25

Wales:	Hennessey; Gunter, A Williams (Capt), Chester; Richards, Allen, Ledley, Taylor; Bale (Vokes 87), Ramsey; Robson-Kanu (King 90+3).
Belgium:	Courtois; Alderweireld (Ferreira-Carrasco 76), Lombaerts, Denayer, Vertonghen; Witsel, Nainggolan; Merterns (Lukaku 46), de Bruyne, Hazard (Capt); Benteke.
Attendance:	33,280
Referee:	Felix Brych (Germany)

Other Group B Fixtures		
Andorra	1	(Dossa Junior 2 o.g.)
Cyprus	3	(Mitidis 13, 45, 53)
Bosnia	3	(Višćć 42, 75, Džeko 45+2 pen)
Israel	1	(Ben Haim II 41)

Group B Table	P	Pts
Wales	6	14
Belgium	6	11
Israel	6	9
Cyprus	6	9
Bosnia	6	8
Andorra	6	0

Round 7

September 3, 2015   GSP Stadium, Nicosia

Cyprus   **Wales 1**
                                        Bale 82

Wales: Hennessey; Gunter, A Williams (Capt), Davies;
            Richards, Edwards, King, Taylor; Bale (Church 90),
            Ramsey; Robson-Kanu (Vokes 68).

Cyprus: Giorgallides; Demetriou, Junior, Laifis, Antoniades;
            Charalambides (Capt, Englezou 74), Nikolaou,
            Economides, Makridis; Mytidis (Kolokoudias 65),
            Makris (Sotiriou 84).

Attendance: 14,492

Referee: Szmon Marciniak (Poland)

Other   Belgium 3 (Fellaini 23, de Bruyne 44, Hazard 78 pen)
Group B   Bosnia   1 (Džeko 15)
Fixtures

             Israel   4 (Zahavi 3, Bitton 22, Hemed 26 pen,
                          Dabour 38)

             Andorra 0

Group B Table		P	Pts
	Wales	7	17
	Belgium	7	14
	Israel	7	12
	Cyprus	7	9
	Bosnia	7	8
	Andorra	7	0

Round 8

September 6, 2015		Cardiff City Stadium, Cardiff

Wales 0   **Israel 0**

Wales:	Hennssey; Gunter, A Williams (Capt), Davies; Richards, King (Vokes 85), Edwards, Taylor; Ramsey, Bale; Robson-Kanu (Church 81).
Israel:	Marciano; Tibi, Dasa, Ben Haim I (Capt); Dgani, Biton, Natcho, Ben Harush; Zahvai, Dabbur (Hemed 46), Kayal (Ben Haim II 46).
Attendance:	32,653
Referee:	Ivan Bebek (Croatia)
Other Group B Fixtures	Bosnia 3 (Bičakčić 14, Džeko 30, Lulić 45) Andorra 0 Cyprus 0 Belgium 1 (Hazard 86)

Group B Table		P	Pts
	Wales	8	18
	Belgium	8	17
	Israel	8	13
	Bosnia	8	11
	Cyprus	8	9
	Andorra	8	0

Round 9

October 10, 2015   Bilino Polje, Zenica

Bosnia 2   **Wales 0**
Djurić 71,
Ibišević 90

Wales: Hennessey; Gunter, A Williams (Capt), Davies;
                Richards, Allen (Edwards 85), Ledley (Vokes 75),
                Taylor; Ramsey, Bale; Robson-Kanu (Church 84).

Bosnia: Begović (Capt); Mujdža, Spahić (Cocalić 46), Šunjić,
                Zukanović; Hadžić (Bižakžić 89); Višća (Djurić 61),
                Pjanić, Salhiović, Lulić; Ibišević.

Attendance: 10,250

Referee: Alberto Undiano Mallenco (Spain)

Other   Andorra 1 (Lima 51 pen)
Group B   Belgium 4 (Nainggolan 19, de Bruyne 42, Hazard 56
Fixtures   pen, Depoitre 64)

                Israel   1 (Bitton 76)
                Cyprus   2 (Dossa Junior 58, Demetriou 80)

Group B Table		P	Pts
Q Belgium		9	20
Q Wales		9	18
Bosnia		9	14
Israel		9	13
Cyprus		9	12
Andorra		9	0

262

Round 10

October 13, 2015   Cardiff City Stadium, Cardiff

Wales 2   **Andorra 0**

Ramsey 51,
Bale 86

Wales:	Hennessey; Gunter, Chester, A Williams (Capt), Davies; Vaughan, Ramsey, J Williams (Church 85); Robson-Kanu (Edwards 23, Lawrence 46), Vokes, Bale.
Andorra:	Pol; Rubio, Llovera, Lima, San Nicolas; Moreira (Riera 12), Vieira, Sonjee (Capt, Ayala 70), Rodrigues; Sanchez, Lorenzo (Garcia 81).
Attendance:	33,280
Referee:	Kevin Blom (Netherlands)
Other Group B Fixtures	Belgium 3 (Mertens 64, de Bruyne 78, Hazard 84) Israel 1 (Hemed 88)
	Cyprus 2 (Charalambidis 32, Mitidis 41) Bosnia 3 (Medunjanin 13, 44, Đjurić 67)

GROUP B FINAL TABLE

		P	W	D	L	F	A	GD	Pts
1	Q Belgium	10	7	2	1	24	5	19	23
2	Q Wales	10	6	3	1	11	4	7	21
3	P/O Bosnia	10	5	2	3	17	12	5	17
4	Israel	10	4	1	5	16	14	2	13
5	Cyprus	10	4	0	6	16	17	−1	12
6	Andorra	10	0	0	10	4	36	−32	0

(c) Appearances: Euro 2016 Qualification Campaign

10 – Bale, Gunter, Hennessey, A Williams.
 9 – N Taylor, Robson-Kanu (8 starts +1 substitute appearance)
 8 – Ramsey
 7 – Davies, Ledley (6+1), Church (3+4)
 6 – Chester, King (5+1), Vokes (1+5)
 5 – Allen, D Edwards (2+3)
 4 – Richards, G Williams (1+3)
 2 – Jonny Williams, Cotterill (1+1), Vaughan (1+1), Huws (0+2), MacDonald (0+2)
 1 – Collins, J Taylor (0+1), Lawrence (0+1)

Unused Squad Members

Dummett, G Edwards, Fox, Gabbidon, Henley, John, Letheren, Matthews, Ricketts, Walsh, Ward, Fôn Williams, Jordan Williams.

(d) Goalscorers: Euro 2016 Qualification Campaign

7 – Bale
2 – Ramsey
1 – Cotterill
1 – Robson-Kanu

(e) Players Capped: 2005-2015

(In order of appearance. Those in *italics* had been capped previously, those in non-italics won their first caps during this period whilst those in **bold** were members of Euro 2016 qualifying squad)

2005   (Manager, John Toshack) *Danny Coyne, Rob Edwards,*
        ***Danny Gabbidon**, Robert Page, Rhys Weston,* **Sam Ricketts**,
        David Partridge, Danny Collins, *Carl Fletcher, Craig Bellamy,*
        Robert Earnshaw, Gareth Roberts, Simon Davies, Carl Robinson,
        Stephen Roberts, *Mark Delaney, John Hartson, Ryan Giggs,*
        James Collins, Craig Davies, Richard Duffy, Gavin Williams,
        David Vaughan, *Paul Parry, Jason Koumas,* **Joe Ledley**,
        Paul Jones, Andrew Crofts, **David Cotterill**, Lewis Price.

2006   Lewin Nyatanga, Jason Brown, Glyn Garner, Arron Davies,
        Gareth Bale, Steve Evans, Mark Jones, Craig Morgan,
        Chris Llewellyn.

2007   Jermaine Easter, **Wayne Hennessey**, **Chris Gunter**,
        Daniel Nardiello, Freddy Eastwood, Neal Eardley,
        David Edwards.

2008   **Ashley Williams**, Boaz Myhill, Owain Tudur Jones,
        Jack Collison, Ched Evans, **Sam Vokes**, **Aaron Ramsey**.

2009   **Simon Church**, **Joe Allen**, **Andy King**, Brian Stock.

2010   Andy Dorman, Mark Bradley, **Neil Taylor**,
        Hal Robson-Kanu, Christian Ribeiro, Steve Morison,
        (Caretaker Manager, Brian Flynn) Darcy Blake,
        Shaun MacDonald.

2011   (Manager, Gary Speed) **Adam Matthews**.

2012   (Manager, Chris Coleman) **Jazz Richards**, Joel Lynch,
        Ben Davies.

2013   **Jonny Williams**, **Declan John**, James Wilson, Harry Wilson.

2014   **Emyr Huws**, **James Chester**, **George Williams**,
        Paul Dummett, **Jake Taylor**.

2015   **Tom Lawrence**, **Adam Henley**, **Owain Fôn Williams**

St David's Press

When Chris, the players, and our amazing fans were celebrating in Bosnia, I just know that Gary was there, chuffed to see the country he loved finally achieve its dream, and knowing that he'd played his part. It's a great story and Bryn is the right man to tell it.'
Roger Speed, from his Foreword

'This diary tells the greatest story the nation's enjoyed since our one and only previous involvement in a summer tournament way back in 1958. A story told by someone who once travelled away to support Wales as a supporter and now travels with the side as a reporter.
Chris Coleman, from his Preface

'Bryn's a fan and he's been as desperate as we have to see Wales qualifying... there's nobody better placed than Bryn to tell the story of how we finally made the dream come true!'
Chris Gunter

This is the book that many Welsh football fans thought they'd never get to read; a tale of outstanding performances at home and away, qualification success and a FIFA Top Ten ranking, and the best thing is...it's all true!

Packed with passion, tinged with sadness, and written with great humour, Bryn Law's diary of the campaign perfectly describes the emotions of following the Welsh national football team; when years of despair vanished in a wave of glorious euphoria to the sounds of Zombie Nation. It will bring a tear to your eye and put a massive grin on your face.

978 1 902719 467 - £13.99 - 320pp - 76 illustrations/photographs

ST DAVID'S PRESS

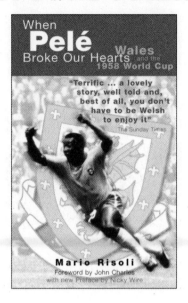

'A beautifully written and expertly researched book, which gives an insight into Wales' greatest football triumph'
Nicky Wire - Manic Street Preachers

"...a brilliant book...a thoroughly good read...I warmly recommend it"
Adrian Chiles Radio 5 Live

'If you were to write a surreal football comedy script tinged with pathos, personal tragedy, heroism, politics, adventure and endeavour, you couldn't begin to emulate the story of Wales in 1958 ... well-crafted ... meticulously researched'
Total Football

'a great tale, diligently researched and well told'
GQ Magazine

'excellent ... an intriguing story, compellingly told'
Four Four Two

'terrific ... a lovely story, well told and, best of all, you don't have to be Welsh to enjoy it'
The Sunday Times

When Pelé Broke Our Hearts is the definitive story of the Welsh team's remarkable 1958 World Cup campaign in Sweden, the first and only time Wales have played in football's premier tournament.

978 1 902719 023 - £9.99 - 180pp - 44 illustrations/photographs